rup

THE ZINE YEAR-BOOK

clamor magazine *presents* a year in the life of the·underground press

VOLUME 8

Printed in Canada by the fine people at Westcan Printing Group (www.westcanpg.com)

Cover Design:
Robin Hendrickson

Distributed by Become The Media | Clamor Magazine:
yearbook@clamormagazine.org
ISBN: 0-9664829-5-6

Become The Media | Clamor Magazine
PO Box 20128
Toledo, OH 43610
www.clamormagazine.org

Inside the Zine Yearbook

Introduction 5
A note about the yearbook process | Acknowledgements.................6

Altar Magazine...7
American Libaries 9
Anti-Up 12
The Beat Within 13
Chainbreaker 17
Chickenhed Zine and Roll 18
Complexification Strategy 20
Cryptozoa 22
Drank Too Much in Milwaukee 23
Fish Piss 24
From Brooklyn to Balata 26
Girls Are Not Chicks Coloring Book...28
glossolalia 30
Go Metric 32
greenzine 36
here...38
Ideas in Pictures 41
Imagine...42
Inner Swine 44
Insubordination..46
kiss machine...52
Kitchen Sink 54
Lady Churchill's Rosebud Wristlet 60
Leeking Ink...62
Letters from a Bicycle 63
Limited Delivery Area 68
LOUDmouth...74
LOVE 77
LuLuLand 79
Mamaphiles 80
Mama Sez No War! 82
Media Geek 84
Merge..86
Modern Arizona 88
Multi-Kid...89
Mutate Zine..92
OFF-Line..94

Pick Your Poison 103
Rated Rookie 106
Ride On 109
Safety Pin Girl 112
Secret Mystery Love Shoes..113
Seedhead 118
Slouch 119
Sobaka 124
This Is Still Not About Your Favorite Band 128
Tight Pants..132
Trouble In Mind 137
With Fire in Our Throats 141
Women's Self Defense: Stories and Strategies of Survival..........143
Zine Librarian Zine..146
Zine World: A Reader's Guide to the Underground Press............148

Honorable Mentions 150

Introduction

"A zine? Is that sort of like a blog? Cuz I LOVE blogs. I mean, I read them all day on the internet when I'm at work, and, like, you know, they're just so, REAL, y'know? Zines are kinda like that, right?"

Um, hell no, and yes — kind of. Plain and simple, right? The zine world is the often-marginalized, never-credited ancestor, contemporary, and forerunner to the electronic media du jour touted as the latest democratic revolution in human communication. Zines are the tangible, real-world material evidence that independent media is alive and well in print and refuses to be outdone by the internet. Don't get it twisted, though. We're not half-assed luddite cranks extolling the virtues of carbon paper over the xerox machine. Nope. We put this anthology together using lots of electricity and more than a couple handfuls of computers. So why do we exploit these technical resources to wave the flag for independent media that can be made by any one with an idea and a desire to share it? It's a silly question, but you asked.

Simply put, written zines are still one of the most accessible forms of self-expression. You don't need any specialized equipment to broadcast over the airwaves or record your ideas, and you don't even need a computer to create or view zines. All you need is a pen, paper, and a couple dollars for the copy machine. All you need to do is walk into one of a many coffee shops, records stores, bookstores, or community spaces to pick up a zine and participate in a vibrant culture that asks a little more of our communities than the mainstream news and entertainment industries expect from us. Because there are no economic barriers to creating zines, they far bridge the digital divide (the gap between those who have access — and how much access — and those do not) as a grassroots and decentralized form of media. You're getting the voices of anyone with the gumption to put their words on paper — not simply those who have have access to a computer. Plus, zines can be read by people on the bus, in the bathroom, behind bars, and in the backwoods — there is no technological limit to where these mighty little pamphlets can travel, and there's a reason why you can trace the history of the zine back to the early tracts of revolution-era Americans like Thomas Paine and Benjamin Franklin.

But perhaps more important than any academic argument about the roots and accessibility of zine cultures, the underground press is about living resistance in an increasingly oppressive world. Zines call into question assumptions taken for granted by so many. They highlight individuals who are defying the odds and creating alternatives in a time when such currency is devalued. They make us laugh in ways we never imagined possible. They reach deep into our emotions and cause us to empathize with one another. Zines are life incarnate on a black and white piece of photocopied paper.

Zines remind us that the world is simultaneously fucked and rife with beauty and potential. We hope you not only enjoy this peek into a year in the life of the underground press, but that you also feel moved to become an active participant in years to follow.

Yours in independent media,

Jen Angel & Jason Kucsma

A note about the yearbook process

··

When we compile each volume of the yearbook, we're consistently reminded that there are thousands more zines out there that didn't get nominated for the yearbook — not because they aren't good enough, but because this book relies solely on zine readers to determine what is good enough to merit nomination for the yearbook. That this year's volume has over 50 pieces is testimony that there are plenty of people out there making and nominating zines to make this collection a worthwhile read. At the same time we'd be more than willing to make a book twice this size if we doubled or tripled the number of nominations we got each year.

So how does it all come together? Throughout the year folks nominate their favorite pieces from zines they pick. They send us actual zines with post-it notes on the pages they want to nominate, or they send photocopies of their favorite art and articles from a particular zine. We collect them all year long — up until the February 1 deadline for the prior year. Once we've got piles and piles of zines spilling out into our workplace and pushing our obsessive compulsive organizational tendencies to their limits, we assemble a crew of underground press enthusiasts to help us read through the nominations to make final selections.

From there we sit down and do work that is not unlike the work done by a lot of zine editors you'll hear from in this book. We compile all the images we have. We envision how it will all come together, and then we set to work scanning, copying, cutting, pasting, and editing until we get to a point where we're satisfied that we have a collection that best represents a collective voice from the world of the underground press. In some cases we'll reproduce actual zine pages. This is especially true with pieces that have an inimitable layout or other original artwork. In other cases (especially longer pieces from full-size zines), we'll re-work the piece using electronic files and any available images so it better fits our format. That said, we still leave the files unedited to retain the authors' spirit and intent — including all spelling slips and grammar glitches. Regardless of whether we reprint the actual pages or rework the layout, we also include the contact information and encourage you to get in touch with the editors themselves. Drop some of them a line and let them know what you thought about their ideas, perspectives, or hard work!

If you'd like more info about next year's edition, visit our website at:
http://www.clamormagazine.org/yearbook/

Thanks where thanks are due

··

This year's crew of underground press enthusiasts was made up of: Jason Kucsma, Jen Angel, Matthew Jaffee, Jenny Lee, Mike Medow, Ruth Lennon, James Marks, Joshua Chamberlain, Sarah Scott-Brandt, Shawn Bess, Keith McCrea, and Elliot Adams.

Infinite thanks are overdue to all of you who took the time to tell us about the amazing zines you came across in the past year. Please keep your eyes and ears open for nominations for next year's book, and we'll make it even bigger and better! And, finally, there would be no Zine Yearbook Vol. 8 if it weren't for the encouragement and financial support of our partner-in-crime, Joshua Breitbart.

Celie's Revenge: Hip-Hop Betrays Black Women
by Jennifer McLune

Indeed, like rock & roll, hip-hop sometimes makes you think we men don't like women much at all, except to objectify them as trophy pieces or, as contemporary vernacular mandates, as baby mommas, chickenheads, or bitches.

But just as it was unfair to demonize men of color in the 60s solely as wild-eyed radicals when what they wanted, amidst their fury, was a little freedom and a little power, today it is wrong to categorically dismiss hip-hop without taking into serious consideration the socioeconomic conditions (and the many record labels that eagerly exploit and benefit from the ignorance of many of these young artists) that have led to the current state of affairs. Or, to paraphrase the late Tupac Shakur, we were given this world, we did not make it. Which means hip-hop did not breed ghettos, poverty, single mothers, fatherlessness, rotten school systems, immorality, materialism, self-hatred, racism, sexism, and the prison-industrial complex that is capturing literally thousands of young Black and Latino males and females each year.

—Kevin Powell

You were given this world, and you glorify it. You were given this world, and you protect it. You were given this world, and you benefit from it. You were given this world, and even in your wildest dreams you refuse to imagine anything else but this world. And anyone who attacks your misogynistic fantasy world and offers an alternative vision is a hater or, worse, an enemy of that world who just doesn't get it. What is there to get? There is nothing deep or new about misogyny, materialism, violence and homophobia. The hardest part isn't recognizing it, but ending it. Calling it unacceptable and an enemy of us all. Refusing to be mesmerized, seduced or confused by what these conditions in hip-hop really are: a betrayal of our imagination *as a people*. Dismissing the sexism in hip-hop as being predicated on socioeconomic factors is a way to silence a feminist critique of the culture: make an understanding of the misogynistic objectification and eraser of black women in hip-hop so elusive that we can't grasp it long enough to wring the neck of its power over us. This argument completely ignores the fact that women too are raised in this environment of poverty and violence but have yet to produce the same negative and hateful representation of black men that male rappers are capable of making against women. His understanding also lends itself to the elitist assumption that somehow poverty breeds sexism or at least should excuse it. White boys can create the same hateful and violent music as black boys and as long as they can agree that their common enemy is female and their power is in their penis. We must not hesitate to name the war they have declared on women.

Hip-hop is sexist and homophobic and any deviation from this norm within the culture and music has to be fought for and still remains marginal to its most dominant and lucrative expressions. Hip-hop owes its success to the ideology of woman-hating and it creates, perpetuates and reaps the rewards of it. The most well-known artists who represent an underground and conscious force in hip-hop like Common, The Roots, Goodie Mob and others still remain inconsistent, apologetic and even eager to join the mainstream Players Club. Even though consumers like me support them because of their consciousness, they still remain on the fence by either playing down their consciousness or giving props to misogynistic rappers. As Talib Kweli said in an interview on the hip-hop shock jock radio show Star & Buckwild, he wants to be cool with artists who degrade women and perpetuate materialism. On another Star & Buckwild Show, Talib's boy Common reiterated this sentiment when he said he also has no problem with sexist and degrading music and just wants his piece this rotten pie. Hopefully, selling out to coca-cola will give him a big enough slice.

I also believe that much of what passes itself off as tackling sexism in hip-hop culture is nothing more than a sly form of public relations to ensure that nobody's money, power or respect is ever really challenged within the circles that benefit from hip-hop's commercial appeal. I have yet to see any of these 'enlightened' interpreters of black culture call for boycotts of cultural productions that degrade black people especially if anyone black benefits from these productions. Instead we are asked to dialogue about, forgive and ultimately celebrate our progress, which is always predicated on a few rappers and moguls getting rich. Angry young black women like myself are expected to be satisfied with a mere mention that some hip-hop music is sexist and that this sexism of a few rappers is actually as Powell calls it, "the ghetto blues, urban folk art, a cry out for help." My question then is whose blues? Whose art? Why won't anybody

contact: 955 Metropolitan Avenue Suite 4R • Brooklyn, NY 11211

help the women who are raped on endless rotation by the gaze of the hip-hop camera?

We are expected to solve the condition of woman hating in hip-hop simply by alluding to it even as we celebrate and excuse its environment of unacceptable misogynistic arrogance, hatred and ignorance. What this angry black woman wants to hear is that Black women are black people too. That any attack on the women in our community is an attack on us all and that we will no longer be duped by genocidal tendencies in black-face. That the black men who make music that perpetuates the hatred of women will be named, shunned and destroyed financially and socially like the traitors of our community they are. That until hip-hop does right by black women everything hip-hop ever does will fail.

If we go by Powell's explanation for why hip-hop is the way it is and why we should continue to consume and celebrate it then, ultimately, we are to accept ourselves as victims who know only how to imitate our victimization and let off the hook the handful of us who benefit from this tragic conclusion. I choose to challenge hip-hop by not feeding its gluttonous appetite for commercial appeal with my money or my attention.

I do this for my own self preservation as a black woman who feels ill and angry every time I'm subjected to the cultural productions of hip-hop. I'm a reluctant member of the so-called Hip-Hop Generation which like the Pepsi Generation or Generation X is a convenient yet completely unexplored marketing tool to get young black folks to channel our hard earned money, energy and creativity into a culture that asks us to obediently consume its mindless, disposable products, media, fashion and messages.

I'm tired of the ridiculous excuses and justifications for the unjustifiable pillaring of black women and girls in hip-hop. If black women experience double the oppression as both blacks and women in a racist patriarchal culture, where is our anger and venom at men and white folks? The black men who make excuses for the ideology of woman-hating in hip-hop are probably the same black men who would have supported the attacks on black female writers whose work went public about the reality of patriarchy in our community. The fact that these black female writers did not create incest, domestic violence, rape and other patriarchal conditions in the black community did not shield them from being skewered by black men who had their feelings hurt by the exposure of their male privilege and domination of black women. Our literature and activism around these issues is taken apart and attacked in spite of its truth by black men and many women for whom ego, privilege and domination supercede reality and who creates it. We were called traitors for refusing to be silent about the misogynistic order of things in our minds and homes and yet women-hating rappers are made heroes by the so-called masses. This is not merely about exposing reality and keeping it real. This is about a particular narrative of reality that sells and gets men hard. A reality in which, as a Wu Tang Clan video shows, black women are dancing cave chicks in bikinis that get clubbed over the head. Or in which gang rapes are put to a phat beat. Or in which working class black women are compared to shit eating birds. As a black woman who views sexism as just as much the enemy of my people as racism I can't buy these apologies and excuses for hip-hop. I will not accept the notion that my sisters disserve to be degraded and humiliated because of the frustrations of black men even as we suppress our own frustrations, angers and fears in an effort to be sexy and accommodating.

Although Kevin Powell blames the negatives in hip-hop on everything but hip-hop culture itself, he ultimately concludes, "What hip-hop has spawned is a way of winning on our own terms, of us making something out of nothing." If the terms of winning are the objectification of black women and girls, I wonder if any females were at the table when the deal went down. Did we agree to these terms of success as being either the invisible or the objectified? Rather than pretending to explain away the sexism of hip-hop culture, why doesn't Powell just come clean: It really doesn't matter how women are treated. Sexism is the winning ticket to mainstream acceptability and Powell knows this, just like Russell Simmons and others. And it's obvious that if these are the winning terms of our creativity, in the end black women are the losers. And that's exactly how these self-proclaimed players, thugs and hip-hop intellectuals want us: on our backs and pledging allegiance to the Hip-Hop Nation. If we were all to condemn woman-hating as an enemy of our community, hip-hop would be forced to look at itself and change radically and consistently. And then it would no longer be marketable in the way that these hip-hop intellectuals celebrate. It's all about the Benjamins on every level of the culture. And black women should expect to be thugged and rubbed all the way to the bank. ★

Sex in the City:
What Happened at the Minneapolis Public Library
by Wendy Adamson

The Internet arrived at the Minneapolis Library in 1997. By 1999 we had approximately 50 Internet terminals scattered around the two public floors of our building. Our commitment to traditional library principles of free access to all information and our optimism about how the Internet would be used by patrons led us to have a hands-off Internet access policy. On our website we had a three paragraph standard statement saying that the Internet was an immense global network, and that "the Library does not restrict use of its materials." All uses were acceptable, including email and chat rooms. We had no signup policy, and only instigated an informal 30-minute limit when it became apparent that we could not keep up with demand.

We were totally unprepared for reality. Our naïve expectation was that people would use the Internet to study history, learn about medical conditions, track stock quotes, do research for college papers, and read their hometown newspapers. Kids would be working on school projects. Voters would seek candidate records to prepare for the next election.

But, when the word got out on the street that there were 50 Internet terminals in our PUBLIC library, and that there were no restrictions on their use, we were flooded with individuals who came to the Library to view sexually explicit materials. They came alone and in groups. In one case, a middle-aged man regularly brought young boys in to show them sites.

Not only did patrons view and display sexual activities, but they often sought attention of the staff, in order to heighten their enjoyment. It seemed to be a thrill to feign trouble with the printer, so one of us would have to go over and be faced with sexual images. They asked for help in logging into sites such as hardon.com. They printed out sexual images, and placed the prints on tables, bookshelves and counters around the building where they would be seen by others. Terminals were intentionally left on such sites, so that the next unsuspecting Internet user was faced with them.

There was a core group of about three dozen people engaging in this activity. Many of them spent hours every day at it. In some cases they came in at 9 in the morning, and were still in the building at 9 at night when we closed. On Monday mornings, after we had been closed on Sunday, they would literally run to the terminals when we opened our doors.

What were the images like? *Warning— this may offend some readers.* We saw lots of women with a penis in their mouth, in their vagina, or in their rectum. We saw horses and dogs mounting women. We saw men mounting animals. We saw women tied upside down, their legs spread-eagled, and men pushing various instruments into their vaginas. We saw children astride men, or with erect penises stuffed into their mouths. We saw torture scenes. (My most memorable was one in which two men held a woman's legs apart while a third inserted a curling iron into her vagina. Her face was contorted in pain.)

It was staff's job to enforce limits—but only time limits. If we approached patrons to point out that their 30-minute time limit was up, they often (not occasionally, but often) called us words like "bitch" and "cunt" and used such choice expressions as "fuck you" or "shove it up your ass." We had many masturbators, some subtle and some not.

We became sex central. Our limited security staff could not keep up with these behaviors. By the time they arrived after such an event was reported, the person would be gone—to another department where they would resume their Internet viewing. It seemed that our viewers were in a constant state of sexual arousal, and we were simply getting in their way.

Anyone who is familiar with privacy screens knows that they are misnamed, and it was easy to inadvertently glimpse a scene of anal sex or fellatio as you walked by on your way to the bookshelf or the Children's Room. Staff had a full view of some terminals from our reference desks. Patrons began complaining to staff, and then to our Administration, where they were repeatedly told that the Library supported unfettered access to information. Many of our regular users abandoned the library for this reason, outraged that they had been repeatedly faced with such unwanted and apparently staff-sanctioned images. Staff members complained to supervisors and the Administration as well. The response was always the same—the Minneapolis Public Library supported unfettered access to information. If we were "good librarians" we would agree with this policy.

We all went to library school, took the course in censorship, were prepared to fight to the death to keep Judy Blume or Robert Mapplethorpe in our collections. But we were not prepared for this. It went on all day, every day, for almost three years. There was

Zine Yearbook **9** Volume 8

no end in sight. Staff was demoralized, depressed, and angry.

In February 2000, 47 staff members signed a letter to the local newspaper, describing the situation in the library, and asking for help from the City Council and the public in finding solutions. This letter drew a published response from the Board, reiterating the responsibility of the Library to offer unfettered access, and offering more general statements about making wise choices when using the Internet.

Two events brought it all to a halt: a legal action and a TV show.

In early April several library staff sought the advice of an attorney on their rights and responsibilities in this situation. What could we do? Were we unreasonable in complaining, on our own behalf, and on behalf of the public? The attorney assured us that we were experiencing an egregious case of third-party sexual harassment, and that most of the materials being viewed in our library (we had brought a thick notebook of printouts) were obscene and thus not protected by the First Amendment. This opinion was confirmed by other attorneys. After much soul searching, 12 staff members decided to file a complaint with the EEOC in the first week of May 2000.

Further, unbeknownst to the staff, a local TV station, spending a week in the Library working on an unrelated story, saw what was going on. They started quietly filming this activity and interviewing some of the people who were viewing sexual material. Some individuals spoke enthusiastically on camera about the material, admitted masturbating as they watched. They went on to say the atmosphere at the downtown library was "more exciting" than at the branches, because a group of people were viewing sex together. The television station then interviewed three staff members, the Library Director, and a member of the Board. A two-part expose aired on our local CBS affiliate during sweeps week in May, the same week when the EEOC complaint was filed. The evidence was incontrovertible and damning.

Our decision to go the legal route was a difficult one for us. We considered ourselves very loyal to our institution and our profession. What tipped the scale for us was our belief that the library was going down the tubes. We were losing patrons in large numbers. We were watching our users repeatedly assaulted by these images, often recoiling in horror, and sometimes literally rushing out of the building.

Even more, we wondered if the very nature of our profession denied us the civil rights afforded to all other Americans in the workplace. Did our status as librarians deprive us of protection from sexually explicit images as we worked day by day in our jobs? We decided not. We were citizens too. Going back into the staff room and crying, and then coming out into the library with smiles on our faces as Hillary Theyer suggests* was no longer an option. Such passive behavior carried the message that we were willing to submit to sexual harassment which no other citizens would tolerate.

Nevertheless, the stress on us was enormous after we decided to proceed. Any employee who has ever filed a legal charge against his or her employer knows what I'm talking about. Fear, anxiety, sleeplessness, inability to eat are all part of the picture. The literature on sexual harassment says that the individual who speaks out is victimized twice, once during the initial harassment and secondly when the incident is made public and coworkers subject the victim to disbelief and disapproval. We were fortunate that in our case, almost all of our coworkers were, and continue to be, very supportive. And once you have filed a legal complaint you are protected from employer retaliation.

Some librarians from around the US, as well as writers in professional journals, have held us up for criticism. We have been portrayed as censors, traitors to our profession, bad librarians with "narrow sensibilities" as Mr. Berry wrote in a passionate editorial in *Library Journal*.

Since we filed, we have received dozens of phone calls and letters from librarians around the US who are facing similar problems, asking for guidance and support as they deal with the same issues. Interestingly, many of the individual calls have included pleas for anonymity, as librarians worried that their employers would disapprove if they spoke up. For some reason, there is a climate of fear and retribution in the library world when the subject of sexually explicit materials on the Internet rears its head.

Within 24 hours of the EEOC filing and the television special, we had a new temporary policy at MPL, with signs posted on each terminal announcing that it was illegal to send, receive, transmit or display materials which were obscene as defined by Minnesota statute. The Library's permanent Internet policy was drastically re-written and made more substantial and explicit, and the MPL sexual harassment policy was also altered to make reporting paths and responsibilities clearer. The security guards were given authority to monitor Internet use and enforce the policy. In less than a week at least 25 of our daily users left the library, and have not been seen since.

A year later, in May of 2001, the EEOC found probable cause for a sexual harassment lawsuit. (Only 7% of complaints to the EEOC receive this finding.) The Library has repeatedly declined to participate in EEOC-sponsored mediation to reach a settlement. Therefore our complaint has now been forwarded to the Department of Justice, and they are currently conducting an investigation.

These events raise so many questions. Can effective policies be written to deal with obscene materials and child pornography on Internet terminals in libraries? Do librarians have a right to a workplace reasonably free of sexually explicit materials? Do members of the public have the right to come into a public library and not see such materials openly displayed on terminals? Should each community decide on what standards it wants enforced in its own library? Were the librarians who filed the complaint responsible and courageous, or cowardly and unprofessional? Can and should obscenity laws which are on the books in various states be enforced in libraries? Should we have separate viewing areas where people can look at sexually explicit materials away from the general traffic in a library? And the "F" word—are filters sometimes useful, appropriate, helpful, at least on some terminals in a library?

And the final question, can we in our profession discuss these issues in a calm, mutually respectful way without criticizing, belittling or vilifying one another? Can a librarian having difficulty with this in his or her institution speak up and ask for help and advice without fear of having her/his loyalty and professionalism questioned? Can we understand that the complex questions the Internet poses are being studied by legal scholars, and that there are no easy, pat, simplistic answers?

At MPL, we succeeded in bringing a problem out in the open. We firmly believe that each Library has a variety of tools to address this problem. Each library will find a different solution. It is our responsibility to take a part in the larger dialog in a search for a variety of answers, rather than putting our collective heads in the sand and resolutely clinging to theoretical principles that may be doing more harm than good. Let's work together in an atmosphere of openness, tolerance, and respect, to explore ideas and craft some solutions that will benefit us all.

Isn't that what intellectual freedom is all about? ★

from New breed librarian *v.2 n.2 (April 2002; http:// www.newbreedlibrarian.org/archives/02.02.apr2002/ feature.html); and from* Off our backs *v.32 n.9/10 (October 2002)*

Endnotes
*The Minnesota staff feel "harassed and intimidated by having to work in a public environment." I'm sure there are many other public library workers who feel they should be able to change something about where they work. Librarians work daily under conditions they would not tolerate in their own homes. Inadequate heat in the winter, abusive patrons, vandalism, unwanted sexual advances, and many more problems have always been present because, by its very nature, a public library is a public building. That is part of how it serves its critical mission. It is therefore also part of our mission to serve those whose tastes we find repulsive. As angry and upset as we may get at the things we see and experience, we shake it off in the staff room (sometimes accompanied by tears) and return to the desk with a smile on our face. That's part of why we are so special and so important. –"A Librarian's Right to Comfort," *American Libraries,* June 2000, by Hillary Theyer, a branch librarian at Torrance (CA) Public Library.

WWBD? What Would Breadfoot Do?

WWBD if he had to get ready for a catfish eating contest?

BF – if'n yer wanting to get into one of them there catfish eating contests what ya gotta do is get to stretching yer stomach out real good like, way ya do it is by eating like nobodies business for 'bout a month before the contest su'posed to happen. it's what you might call one of them see-food diets. eat anything that ain't nailed down. if it ain't on someone else's fork, eat it. fuck 'em if they still be hungry, you wanna win or what? then come the day of the contest you don't be eating nothing all. that a ways that big ol' stretched out stomach is real empty and you can 'bout fit a barn in there. and sure enough yer gonna win. jus' you don't set 'cross from me, ya here?

WWBD if he was stuck in an elevator with two claustrophobics and a republican?

BF - probably be inclined to do somptin' that would end end to be awful darn messy. ya unnerstand how how a fella wouldn't have much choice at all.

course if'n yer a thinkin' man might be that you take out them claustrophobics figuring that maybe that republican would wise up. got to bed that faced with the same fate that he'd be promising just 'bout anything. course than what ya do is think some more 'bout what those promises are worth and well, guess ya got the elevator to yer self after that.

WWBD if he had three wishes?

BF – well this kinda relates to that elevator one don't it? on account of the fact that one of my wishes would be for an open season on republicans. be just like deer season. you'd have to get a license and all. and there'd be a bow and a black powder season. 'course lot of them democrats ain't much better off so maybe it oughta just be open season on politicians.

uhm,, let's see might have to wish that them female types would stop trying to explain what kind of green "heather" is and just fuckin' show it to ya. guess maybe that's like wishing that they might be able to tell ya 'xactly what they mean to say, hmm might be in trouble with this one. was wondering if a wish can't be granted do ya get another?

and ya know what else i'd wish for is for folks to stop being so darn greedy. gotta figure if folks didn't want more than they need then a whole lot less folks

would be getting fucked. another thing to think about is what we'd do in the fall if'n we didn't have to hunt politicians. would have to imagine for a moment, (yep this is a tough one), theiving bastards that they might be pretty alright folk and we wouldn't be wanting to hunt 'em down.

WWBD if asked how to write a love letter?

BF- writing one of them love letters is kinda like opening up one of them cans of nuts that has the springy snake in it that pops out at ya. ya know it's in there but ya open it anyways. believe it was ol' albert e. who said, only two stupid things are infinite: the universe and human stupidity, and i'm not so sure about the universe.

still wanting to go ahead with this? boy you are dumb, well, okay then, first things first. what you oughta be doin' is getting good and lickered up. yep, get yerself stinking drunk. cause if yer figuring to get yerself all tangled up with one of those female types. well brother good and lickered up is what ya wanna be most of the time. ya see it not only makes 'em look more pretty, but it makes 'em easier to deal with.

alrightiethen, presuming yer properly medicated. go on ahead and write down abunch of that lovey dovey stuff that you think she'll wanna read.

here's a tip for ya the more live stock references you can cram in there the better your changes are, (really, just trust me on this one). course though it might be that she's not even half as nice to look at as that sow that you won a blue ribbon with at the fair, so in that case you kinda might wanna hope that yer so drunk that yer writing looks like chicken scratch and she won't be able to read it anyhow. and how ya like me now?! you'll be off the hook, but if yer not drunk enough well than you'll probably figure to send her some flowers too, and well, dag, brother its yer funeral. Don't say i didn't warn ya.

contact: PMB 250 | 15105-D John J. Delaney Dr. | Charlotte, NC 28277

My Experiences on Drug Addiction

by Steve Farley, Pelixan Bay State Prison SHU

I can relate and understand the haunting shadows that our society and youth face today in this world of drug addiction. This epidemic has long existed throughout history. It has been the quiet demise of many before us. It's like the roots of an old oak tree that's long been embedded in the hearts and minds of our forefathers' generations that faced the same evils that go hand in hand with the masquerades of drug addictions.

I hope to share the raw realness of my story, the reader will hopefully gain a better understanding about the depths that drugs can traumatize and taint your life and its surroundings, and those who've been through these struggles and rose above its destructive ways, I salute you . . .

Even before I was born, my parents were going through the effects of drug addiction. It seemed in a sense it had become a hereditary thing passed down from my parents' parents. My father, who now is at peace (RIP), had committed suicide when I was at the young age of four. It has become a faded memory, but I, as an infant, had watched my own father blow his brains out in front of our trailer house door. My mother had left him from the constant abuse he inflicted on her, and after about eight years, she left him. Even his drug usage couldn't shield the sorrow it put on his soul when my mother left him. So the only peace he found was in the end of his sufferings . . .

My mother was a lovely soul, and in her own way meant the best for us, but someone who is a drug addict shows it in funny ways. Her way of dealing with life's adversaries came in the form of heroin. I remember me and my two brothers living wherever we could find a space to lie down at as my mother chased the dope sack. We lived anywhere from hotel rooms, other people's houses, on riverbanks bathing in the river. As a matter of fact, growing up in the care of my mother, we only had actually had our own apartment twice. We were always going where the dope connection was at, and depending on if she got the right amount of dope in her veins, she might be in a loving mood. I used to hate the fact I had to fight for my mother's affection and attention. Don't get me wrong, my mother loved us with all her heart and we knew this without a doubt. It's just that the drugs had made her dependent on them, and in these times, she wasn't herself, and as a child, I couldn't understand why she chose drugs over her own children, but I would come to understand the grasp it could have on a person's actions . . .

I remember when our SSI checks on every first of the month would run out she would get sick from not having money to come up on a fix. So we would go out in front of stores and make "Will Work For Food" or money signs and hustle up some money for our mother. I remember hating to see my mother like this and I would try to do anything I could do to get her a fix, because when she had her fix, everything was all good!

I hated all the men she would get with. How these strange fools would try to act like my father. It seemed like every man she got with would do the same old thing in all her relationships with men, beating on her every day — a couple of times she would get beat on so bad she would be laid out on the floor and we would run up scared that our mom was dead and she would whisper to us, "Shhh, I'm playing dead so he'll leave me alone, honey." When this would happen, we would jump on him and try to save our mom from another beating. We learned easy that a drug addict's hardened heart has no mercy on children. We would get whooped with belt buckles, wire hangers, anything in hand's reach. I remember as a kid wishing they always had dope, because

> I remember when our SSI checks on every first of the month would run out she would get sick from not having money to come up on a fix. So we would go out in front of stores and make "Will Work For Food" or money signs and hustle up some money for our mother. I remember hating to see my mother like this and I would try to do anything I could do to get her a fix, because when she had her fix, everything was all good!

contact: 275 Ninth St. | San Francisco, CA 94103.

when they had dope, that means they wouldn't fight, and when they wouldn't fight we weren't always scared

We hardly ever had any food or clothes when I was growing up. We would always go to the Salvation Army for clothes. I remember hating having to wear old hand-me-down clothes and the hands of poverty's despair. It was like a scar that wouldn't go away. The constant fear, depression and sorrow that drug addiction had brought upon our youthful hearts.

I remember looking forward to the third of every month. This is the time when me and my brother's SSI checks would come rolling in. We all got happy. My mother's whole personality would brighten up knowing for at least two weeks she would be able to get her fix. We loved it because she would take us places, buy us things. We would go into the store and she would say, get whatever you want boys. Us running around with grins on our faces picking out our favorite candy while she got a couple of cartons of smokes and some good ol' cheap man's wine. It was those times when her eyes would look sleepy, that slowed speech and the beads of sweat on her brow. When she was in a sense of tranquility then we knew everything was gonna be okay for a while.

This would never last though; it never did and once the dope ran dry so did her attitude, always falling into depression getting angry over the smallest things. I remember a couple of dark moments when she was in an abusive relationship and didn't have dope she would fall so deep into her pit that she would threaten to commit suicide as my father had done. I think it was these experiences that led me down the same cycling path of drug addiction.

The User and The Used

The "used" is what my old lady quickly turned me into, not that I cared about putting up too much of a fight in those days. The "user" is someone who casually uses. I think everyone tries dope, or does it every now and again with their friends. Going to a party not really looking for it but it being there so they do a little to have fun. The user can do it just long enough to not get hooked with it becoming a dependency that he or she needs it to function properly or get by. Even though the user doesn't become dependant on it to live, it always imbeds its roots within some depth of your life, eventually showing its wrath.

Me becoming the used, I couldn't resist its daily temptations. Going from just doing it a day or two out of the week, to doing an eight ball by the time I was fourteen on a daily basis. The more I used, the more malcontent I would get towards my family. The more

I used, the more depressed I would feel when I was coming down and didn't have it to numb my demons. I couldn't think right when I wasn't high because I was always angry and frustrated about all the drama that was going on around me. I needed my old lady's high so I wouldn't have to confront and deal with the psychological trauma that my father's demise had inflicted upon my young soul.

So I took the easy way out! I started roaming the streets more and more, getting involved with my neighborhood clique that would lead to violence, robberies, home invasions, to support my old lady and her evil ways. It was then that I had turned into the "used." She strips you of your morals and values, lowering you and your pride to as low as she commands you to do so. I was stealing from anyone to support my habit. Age didn't matter — old or young, if you had something I wanted, I was taking it. Family or relatives it didn't matter — my old lady makes sure she numbs all areas of feeling. Her ways are ominous beyond any human understanding unless you've been the used . . . She (drugs) will turn family members into enemies. She will turn a respectable woman into the next hooker, turning tricks, selling her body for the next fix. She will take the food from an infant's mouth. She loves to spread dirty diseases. She makes people lose their minds from her mastered skills of deception. She poisons your soul, casting a paranoia over your mind, thinking no one understands you besides her. Everything and everyone else is there for being against you.

I think about all the times hearing about another homie's overdose. The homeboy who was found OD'd in the park. My dawg getting stabbed to death over a twenty-dollar dope debt. My sister-in-law's overdose and the image of my mother giving her CPR to keep her breathing, realizing she would be dead two minutes later. I tripped off how I was getting high with her one minute having a blast and the next feeling scared and stunned that she was actually dead. I remember getting shot at one time while I was breaking into someone's house trying to come up on someone's dope. I remember tripping off all this and the thought of a black widow jumped into my mind one night while me and one of the homeboys were tweeking, talking about one of the homeboy's overdosing and how we missed him.

A black widow is kind of like speed or drugs, period. It has a dark nature but possesses a beauty at the same time. It is a master at deception, tricking her prey into its web of entrapment, always patiently waiting for its next victim, and that's the day I started calling my dope the "black widow." She tainted my young childhood. I did things and said things that I never would have done or said without the black widow. I was loyal to her as she left me broken, shredded of all dignity, prideless, crippled on the pavement, a hopeless soul as I wandered about, chasing her shadow, longing to feel the numbness of her glass passions.

The black widow wasn't able to totally consume my soul, and I now am thankful for the safety of these prison walls — even though in the beginning when I first got locked up in prison, I did a little heroin to try to substitute my high of speed, which was hard to get back then. I hated it and was able to be put in an environment without her potent grasp, and this gave me the opportunity to open my eyes to her true demise. Many people have to really look in the face of death before they realize the face they're looking into could be their own if they continue down her destructive path. I turned against family and friends when all they were trying to do was help me; I hurt people and robbed them just to be able to feel her high. She played me with the Hepatitis C virus. This is how wicked she is: while she destroyed my young life, I sat back and tried to justify the means, asking, "What did she do for me?"

Now that I am cleansed of her poison, I can sit back and view it from a clear perspective. I'm trying to pick up the pieces of my life that she scattered through my memories. Even though free of drugs and the black widow's influence, she still found ways to bring me down. My mother, who I loved with all my soul, regardless, was found dead of an overdose two years ago (RIP). Losing my mother truly shattered the essence of my being to the core. These drugs took my parents from me and it tore me up to know that I was continuing this cycle of evil. I'm only in my early twenties and I've seen many homies and homegirls die due to her ways. Above all, I've outlived both my parents, and all it took was twenty-three years to do it. Even though I made it through those dark moments of my mother's death and faced these demons in the eye, I can't help but wonder who really wins in the end if the drugs continue to pass from hand to hand.

I struggle with these thoughts every day, but all I can do is take it day-by-day. I'm living a clean life and will continue to do so, not only for me, but for my lost loved ones who would want to see me live me life clean and free of drugs and their ominous ways. While it's a constant fight confronting your demons as an addict, it is truly a fight worth fighting for.

Our society today is being plagued with the greed for money, which manifests into drugs and violence. Our children are being raised by a cycle of addicts that's neverending. With this lack of parental guidance, they slowly build their morals and values off the facades of a TV screen. Our media has no conscience as it decays the minds of our youth with the widespread promotion of sex, drugs, and violence. Only through the parents of today leading by example, becoming positive active role models within our youths' lives, can we flush out the deep-rooted seed that has, for generations, imbedded its roots into the core of our humanity.

A Drug Policy

A drug policy. This is a very difficult and complex problem, which I don't claim to have the answer to. All I can do is express my thoughts on a drug policy through my own recovery as an addict.

I don't think imprisonment works in the way it did for me with most individuals. There have been efforts put forth by the system, though, by trying to give an addict open opportunities like drug programs before prison terms. I also think most drug programs fail in their attempts to recover an addict because they have no true dedication in sticking with the addict through hard times. As I like to say, you can take the drug away from the addict, but the addiction never leaves, always lingering in the back of an addict's instincts.

So in my view, I think recovery from drug use is each to his own, but there are three steps that I think you must take if someone is gonna stay drug free and away from its destructive dependency. These three factors are as follows:

Wanting to really change:
You have to come to that point where you really and sincerely want to change with all your heart and mind. Not because you don't like being locked up, not because others want you to, but because you want to overcome this sickness that has plagued your life and made you dependent upon it just to get b. You have to be tired of suppressing the pain and the struggles with the false realities drugs put you in. You have to be ready to put all you got into exposing your past and present, confronting your demons with the seriousness it takes to understand your fears and reasons for turning to dope for all your answers. Once you can do this, it's the first of many steps in recovery . . .

Uncovering the depth of your issues:
You have to face your issues in the eye! Travel back in your memories and deal with your pain by opening up those old scars that were concealed by drug addiction. Come to understand why you used and how it kept ahold of you for so long. Understand your feelings and explore their reasons for your sorrow and how you can turn them into a positive growing process. Let yourself be vulnerable to being hurt if it helps you deal with the child abuse, neglect, poverty, lack of love, whatever, you've gone through in life. Once you can channel these

emotions and learn to be a peace with them, you're well on your way to kicking drugs to the curb.

A positive environment and positive people:
Once you've gained the tools to face your reasons for using and built the dedication it takes to overcome this addiction, that's a big step on your way to a drug-free life, but, in a way, it's only a small part of the long road ahead. Just as you've lived your life in building up your habit, it's gonna take even longer to overcome those temptations when times are hard. It will be a long process in learning to not hold onto your problems and fall back into your old ways when confronting a stressful situation. There will always be times when life is extra hard and you feel like giving in to you trials and tribulations, but you got to remind yourself that in anything you do, you're going to face these struggles sooner or later. It's learning to find ways within yourself to keep your head up and know that it only makes you a stronger person in dealing with those problems and coming out of them with your head held high because you faced and overcame them on your own.

Disconnect yourself from old friends who are addicts, or anything that has to do with the cycle of drugs — gangs, violence, and even any family that hasn't stopped his or her drug use. Even though it's a loved one, they're not themselves while under the influence, and can try to pull you back into that lifestyle. Surround yourself with a positive environment and living area. These positive aspects will help you maintain the desire to overcome drugs.

These are some of the many things you can do to break the hold drugs have had on your life. It is possible — you just got to want to change. I don't believe in programs, though as I said before, it's each unto his own on the passage to true recovery. It's a hard road, but life is too special to waste away in the darkness of drugs. In the end, you and only you can decide your fate. People will help you in your recovery but no one can change you but yourself!

Only through this generation's actions to stand fast and face this epidemic with strength and dedication that it must take to beat this battle of addiction to drugs. If we don't, this cycle will never stop giving me the doubt that we may, in our own individual recovery, water down the problem, but I fear we will never flush out its seed that has rooted itself within the cycle of life! ★

Vice-Grips*: ENEMY OF BIKE-KIND!

ALLRIGHT, KIDDIES, LISTEN UP! I DON'T KNOW IF ALL PLACES ARE LIKE THIS, BUT, SOMEHOW THE GENERAL CYCLING POPULATION OF NEW ORLEANS HAS GOTTEN THE IDEA THAT THE ONLY TOOL THAT YOU EVER NEED TO FIX YOUR BIKE IS A PAIR OF VICE-GRIPS. THESE MIS-INFORMED D.I.Y. MECHANICS SOME- TIMES EVEN RIDE AROUND WITH A PAIR OF VICE-GRIPS CLAMPED ONTO TO SEATPOSTS. GOOD THEIR SURE, BUT, THERE'S STYLE, A PROBLEM, SEE:

GRRR!! I KILL YOU BIKE! I MANGLE YOUR AXLE NUTS!! AARRRR!!!!

9 TIMES OUT OF TEN, THEY ARE THE WRONG TOOL!!!

VICE GRIPS ARE MEANT FOR REMOVING STRIPPED, THREADED, OR OTHER-WISE STUCK BOLTS. **PERIOD!!** OFTEN THE REASON CROSS- STRIPPED IN THE FIRST PLACE NUTS & PEOPLE USING VICE GRIPS ON NUTS ARE CRUSH STUFF. HENCE THE IS FROM COMMUNITY BIKE PROJECT THEM. THEY POINT WHERE WE WERE LOCK- NAME. AT THE **USE A WRENCH!!!** IDEALLY A IT GOT TO THE ING THEM UP.

NON-ADJUSTABLE ONE THE SAME SIZE AS YOUR NUT/BOLT.

OKAY, WORD! - ETHAN °⁴/₀₃

* OR, AS THEY ARE KNOWN IN NEW ORLEANS, "GRIP-PLIERS".

contact: 621 N. Rendon | New Orleans, LA 70119

by Josher

When Fred Left town,

HE LEFT ME WITH SO MUCH MORE THAN A CAN OF REFRIED BEANS IN the PANTRY AND THAT POUND OF TOFU IN the FRIDGE. NO, THERE WAS SOMETHING MORE, I REALIZED AS I DRAGGED MY FEET ON the WET PAVEMENT, WALKING TO the POST OFFICE. NO NO, HE LEFT ME WITH the MOST ABSOLUTELY FANTASTIC INFERIORITY COMPLEX. I DON'T MEAN THAT IN A BAD WAY... ODDLY ENOUGH. ✳

BUT I WAS FEELING DOWNTRODDEN AS HELL, AND the DREARY WEATHER REFLECTED THAT, EMBRACING ME IN ITS GREY SKIES AND WHISPERING WINDS. FRED HELPED ME TO ADMIT TO MYSELF THAT, YES, I AM DEPRESSED. FOR SO LONG I WAS AFRAID TO DO THAT, BECAUSE A LOT OF NORMAL PEOPLE AND MAINSTREAM PSYCHOLOGY-TYPES SEEM TO THINK THAT BEING A PUNK ROCKER IS A SYMPTOM OF DEPRESSION OR MENTAL ILLNESS. TRUTH IS, PUNKS ARE JUST MORE SUSCEPTIBLE TO DEPRESSION BECAUSE WE CARE ABOUT & THINK ABOUT ALL the EVILS IN THIS WORLD, INSTEAD OF BEING APATHETIC & SIMPLY LYING DORMANT. WE'RE MORE SENSITIVE.

LIKE I SAID, I WAS FEELING DOWNTRODDEN AS FUCK, AND IT WASN'T JUST CUZ I WAS SAD THAT FRED WAS GONE. SEE, FOR SO LONG I'VE BEEN WANTING TO LIVE THIS EMPOWERED LIFESTYLE; THIS ACTIVIST LIFE, AND FOR YEARS I'VE BEEN TAKING BABY STEPS TOWARD THAT GOAL, ALWAYS LOOKING FOR OTHER PEOPLE TO HELP ME. AND HERE FRED WAS— JUST LIVING the LIFE. HE HAD NO COMPLAINTS ABOUT IT, NO QUESTIONS, NO PROBLEMS WITH IT.

HE WAS JUST DOING IT.

contact: 2915 Kenmore Ave I Dayton, OH 45420

HE HAD SO MUCH SELF CONTROL;

WAS SO DISCIPLINED. HE HAD BOUNDLESS ENERGY. WHEN THE MAN WANTED SOMETHING DONE, HE FUCKING DID IT. HE DIDN'T BITCH ABOUT IT OR ANYTHING. HE COULD TAKE A CHORE LIKE TAKING THE RECYCLE TO THE DUMPSTER ACROSS TOWN, AND MAKE IT SEEM LIKE AWESOME PROJECT- A 10 MILE EXCURSION TO LISTEN TO HANGCORE AND SMASH BOTTLES. HE WASN'T AFRAID TO ASK FOR HELP, OR GO OUT IN PUBLIC, OR ASK A PRETTY WAITRESS FOR SOME NAPKINS. MAYBE HE DID HAVE TEN+ YEARS ON ME; BUT STILL, GIVEN THAT TIME & EXPERIENCE, I DON'T KNOW IF I COULD BE LIKE THAT.

AND DID I MENTION THAT FRED WAS SMART, TOO? SHIT, FRED SEEMED TO KNOW EVERYTHING ABOUT EVERYTHING ABOUT EVERYTHING, ESPECIALLY MUSIC. HE COULD NAME LINE-UPS OF BANDS FROM THE '30s THAT I NEVER EVEN KNEW EXISTED. THEN HE'D SWITCH GEARS AND TALK ABOUT JAPANESE POWER VIOLENCE, AND WITHOUT MISSING A BEAT COMPARE IT TO '60s GARAGE ROCK, AND THEN RELATE THAT TO (::GASP!::) TECHNO, OR SOME EQUALLY UNPUNK FORM OF ELECTRONIC MUSIC. → BUT HIS KNOWLEDGE WAS BY NO MEANS SUPERFICIAL. LIKE I SAID, HE KNEW EVERYTHING ABOUT EVERYTHING — BOOKS, MOVIES, SPORTS, HISTORY, GARDENING, GROUNDHOGS... FUCKING NAME IT.

BUT HE WAS GONE IN A FLASH, AND I WAS

LEFT TO WONDER IF HE'D EVER EVEN EXISTED. AND WHEN I GOT TO THE POST OFFICE, MY MAILBOX WAS EMPTY. ERG-A-LERG, ALL THIS WAY IN THE RAIN FOR NOTHIN'. BUT I THOUGHT OF FRED, AND HOW HE'D HAVE SAID SOMETHING LIKE, "BUT IT WAS GOOD EXERCISE! AND YOU GOT TO LOOK THOSE HUMONGOUS HOLLY BUSHES THAT DON'T GROW TO BE TREE-SIZED IN MY PART OF THE COUNTRY!" AND, THOUGH I'M TALKING ABOUT HIM LIKE HE'S DEAD, I JUST HOPE THAT PASSING TIME DOESN'T MAKE HIS INFLUENCE LESS POTENT. HE WAS THE MOST FASCINATING PERSON I'D EVER MET IN MY WHOLE LIFE. HE MADE ME WANT TO TRY HARDER TO BE A BETTER PERSON.

BUT WHERE DO I START....... ✖

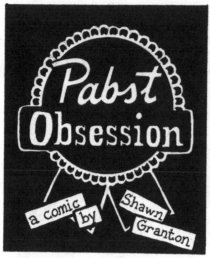

Pabst Obsession

a comic by Shawn Granton

I FIND MYSELF LIVING IN *PORTLAND* (OREGON, OF COURSE!) THE FABLED "CITY OF ROSES." THIS TOWN IS GREAT N' ALL, BUT THERE'S ONE THING THAT STILL HAS ME PUZZLED: *WHAT'S THE DEAL WITH PABST BLUE RIBBON?*

THIS CITY (OR TO BE MORE SPECIFIC, THIS CITY'S PUNK/INDIE/HIPSTER/MOD/ ROCKERS/ZINESTER/CARTOONIST/FILL IN THE BLANK *CROWD*) HAS SUCH A FIX-ATION ON THIS PUNGENT PILSNER. BARS ARE RATED ACCORDING TO HOW CHEAP YOU CAN BUY PABST IN IT!

The Jockey Club - $1.50 a pint

TO ME, PABST IS JUST ANOTHER CHEAP, PISSWATER BEER. I DON'T CARE FOR PISSWATER BEERS. MAYBE IT'S DUE TO MY "REFINED PALETTE," BUT I TEND TO STICK TO MICROBREWS. AND THERE'S SO MANY GOOD BEERS IN THE PACIFIC NORTHWEST! BUT ASK A DIE-HARD PABST DRINKER WHY *PBR* * AND NOT A LOCAL BEER AND HERE'S WHAT YOU'LL GET:

* Pabst Blue Ribbon.

Man, fuck that pretentious bourgeois "micro-brew" shit. Pabst is union-made beer brewed for the working class! It was selected as "America's Best" in 1893!

YEAH, PABST IS MADE "BY THE PEOPLE, FOR THE PEOPLE." BUT SINCE WHEN HAVE *YOU* BEEN *WORKING CLASS?* DID YOUR PARENTS (OR YOU, FOR THAT MATTER) EVER WORK IN A FACTORY, ON A FARM, OR IN CON-STRUCTION? OR IS DRINKING PBR YOUR WAY OF "SHOWING SOLIDARITY" WITH BLUE COLLAR FOLK? DOES PABST = THE MASSES?

contact: Shawn Granton/Ten Foot Rule | PO Box 14185 | Portland, OR 97182-0185

WHAT I FIND FUNNY (OR IRONIC, IF THAT TERM *HASN'T* BEEN DRIVEN INTO THE GROUND AT THIS POINT) IS THE DAYTIME BEHAVIOR OF MR./MS. "WORKING CLASS" WHEN THEY ENTER ONE OF THE CITY'S NUMEROUS COFFEEHOUSES:

Can I have a White Mocha with Soy Milk, Half-Caf? And can you make it iced?

OR, IS IT BECAUSE SOMEONE SOMEWHERE DECIDED THAT PABST WAS GOING TO BE THE "HIP" BEER OF THE "IN" CROWD, AND IT CAUGHT ON? IF THAT'S THE CASE, I HOLD *OLYMPIA, WASHINGTON*, THE EPICENTER OF THE ÜBER-HIP, ACCOUNTABLE (DESPITE NO EVIDENCE TO BACK UP MY CLAIM.)

Perfect! This'll fit in with the whole "Ironic White Trash" look!

"PBR"

GRASS GAS or ASS Nobody rides for free!

The Evergreen State College

Born to Ride

AAH, WHAT DO I KNOW? I'VE BEEN KNOWN TO DRINK PBR FROM TIME TO TIME. HELL, IT'S DIRT CHEAP! THOUGH, IF GIVEN THE CHOICE, I'D DRINK *OLYMPIA*. YEAH, I DO REALIZE IT'S PRETTY MUCH THE SAME AS PABST (MADE BY THE SAME COMPANY, NO LESS), BUT THEY COME IN THOSE CUTE LI'L BOTTLES (STUBBIES) THAT HAVE WORD PUZZLES ON THE CAP!

SHAME

BUT STILL *WHY* PABST, AND NOT *HAMM'S*, FOR INSTANCE? WHAT IS THE PARTICULAR NOVELTY IN PBR? IS IT BECAUSE IT CAN'T BE FOUND EVERY-WHERE? IS IT BECAUSE OF THE TASTE? IS IT BECAUSE THEY USE "ONLY THE FINEST OF HOPS AND GRAINS"?

IN-DUL-GENCE

MAYBE IT'S DEEPER THAN THAT? MAYBE PABST THEMSELVES IS BEHIND IT ALL? DID THEY FIND AN ANGLE TO GET THEIR PRODUCT CONSUMED BY A DEMOGRAPHIC NOT SWAYED* BY TRADITIONAL ADVERTISING? TOO FAR FETCHED? THEN WHY DID MY FRIEND NICOLE GET A LETTER FROM PABST'S MARKETING DEPT. ASKING ABOUT AD RATES? *HOW* DID THEY FIND OUT ABOUT HER?

Dude! I write a *"Personal"* Zine!

*Okay, maybe I'm giving too much credit here

I THINK THE BEST ARGUMENT FOR PABST CONSUMPTION COMES FROM MY FRIEND PAUL, WHO SUMS IT UP SO:

DUDE, IF YOU'RE GOING TO DRINK SHITTY BEER, IT MIGHT AS WELL BE THE CHEAPEST! BESIDES, THEY ALL TASTE ALIKE!

granton ✶ aug 2002

AMEN, BROTHER! I'LL DRINK TO THAT!

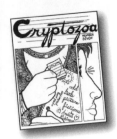

Cryptozoa

by Androo Robinson

She's kept a journal for most of her life. When she broke her right hand in a gardening mishap (don't ask), she was obliged to switch to the left for a while.

She discovered, to her surprise, that her left hand harbored a rich inner life she knew nothing about.

When we were kids, my cousin showed me the imperfectly preserved skeleton of a gnome he'd found in his mom's garden. This resolved the question of magic for me; if a thing could die, it was real.

Years later I discovered that he'd fabricated the whole thing from tiny bones and toy fragments, but this simple prank enriched my life more than any other work of art I've encountered since.

contact: 2000 NE 42 Ave #303 • Portland, OR 97213

Drank Too Much in Milwaukee

DEFINATELY NOT RICKI RICCARDO
BY CHRISTIAN

Poison and Quiet Riot played at Summerfest a couple years back, they had a ride that costs $25 to get on and it looked like fun. Six or so wine coolers later (they were cheap) and being excited by Poison's version of rock'n'roll, I told the guy who ran the ride that "I'm the drummer for Poison, Rikki Rocket, we just got done playing and I would like to go on this ride now." Fully expecting rejection, he stopped the ride, brought me and my friend Ruby to the front of the line, and strapped us in. While we were trying to hold back laughs, waiting for the ride to start, two kids came running up with Cds and asked me to sign them. I really wanted to go on the ride and not blow my cover, so I signed the kids Cds. I think I signed Rikki Rachman instead of Rikki Rocket, being drunk and everything. The ride was fantastic.

FEARED WORLDWIDE
BY MARKCHEREK

My friend "The Gouge" is in the merchant marines. Originally from Milwaukee, he's been in Williamsburg for the past, I don't know, eight years. Anyway, that's beside the point, a couple of years ago he's in Singapore on shore leave. Drinkin in some shitty, wharf, sailor dive (think Tom Waits). So he's sitting there minding his drink, missing his girl, when the bar door flings open and some nasally, loudmouth, little, Texas dick walks in exclaiming, "I'LL DRINK ANY OF YOU MOTHERFUCKERS UNDER THE TABLE!" Nobody says anything. The Gouge leans forward, to look down the bar and back, to see if there are any takers... Pushes himself upright in the stool and gruffs, "I'm in". The Texan gets right up in his face and asks, "WHERE YOU FROM"? "Milwaukee". Says, Gouge flatly. The Texan takes a step back, points and shouts, "I'M NOT DRINKIN WITH YOU"!!!

THE END!

...and then there was much rejoicing.

BACKSTAGE PASS... PASS OUT
BY CHRISTIAN

At Motorhead at the Rave, I told the bouncer that I was in the first band, Havichate. He said he had just started, so he let me backstage. I got to watch Motorhead from on the stage. After five songs or so, I decided to see what the dressing rooms were like, so I walked in to find Anthrax sitting on the sofa, talking and drinking. I gave the head nod and went to their buffet table and proceeded to eat their food. After a while, a bouncer asked to see my pass. I told him it was in my dressing room. He responded by telling me I have to leave and escorted me out. I took a turn into the bar, drank one of my "free" drinks, then sat outside and waited for everyone else to get outside.

contact: iliketodrawpictures@hotmail.com

Fish Piss

Twenty-Five Irrefutable Arguments for the Superiority of Vinyl
by Ian McGillis

1.) Records just SOUND better. Don't argue, okay? They just do.

2.) Twenty years after the egregious imposition of CDs, people still say "record store," even when the store in question has no actual records.

3.) No one has ever sat staring for hours at a CD cover.

4.) Remember when double albums used to be configured with sides one and four on one record, and sides two and three on the other, so you could listen to concept albums like Tommy in sequence with a stacker, even though hardly anybody used stackers? That was so cool.

5.) Yes, records sometimes skipped, but the possibility of their skipping added a certain frisson to the listening experience.

6.) Records were much more often defective than CDs. That meant you would go back to the record store, talk to actual human beings(often about music)and end up buying more records.

7.) Some label logos (Vertigo, UNI, Charisma) were actually designed to do neat swirly things as you watched them spin. This meant that suburban children born too late for the 60s could approximate the LSD experience, with none of the brain-frying risks, in the safety of the rumpus room.

8.) The Ohio Players' sequence of album covers in the 70s. I'll say no more on this matter.

9.) True aficionados could learn to recognize different import vinyl BY SMELL. British pressings had a certain liquorice-like scent, German was more oily. There was a Raspberries album that smelled, a bit too strongly perhaps, of raspberries. CDs, lamely, have no smell at all.

10.) Carrying records on a windy day, you had to hold them at just the right angle.

11.) I once bought a Jamaican 45 (Uptown Top Ranking, Althea and Donna, Joe Gibbs label) that had a piece of hemp accidentally pressed right into the vinyl. That just would not happen with a CD, and the world is a poorer place for it.

12.) Walking around on the street or at school with unbagged albums, you were making a statement about yourself to the world. Carrying a Kraftwerk album, for example, said "I am the possessor of dark Teutonic secrets. You really should consider sleeping with me." CDs are more like business cards. Boring.

13.) The liner notes in a CD booklet are so fucking small you can't even read them half the time.

14.) The vinyl LP was an organic artifact. It aged in interesting ways. If you wanted it to sound good, you had to take care of it. It was almost like a pet. CDs don't DO anything. They'll be choking up landfills until eternity.

15.) Who didn't love the tactile, diamond-cutter delicacy of placing a tone arm on a record? You felt, in a very small way admittedly, that you were part of the creative process.

16.) Two words: gatefold sleeves. (Often with paintings of vaguely Tolkienesque tableaux. Even boogie bands like the Allman Brothers did this.)

17.) Somehow, punk rock has just never looked right or sounded right on CD. Admit it, all you punks. There's just something inherently non-snotty about the CD format. The same goes for reggae. The mere idea of reggae on CD is ridiculous.

18.) The poster of Bob Dylan with psychedelic hair, included in his Greatest Hits LP, is a high-water mark of 20th century culture. So is the Mothership poster included in P-Funk's double live album.

19.) What would kids in the 70s have covered their bedroom walls and the inside of their lockers with if they hadn't had those Dark Side Of the Moon posters and stickers?

20.) Record store clerks used to look a bit like rock stars sometimes. They weren't always geeks, that's historical distortion.

contact: Louis Rastelli | Box 1232 Place d'Armes | Montreal Que. H2Y 3K2 | Canada

21.) Warped records made cool woozy sounds. Some music (my brother's Yes albums) sounded better when the record was warped.

22.) Two words: backward masking. (Everybody denies it, lots of people did it.)

23.) There was so much scope for righteous snobbery with vinyl. You could show your superior commitment by buying accessories like inner sleeves, outer sleeves, dust brushes, anti-static spray. (Alternatively, you could melt records down into ashtrays and expressionist sculptures influenced by those Dali and Munch prints you saw in art class.)

24.) If you weren't careful you could get a nasty paper cut opening a new album. That meant feeling like you had passed a small test of courage and could listen to your new album with an extra sense of entitlement. CDs are such a pain in the ass to open that by the time you're done you're too pissed off to listen to them.

25.) Don't even get me started on downloading.

From Brooklyn to Balata

From Joseph and Sean

June 25, 2003 9:00 pm, Balata Refugee Camp

Dear Friends,

I have been here five days and I am not adjusted to seeing soldiers with guns pointed at people trying to go home, crossing a checkpoint across a road in their country.

Here is what I learned:

Palestine has a gun held to its heart. Tanks, APCs, jeeps, hummers, f-16, Apaches, checkpoints, new road blocks daily, settlers, snipers, bulldozers, colonial kids with guns, all of it one big gun, the heart of Palestine in the crosshairs, the finger of Occupation caressing the waiting trigger. Today, and yesterday no one is allowed to leave Nablus if you live in Nablus, and no one is allowed into Nablus unless you live here.

We woke up at 4 am today to try and make it to a nearby village before the soldiers could block the road; we were going to start clearing the 8 or 9 road blocks cutting the village off from the surrounding area. Around 5 am after walking for a while on the early morning sand roads we came across a large APC. They told us the internationals could pass, the Palestinians with us could not. The soldier said he knew we are not a part of the "conflict," that our Palestinian friends are not a part of the "conflict," but orders are orders. We went back to Balata, tired and disappointed.

Today we approached Aseria checkpoint, walking over a hill in the searing midday sun when up the hill, from around the bend, on the dusty dirt road came a hummer. It stopped sixty feet from us and two soldiers got out immediately yelling at us in Hebrew. We told them we did not understand. They told us to walk forward and give them our I.D.s and we turned around ignoring their shouts, trying to avoid being detained. A Palestinian man who walked forward with us walked towards the soldiers and gave them his I.D., after several minutes he was released and turned around following us up the hill. Their guns were aimed at us the whole time, their angry words pressed on our backs like the black hole barrels of their weapon, like the uninterrupted sun. I have not gotten used to this yet. I constantly fight my urge born from heavy exchanges with NYPD to do what the soldiers say. I constantly have to remind myself,

overcoming the slowly churning mess of my stomach, that, as an international, I can ignore them to a point.

Later in the day we went to Biet Iba; another checkpoint hemming in this ancient city. No one was allowed past the young Israeli soldiers in drab green, hidden behind squat concrete checkpoint huts, squinting through sniper sights at old ladies fainting in the sun trying to get home from the city with small children hanging on wind worn fingers. Again they called for our identification, again we walked away hoping to be useful here in the future.

Here in this prison city the old walls raise up to the unforgiving sun, the dust of history filling the cracks between the ancient stones. When you see the market center here tucked into the alleys that have held vegetable stalls, butchers and clothing shops for centuries you understand why this war of erasure against the Palestinian people is so centered on land. These homes, these places of worship, these shops are all heritage, they are not the same as contemporary U.S. homes made of plastic and concrete, ready for resale, release, re-rent. These are centers of community, homes, and hearts. There is a bulldozer at the front door of these homes, the gnarled metal teeth crusted with the dust of broken history and the dried blood of family legacy are paid for with U.S. dollars, my dollars.

Later in the afternoon we went to Huwara checkpoint (the same one I was turned away from five days ago). The checkpoint was closed when we arrived but through some negotiation with the captain we got it open for people headed into the city with Nablus I.D.s and headed out with outer lying village I.D.s. The negotiation took a little while. We had to deal with a soldier who was holding a bullhorn up to people's ears and shouting into it to go away. He also walked over to a cab and was about to plunge his knife into the tire when we and several Palestinians intervened. This soldier continued to pull his gun up keeping it at chest level with everyone he was talking with, yelling at. This one soldier is not an exception; he seems to be the heavier end of the rule. We have encountered some soldiers a little more sympathetic and hating their jobs, but doing it nonetheless.

I met a young man here who has one year left to study at Bier Ziet University. He is studying science. He is a refugee; he wants his land back, a single

Palestinian state. He wants his families land back. He hasn't been to university in three years, it's a thirty-minute drive but he can't get there.

The gun is cocked; Israel's finger is playfully tugging the trigger. Every night there is the hum of drones flying across the star full sky. Every night a family's house is occupied nearby, every day we wake up to new roadblocks. Here the gun is pressed lightly against Palestine's chest, pushing to the heart. The gun has bullets built on fifty–five years of evictions, land stealing, humiliation, torture, and murder.

I feel like this gun is fired every second, every moment there is the chance of death and the only thing shielding this heart is daily resistance, daily push to live and make a life. People continue to have tea with friends, study, argue, love and live. I am amazed, as my guts turn to nervous at the sight of a soldier walking towards me his gun swaying with his swagger. I am amazed by peoples' will to live and resist.

In Solidarity
Joseph Phelan

June 26th 2003, Balata Refugee Camp

Dear Friends

I've never seen anyone who'd been shot before, and to be honest, I can go a lifetime now without seeing it again. He was maybe fifteen years old, maybe a little older, I don't know, and when I saw him he was on the ground crowded by Shabob (local teenagers) who lifted him up on to their shoulders and rushed him to the ambulances that had gotten through the APCs and the tanks and then rushed him and the other boy away to the hospital. When it's rifles versus rocks, rifles win every time.

The boys had been throwing stones at an APC, a heavily armored small tank of sorts, that had parked itself at the end of Market St., where I am staying, for no reason I can understand. After about fifteen minutes of kids as young as eight throwing rocks at the APC, the soldiers fired two shots dropping two kids to the ground. There were no warning shots, no tear-gas, no rubber bullets - just two kids on their way to the hospital.

Joe said this earlier, but I've been thinking it since this happened. I'd like someone to explain to me how exactly a dozen kids with rocks are a danger to an Armored Personnel Carrier and deserved to be killed. I'd like someone to sit down and tell me honestly that they think any of this makes sense, or that any good will come of another couple Palestinian boys joining the masses already walking through Balata camp with scars that they show me when I go to the store, and ask me what Americans think of all this, and I have to say that most Americans don't care.

I leave Balata tomorrow; go past the same soldiers I've been arguing with for days, and head to Jerusalem. I will write again from there.

My love to you all,
Sean Sullivan

Girls Are Not Chicks Coloring Boook

by Jacinta Bunnell & Julie Novak

We pledge allegiance...

to all-girl bands, pro choice rallies, witchcraft and voodoo.

contact: PO Box 325 | Rosendale, NY 12472

Don't get trapped inside someone else's pumpkin.

glossolalia

What I remember ...
by Sarah McCarry

What I remember most about that week, the week we went back to war, was living with the awful knowledge that ten million voices in the streets of all the countries in the world meant nothing, that all our hope and rage and love meant nothing, all our organizing meant nothing, the largest protest in the history of the world meant nothing. Now, watching this pretend administration collapse into its own lies, we get a bitter little laugh out of it; but nothing will stop this nightmare. I fight for what I love now not because I think anything will change but because I have no other choice, because to let go of fighting means to let go of living. Because what I am fighting for matters. Such basic, basic things; love, safety, shelter, community.

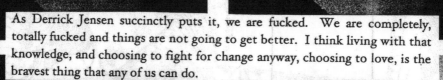

As Derrick Jensen succinctly puts it, we are fucked. We are completely, totally fucked and things are not going to get better. I think living with that knowledge, and choosing to fight for change anyway, choosing to love, is the bravest thing that any of us can do.

It's been hard lately to write things down. Little pictures and ramblings about crushes and bike rides seem hugely unimportant. But these are the stories I tell because these are the stories I know. Our stories may not shift power or change worlds but they are ours, all our voices combining to say *another world is possible, another life is possible*. All our voices combined may be only a whisper but even a whisper is something, even a whisper is more than silence. We tell each other stories and remind ourselves to be strong.

contact: 5711 NE 24th I Portland, OR 97211

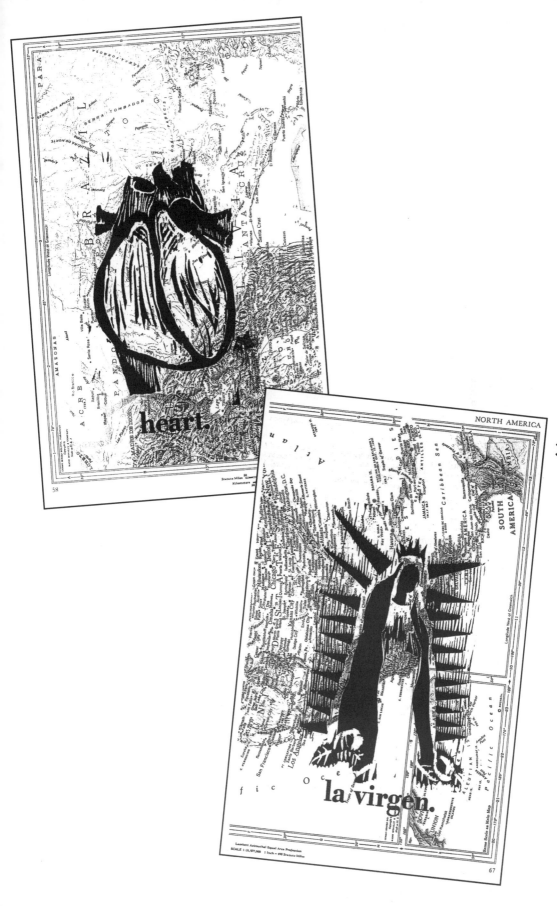

heart.

la virgen.

Tribute bands? What the f**k?

by Mike Falloon

Tribute bands?
*What the f**k!*
aka, A GM! Interview with
Russ Forster

Filmmaker Russ Forster has a knack for examining easy-to-ridicule subjects. With So Wrong They're Right, he chronicled the world of 8-track enthusiasts (see GM! #12). With his latest documentary, Tributary, he tackles an equally vulnerable subject: tribute bands. And again he's created a fascinating movie using humor, intelligence, and curiosity to show that there's more than meets the eye when it comes to tribute bands. And even when there's less, Tributary still entertains.

(Listed below are the four categories Forster devised to organize the bands presented in Tributary, along with the introduction from the movie. The interview follows. Questions by Mike Faloon.)

1. Post-modern tribute bands
"I call the first type of tribute bands in this video post-modern, because this type is extremely self-reflective, sometimes to the point of becoming an elaborate in-joke."

2. Working tribute bands
"Working tribute bands have gotten popular enough so that gigs are lucrative and common. They love the bands they tribute, but they are in it for the money as well."

3. Social tribute bands
"Social tribute bands are similar to working tribute bands if you substitute hanging out with friends for money. Some do make decent cash, but the emphasis is on community."

4. True love tribute bands
"Finally, true love tributes are the one which best live up to the name tribute. They are driven by a burning passion for the music and band they emulate and elevate those bands to the level of mentor. It's hard not to get caught up in their energy and enthusiasm."

(From the introduction to Tributary) *This is the weird, wild, and wonderful world of tribute bands, and welcome to it. Scoff if you will, but while shooting this video my opinion of the tribute band world completely changed. I used to think of tribute bands as degenerate off shoots of real music, a refuge for the unimaginative and untalented. Four years after embarking on this video adventure, I feel that tribute bands are a sincere if naive art form of their own. And, art form or not, they sure are a lot of fun, and nice people too, save for the Jim Morrisons and Eddie Van Halens I ran into. So brace yourself for an exhilarating ride with some backwards looking bands who are part of this culture's end of the century reassessing process.*

Go Metric: What initiated the project?
Russ Forster: Well, it was an idea from a friend of mine, Jean Lotus. She actually was co-editor of a magazine called *The White Dot* that was encouraging people to turn off their televisions sets. She had been going to see some tribute bands in Chicago, and was completely floored by a few of them. I think there was a Motorhead tribute and a Ramones tribute that particularly excited her. I had already finished *So Wrong They're Right*, the 8-track film, and a lot of people were giving me ideas about what my next project could be, so that was her idea. And actually the first few times she brought it up, I wasn't all that enthusiastic because it seemed that tribute bands were a suburban phenomenon that just wouldn't appeal to me. In the summer of '96 some friends and I went to a tribute band show that happened to be near their house in Chicago, it was an outdoor festival. There was an AC/DC tribute and there was a band called War Pigs, a Black Sabbath tribute, and the show completely blew me away. It was one of the weirdest experiences I ever had. It was the strangest mixture of old time rock'n'roll type people, middle aged rockers who are well past their prime. There was definitely this sort of trailer park aspect to it, too. I saw this one mother/daughter tag team where they were both interested in the same guy, battling each other for his attention. It was way beyond anything I'd ever seen

before, and the bands were just goofy. They didn't get it right exactly, but the audience didn't seem to care. It fascinated me. I thought, Wow, this really is a bit of Americana here, maybe not what most Americans would be proud of, but it was something quintessentially American. It sparked my interest in trying to do a project.

I was struck by how realistic a sense they have of what they're doing, and how they're perceived. One of the guys in one of the Rolling Stones bands was saying, My original songs were only okay, but these songs (by the Rolling Stones) are better. It's seldom that you hear musicians say anything less about their songs than, My stuff's amazing and the world just doesn't get it.

You're talking about the band Sticky Fingers, I think, in Los Angeles. They had a big effect on me too. They were an odd case, because they were in it for the money and they became pretty big. They still are playing around Los Angeles, and the last I heard they were commanding three or four thousand dollars a gig. They were on the cover of a bunch of musician magazines in the late 90s and became quite a big deal, became quite a symbol of what journalists started seeing as a trend. They had their sort of working ethic that was very appealing. They really wanted to make you feel that you were seeing the Rolling Stones circa 1972 in every way that they possibly could. And yet, they were clearly fans of the music. It wasn't just a put on; it wasn't just a day job. They were an amazing interview; they just went on for hours and hours. Actually, it was two members of the band Sticky Fingers that I ended up talking with the most. One was with his girlfriend and they were having sex in the bathroom so he was kind of preoccupied. Ironically enough, he's the Billy Wyman. It's one of these weird cases where the person kind of mimics the behavior of the person they're portraying. But the Keith Richards guy and the Mick Taylor guy, those two guys wanted to tell their story. They really wanted people to see them as something other than loser hacks. I think they did a really great job of portraying themselves as intelligent, dedicated musicians who are doing the Stones thing as sort of a job but, again, it's not out of desperation. They sort of fell into it and they really, honestly enjoyed what they were doing and wanted to do a really great job of it, and could make the house payments with the money they were making.

With *So Wrong They're Right*, you knew the people you were interviewing. With *Tributary*, you were getting to know the bands as you were interviewing them. Were there cases where you had to convince someone that you were sincerely documenting tribute bands and not making fun of them?

Surprisingly enough, the bands were extremely open to me for the most part. The only real trouble I had were the Jim Morrisons and the Eddie Van Halens I ran into. The Jim Morrisons seem to be completely out there; they thought they were Jim Morrison. They wanted contracts, they wanted to see raw footage, and they wanted the rights to re-edit, if necessary—all this crap. It was just unbelievable. I talked to one guy, I think he was with Soft Parade, in New York, I wish I had had the presence of mind to record that conversation because it was just

absolutely surreal and completely hilarious, although at the time I'm not sure I was catching the humor. I'd had such a good experience with all the bands I'd talked to up to that point. This Jim Morrison guy was absolutely impossible from the word go. It was just surreal that he could believe that he was channeling the spirit of Jim Morrison. One of the first things he said was he wasn't sure he wanted to be associated with the tribute band scene because he was getting ready to release a solo album that would be like the solo album Jim Morrison would have recorded had he lived long enough to do so. I was just like, Holy crap, this guy really is out there and not in a fun way. Then he got really demanding. He wanted to see all of the stuff I had already shot and he wanted all these stipulations about how he could change his segment in the film, and maybe other aspects of the film. At a certain point I was so in shock I just said, I don't think this is going to work out; there are other Jim Morrisons I could talk to.

That's such a funny phrase.

And the Van Halen thing, that I couldn't really get either. I don't know that much about Eddie Van Halen. I don't know if he is litigious himself, but the two Eddie Van Halens I talked to wanted contracts. The one, he wouldn't sign a release and he wanted a stipulation where I would use the footage only for my own personal use and I wouldn't use it in any other forum. So we ended up not being able to do any Van Halen. Those are the only bands that I got that from. Every other band was so willing to share everything and so willing to turn me on to other bands in the same city that I could talk to. There was no sense of competition, or very little that I came across.

That reminds me of the Kiss band who was saying that they didn't compare themselves to the other Kiss bands. They just want everyone to have a good time.

That was Dressed to Kill, I think. I wouldn't necessarily believe them 100% on that, they're a little more competitive than they let on. But basically, if you're a Kiss band, you're in a pretty good situation because Kiss fans are insatiable. They'll go to see Dressed to Kill and then if Strutter is playing the next weekend, they'll go see Strutter, too. Most of the fans of the Kiss bands that I saw could list off five or six Kiss bands that they'd seen; they cannot get enough Kiss.

It sounds like there were a lot of surprises in making *Tributary*. Are there others that haven't come up yet in our conversation?

Well, I never thought I would run into one Guided By Voices tribute band and now there are four on the West coast. I do sort of understand where that's coming from. I came up with the idea of true love tributes as a motivation, where you're just such a great fan of the band that it's sort of your way of being a fan, to play their music live. That seems to be the motivation for that kind of expression because none of the bands are getting huge audiences or making lots of money. But there is a social thing though, not only do you get to pay homage to your heroes, but it's sort of a convention—whenever a Guided By Voices tribute plays—of Guided By Voices fans. So in some ways you could make an argument that they fit into both of those categories (true love and social). The categories are sort of arbitrary, any of the bands could theoretically fit into any one of those categories. We were talking about stuff that blew me away, that changed my mind about what the tribute scene was like. I guess you could say the fact that you could come up with different categories for reasons for doing a tribute band was something that I didn't expect in the very beginning. When I started cutting the bands together I realized I felt more comfortable letting the bands talk for themselves, letting them contradict themselves and each other, and letting there be a certain amount of ambiguity, rather than trying to force fit these bands into these slots. I didn't want to be pedantic about the categories. So I threw them out, not half-heartedly, but as ideas to think about when you're watching the bands. I sort of expect the audience to sort their feelings out about, Well, is this a reasonable category, are the bands speaking toward this or are they not?

I love how the movie offers glimpses of so many bands. I especially like the self-effacing bands, like the Judas Priest band that said, We're #2, we're #2! Or, the Motley Crue band that talked about how they got their bio-rhythms matched up to the bio-rhythms of the original Motley Crue at the time they made *Too Fast for Love*—bands like that don't require additional comments.

I agree with that, and that's perhaps why I'm a little less present in *Tributary* than in *So Wrong They're Right* in some ways. And actually the issue of whether the filmmaker should be present in the film was one of the things that split me and the people I'd been working with in Chicago apart.* They were really strong about, No, should be presented as an objective view, and the bands have to be completely speaking for themselves. And I felt like, No, we sort of become experts on the topic and why shouldn't we put our two cents in? I think I wanted it to be a little more issue oriented to deal with questions like what is the difference between a symphonic orchestra interpreting the works of Beethoven and a tribute band interpreting the works of Led Zeppelin? Is there a difference? I wanted to deal with issues like that and where do you separate art and interpretation? Are the tribute bands less artists because they're interpreters other people's work?

Something you've said brings to mind Voodoo Child, the guy who does the Jimi Hendrix tribute. To me, he stuck out because he was saying stuff that made me wonder. Like, he claims to have been doing this band since 1968, and he knew Jimi Hendrix, and he said that Jimi wasn't all that good live—never heard that before. What was your take on him?

He is definitely a case of someone who is sort of, hmm, he's sort of lost himself in his character. I don't think he's as bad as the Jim Morrisons I was talking about, but I think he's a very intriguing character because it's almost like a split personality where you're talking with him and he seems very reasonable and he seems to understand that he's just a performer, an entertainer, and this is his shtick and that's pretty much the end of it. But then he starts to go into this whole thing about, well, I'm the only authentic Jimi Hendrix tribute and authenticity is what it's all about and I play left handed, and I do this and I do that. Then he starts talking about the spirit of Hendrix and hanging out with Hendrix, the conspiracy theories involving Hendrix. I started to realize, well, there are two guys here. There's a guy I can deal with who's pretty much on the same level as most of these other tribute bands. Then there's this other guy who's kind of gone off the deep end, but he would always come back. He would always go to the cliff's edge and you'd be thinking, I can't believe he's saying this, and then somehow he'd come right back and then he'd talk about, well, he was playing guitar with Cleopatra and he had these other side gigs. He's like an actor who's completely into his character, to the point where you could probably go up to him and say, Oh, Mr. Hendrix can you sign this autograph, and he'd sign 'Jimi Hendrix.'

Reminds me of an actor, who doesn't write their own material, interpreting someone else's written work. What's the difference between that and five

*At the start of the project, Forster was part of a group working on the documentary. The group split during the making of the movie. The rest of the group went on to complete a documentary called An Incredible Simulation.

guys who want to play *Sticky Fingers* or *Get Yer Ya Ya's Out* all the time.

Yeah, right, or even more intriguing is a band that does Devo as sort of this, what would I call it, almost guerilla art performance trying to get people to quit their jobs, and drop out of society. It's amazing to find bands that would go to that length, where they're almost talking in religious terms about it, educating audiences or converting audiences.

Is that Mongoloid you're talking about?

Yeah, Mongoloid is the band I was referring to. I don't think it's a post-modern thing with them. Yeah, they're in on the joke, and they understand that Devo was an elaborate joke, in a sense. But at the same time, there is

something about the message of Devo that really captures the singer, to the point where he sees himself as sort of a missionary for the band.

I didn't pick up on the extent to which he was invested like that.

It may be more subtle in the way it's edited than the way it was in talking with him. But he does talk about getting people to quit their jobs, he's not being completely facetious about that. Maybe a better example is the Guided By Voices band where they actually talk about evangelizing Guided By Voices and turning people onto Guided By Voices, as part of what they want to accomplish with the band.

At one point, they said they felt they did some of the songs better than the originals, which I thought was funny.

Most of the bands were too humble to go that far. It's sort of like stabbing Caesar to say that for most of these bands. It's kind of ironic that the band that says they're evangelizing for the band they're emulating, also commits the ultimate sacrilege of saying they do it better.

That reminds me of another great quote from the movie: We play Black Sabbath the way Black Sabbath would if we were them. These bands seemed to have a great sense of humor.

Yeah, that was very appealing, just the down to earth-ness, the sense of humor, that's what kept me going. I don't think I would have lasted through the project if those weren't major aspects of the scene.

I also noticed that with all the Elvis acts out there, there is only one presented in *Tributary*, the Brothers E. How did that work out?

I did consciously try to make a distinction between tribute bands and impersonators or tribute acts. It's sort of the difference between pop music circa 1940s and 1950s versus pop music circa 1960s, 1970s, where the Beatles changed everything. In the tribute world Beatlemania changed everything. Before Beatlemania you had tribute acts—you'd have a Billie Holiday sound alike and a Patsy Cline sound alike and Elvis sound alikes and maybe some Sinatra sound alikes; it was always one person doing one other person—with the Beatles everything changed. You now had four different people in a band with four different identities but playing together as a band. It wasn't just one specific person with a bunch of faceless musicians behind them anymore, and that's where I wanted to make the distinction, that tribute bands are doing the whole band, not just singers with anonymous musicians. So that's the distinction I wanted to make. I figured there are already films doing the Las Vegas impersonator thing and I wanted to narrow the topic, the scope. Technically, the Elvis band (the Brothers E) doesn't really fit according to my arbitrary rules. But I felt like, this is such a weird take on Elvis, and it really is sort of a band and it does deal with a lot of the issues of interpretation and putting your own personality into the act that I felt that it did fit. I don't think I would have wanted to put any other Elvis impersonators, though. It had to be something that was completely out there like the Brothers E.

(From the closing to Tributary*) So we're left with the question of whether tribute bands are part of a musical devolution or evolution. My feeling is that they represent a brief look back to fuel a giant leap forward. But who's to say what the future will bring.)*

greenzine

by Christy Road

contact: 14222 SW 83 St. I Miami, FL 33183

here

Scenes from a War (excerpts)
edited by Neil DeMause

On March 19, 2003, we sent out an e-mail to HER-Ereaders, friends, and random acquaintances, asking:"What does the war look like from where you are?"These are some of the responses.

Mar 19, 2003 11:19 PM GMT
Spring arrived at long last in New York this week: birdsong and shirtsleeves replaced snowdrifts, as clear skies and balmy temperatures had everyone out on the streets, in the parks. Today it's turned colder, but still crisp and sunny. And all the while, part of me keeps looking to the skies and expecting to see something else — but unlike that beautiful autumn day 18 months and eight days ago, today there's no rising grey plume to remind us of what's taking place, out of our direct line of sight.

On the cable news channels, meanwhile, they're playing with Telestrators like it's the NBA Finals, and talking endlessly of "sorties." I don't think I know a single person who could say just exactly what a sortie is — which is probably the point.

Neil deMause, Brooklyn, NY

Mar 20, 2003 12:05 AM GMT
What does war look like from where I am? It depends on when you ask.

Sometimes it looks like Ricki Lake, Good Day NY and Joe Millionaire... all the crap television that we drug ourselves with when we can't find the energy to leave the house. It looks like activists giving in to the depressive drumbeat of, "Why are you even bothering, when the fundamentalists in power are willfully ignoring millions of people in the street every month. Why take to the streets when They (the capital T 'they') are hearing our voices, but They just don't care?"

It looks like a street theater performer known for making people laugh at tragedy, forgetting how to smile.

Other times it looks like solidarity, rebellion, an aggressive thirst for peace and unending outrage at the subversion of justice. It looks like thousands of people walking, marching, chanting, screaming, pushing empty strollers while holding posters proclaiming "Thou Shalt Not Kill (Children)," using everything from feather boas to Gollum masks to our own bodies to make visual, verbal and powerful statements against unjust military attacks. It looks like me forgoing my quiet magazine-reading commute in lieu of debating strangers on the F train about the immorality of preemptive strikes, KO'ing the arguments of smug Wall Street types on the Q train when they claim "the price is worth it," and offering a polite, smiling, "God helps those who help themselves" retort when the fundamentalist Christian lady who, after being informed of the Pentagon's stated plans to drop 3,000 bombs on an urban population, says that what she plans to do to prevent the deaths of thousands upon thousands of innocent children and adults is... well, pray, of course.

In brief moments, war looks like hope: US ambassadors and diplomats resigning their posts, tax resistors refusing to subsidize the machinery of war, Southern and midwestern students hungry for lefty insight, country singers denouncing their hometown idiot-savant-turned-President, UN vetos, FRENCH fries (dammit!), and good, old fashioned, American dissent.

War looks like heroism: like a 23-year-old American student who, staring eye-to-eye with the driver of an Israeli bulldozer advancing to demolish the home of a Palestinian doctor, refused to back away. It looks like a peace activist willing to put her body, her life, on the line to defend the human rights of people she hardly knew in a country that was not her own.

And as we all know, war looks like death: like the crushed body of Rachel Corrie, murdered by that same tank driver who ran over her not once, but twice. It looks like death.

Finally, from where I sit right now war looks like typos and tears, neither of which I have time to clean up (ie., forgive the misspellings and run-on sentences — there's no time for spellcheck when I have five more media outreach calls to make before the close of the business day).

Jennifer L. Pozner, Brooklyn, NY

Mar 20, 2003 12:10 AM GMT
We live in lower Manhattan. There may not literally be a smoking cloud of ash over my neighborhood today, but from where I'm sitting the war looks like a black and acrid swirl of noise and stupidity, a frightening toxic cloud gathering all around, trying to suck us

contact: PO Box 300743 | Brooklyn, NY 11230 | heremagazine.com all up in its darkness. It creeps just outside the door to the room where my 6-week-old daughter sleeps. And I'm doing my damnedest to keep it out of her room. She'll have a lifetime of wars, just like her Daddy and her Daddy's Daddy — let it not start now. And every time I change her diaper, rock her in my arms, or lift her up for a burp, I feel like my body is the only thing that's keeping the war from her, and I pray that my body's enough. And I hope, as I'm sure my parents once hoped for me, that there's still a place in this world for the mundane business of life's joy.

Peter Cenedella,
Lower East Side of New York City

Mar 20, 2003 01:27 AM GMT
I was walking down Broadway this morning, beneath the el tracks at 125th Street, about to climb up Morningside Heights. Two large men walked downhill towards me. One of them was talking loudly. "It's like Rome," he said, and waved his hands. "It's like Rome or anything. The Romans, they kept conquering people. You have a little run there, you're going good for a few hundred years, but then in the end, what have you got?" I kept walking downtown and uphill as they walked uptown and downhill behind me and their voices faded away.

Tim Morris, Great Neck, L.I.

Mar 20, 2003 01:28 AM GMT
In Seattle, we can get a Canadian TV station on cable channel 99. The news on the CBC is dramatically unlike ours, with real reporting rather than regurgitated White House talking points, and in-depth analysis of not only what's going on now, but also what has led up to this — what's been going on with our unelected ruling junta since before the 2002 elections. What's scary is not just the war, but how obedient and pliable our news media are at a time when they should be particularly informative and critical.

To repeat a cliche, it looks as though the terrorists have already won. This is absolutely the low point of American civilization.

John Pastier, Seattle

Mar 20, 2003 04:11 AM GMT
In Fort Montgomery today, war looks like a thing from the past. I live on the outskirts of the old fort and from my home you can see the river, the Bear Mt. Bridge, just about where the first chain stretched across the Hudson 230 years ago, and evidence of the battle (redoubts, stone walls) surfacing beneath the melting snow. Taking a short walk through the back-yard you can tour the restoration of Fort Montgomery, a Pataki pet-project that opened last fall. (On the weekends you can witness visitors from Westchester and Jersey parking their SUVs along 9W to take in the site.) This time of year you can even see bald eagles nesting on Iona Island, they still exist here.

Even after 9/11 (I wasn't alive during Vietnam) it's hard to really imagine war. I've got a warm home, a soft chair, a wall of great books, a refrigerator full of food, and a majestic, if not unforgivably sheltered view.

Pamela Nugent, Fort Montgomery, NY

Mar 20, 2003 04:12 AM GMT
I'm watching NBC. Tom Brokaw drones on and on. Some retired general drones, also. The oddly legendary Peter Arnett joins the chorus of monotony. Pictures of dawn breaking over Baghdad, punctuated by occasional anti-aircraft fire, repeat themselves endlessly.

Is the sheer overwhelming boredom of this coverage supposed to make me forget what's happening?

I am confused and sleepy and desperately sad.

David Dyte, Brooklyn

Mar 20, 2003 04:18 AM GMT
I've got a pinched nerve in my neck, so the past few nights I've been jarred awake at about 4:00 a.m. as pain shoots through my arm. And the first thoughts I've had upon awakening each night has been about the impending bombing. Last night I wondered how terrifying aerial bombing must sound, how it must feel to have these huge, concussive explosions going off everywhere around you. How our smug military people talk about "precision" and "surgical" bombing, as if that were ever possible. And I wonder how things would be if any of these gung-ho Rumsfeld types ever experienced that kind of terror, that kind of horror. Bombing is such a cowardly act, orchestrated by grandiose men isolated in bunkers and command centers far away from the destruction. Perhaps that's why the French and Germans wouldn't be part of the "coalition," because they know what aerial bombing felt like sixty years ago. Which makes you wonder whether Tony Blair and his British cohorts have no sense of history whatsoever.

My son and I came home from an afterschool event and he turned on the TV, wondering if there was a sports event he could watch for a few minutes before going to bed. Every channel had that grim view of Baghdad, awaiting the bombs falling. I told him to shut the TV off.

Tom Goldstein, St. Paul, Minnesota

Mar 20, 2003 04:19 AM GMT

A short, blood-red sign spears the muddy ground near the county library in Durham, N.C. "Stop War," it says. I love its ambiguity. This war. That war. Any war. Stop it. Stop it all.

North Carolina is a conservative state, meaning it didn't take long for people here to rename French fries. Everyone seems to know someone who's "over there in the Middle East," and to hear people talk, it could be another galaxy, far, far, away.

The pictures on TV show blowing sand instead of yawning irises, rumbling tanks instead of the gas-guzzling SUVs that today are waving flags in red and white and blue and white — for the basketball teams at N.C. State and Duke. For about a day, the newspaper and television reported that the NCAA basketball tournament could be postponed in the event of war.

It won't be. People want life to go on as normal.

And so it does. The squash-colored school bus chugs along Route 54. At the Harris Teeter, people buy bananas and soy milk and rotisserie chickens.

Dinner time is still 6 o'clock. In my house, we're having quesadillas. Our neighbors are having pork chops and onions.

The sun sets and Saddam Hussein's deadline comes. Then it goes.

"Time's up," they say on the news, and I think of that perky woman on "Trading Spaces" saying the same thing.

Time's up.

The air outside is damp and the birds have settled down for the night, fat on our grass seed.

So far in Durham, war remains something we hear about, but nothing we see.

Madelyn Rosenberg, Durham, N.C.

Mar 20, 2003 01:49 PM GMT

Woke up with a tight heart. Usual routine, shower. Lit a prayer lamp to God, and prayed; saying this world is yours and I have no idea what's your plan. got ready for work: 8am after breakfast, the countdown showed 1 hour 15 minutes.

Vijay, Singapore

Mar 20, 2003 01:50 PM GMT

Early this morning, riding on the trolley with all of the glum faces (probably half asleep and not wanting to go to work, like every morning), the clear and chipper voice of the driver/conductor announces the available pamphlets on what to do in case of a terrorist attack. Eyes roll, as if work wasn't bad enough.

It is almost a strange flattery, that somehow our lives could be in danger when people are most defi-nitely being killed in other countries. The past thirty years have basically been the businessmen and politicians bombing tired people in little countries that have never done anything against the tired people riding the trolleys early in the morning.

Darin Prey-Harbaugh, Philadelphia

Mar 20, 2003 02:15 PM GMT

The view from here is bright yellow. That's the color of the mucus I'm expelling from my system this Thursday morning, the night after the U.S. military began expelling its bombs and missiles upon the country of Iraq. I imagine these incendiary projectiles produce explosions similar in hue.

I usually get sick two or three days after I'm exposed to whatever virus or pathogen is going around, and I have a very strong suspicion that, in this case, the toxin in question was Monday's speech by President Bush. When I learned that he'd decided to abort the United Nations Security Council vote on his war resolution — just a week after he had publicly promised to make nations "show their cards" whether they were for or against — I felt my blood pressure spike and sweat stain my palms. I stalked into my boss's office and spat, "That piece of shit lied again and is going to start the war!"

And now my psychological stress has translated into a physical illness — a minor thing, really, compared to the cries of terrified Iraqi children, or the silence that follows the rumble of collapsing walls when a stray missile strikes a Baghdad home. Yellow for me indicates my body is fighting its infection, and I'll probably feel better in a few days. For President Bush, the military and paranoid patriots, yellow reflects the caution that led to this pre-emptive war, which will save our country from "grave danger" through ridding the world of the disease that is Saddam Hussein. It's a Code Orange terrorist alert in the United States right now, but for my runny nose and the Iraqi people, it's nothing but yellow.

Vincent Romano, White Plains, NY

Ideas in Pictures

by Colin Matthes

when you give an animal a number instead of a name essentially you are denying the animal's existence. it becomes an object.

a line on an inventory list.

this beautiful calf is number 18.. number 18 is a lot easier to lock up (and sw slaughter) than davey or little sniffles. numbers contribute to giving us the distance to x be inhumane....just as a prisoner is #4637, not sam anderson. when a living being is given a number i cannot help but fear for xxsxxkxxx it's existence.

contact: PO Box 510214 | Milwaukee, WI 53203

Imagine

Imagine

Enforcing the laws of irony

Douglas Stanhope on America (excerpts)

Doug Stanhope is one of my all-time favorite comedians and probably the best on the standup circuit today. He's recorded a number of his shows for television, even cable, but executives always get cold feet and block broadcast before they air. He's got four CDs out. I personally give my highest recommendation to "Sicko," "A Little Something to Take the Edge Off" and "Die Laughing." (You can safely skip his first album called "The Great White Stanhope.") The following transcript comes from his new DVD "Word of Mouth," recorded May 2002 in Austin, Texas. To order any of the CDs, send a check or money order made payable to Doug Stanhope for $15 each or $35 for all three to Doug Stanhope, 1200 N. Curson #7, Los Angeles, CA 90046. The DVD is $23 postpaid from Sacred Cow Productions, P.O. Box 300123, Austin, TX 78703 or (888) 903-SACRED. Reprinted with permission from Doug.

Airport security

It was either me or Confucius who said, "A journey of a thousand miles begins with a vicious ass raping at airport security." I think that's how the saying goes, isn't it?

But I feel safer that's all that counts. I feel safer being stink-eyed and finger-fucked and made to roll over and take off your shoes and sit up and play dead. "Hang on, we're gonna pull every third grandmother out of line and make her open up her piss bag on a long banquet table just to make sure she didn't pass a sharp stone at some point during the night. It's for your safety."

You can't keep knives out of prison, and in prison they look in your ass. How far are you gonna go with this bullshit?

... This is what pisses me off. I don't know if you've seen it. It's at Phoenix and LAX. I'm sure there are other airports where they have "first class" security. Have you seen that? You go through security [demonstrates long, cordoned-off lanes] and they have the big cattle troughs with 45 people in a row, seven rows deep and then they have "first class" security with eight people.

Security has nothing to do with the airlines; they're not connected. Fuck you. It's like having a DUI roadblock and then having an express lane for Mercedes. Fuck you. "Nice car, sweet. Go ahead. You, poor guy, you fucking wait in the trough. Wait with the other cattle." Fuck you, that's why I don't care if they blow

shit up. Go ahead, make your terrorist alert, I don't give a fuck. This country is a big, bloated celebrity that thinks it doesn't have to pay the cover charge.

Does Osama exist?

... Do you think Osama bin Laden even exists at this point? I think he's completely invented. He's like a WWF anti-hero that was created. They made him up so you didn't have to pull your "Fuck the Ayatollah" T-shirt out of storage. Now you've got something else to buy. Not only have you got an enemy with a face on it, you've got something else to buy. It keeps people in business.

Terrorists are jealous of America

... People are just retards. "You know, they blew up the World Trade Center because they're jealous of the way we live." No they're not. They want us to stop fucking with them. Why are we over there negotiating peace in the Middle East? Who the fuck are we? We've got problems in this country. We had a big election dispute with Gore and Bush. You didn't see the emperor of Tunisia coming over here: "I'm over here to help you guys work it out. You sit here and you sit there, and we're gonna have to come to a resolution." Who is this fuckin' guy? Get him out of here; go blow shit up in HIS country.

It's the arrogance that gets shit blown up. "No, they're jealous." No, they're not jealous. That's like the fat, skanky, unwashed girl on "Ricki Lake" who gets booed and she goes, "You're just jealous is all. You're jealous of my spandex and my dirty ass." They're not jealous. You have to stop fucking with people.

But we have to fuck with them because they have all the oil. That's the only reason. Shit goes on all over the world that we don't give a fuck about, but when there's oil, we all of a sudden have to negotiate peace. Blow me.

But everyone's fat and has cable so they don't pay attention. Wrestling's the Number 1 show on cable television, and you expect people to know what's going on?

They got all the fucking oil. We've got all the toys but they've got all the batteries so let's go negotiate peace and let shit blow up.

"Drugs support terrorism." No, your fucking SUV does. If you're driving an SUV, you killed people in the World Trade Center.

America is not free

... Free country my ass. This country isn't free at all. You believe it because you spent 12 years in public school going [raises hand, uses robot voice] "I pledge allegiance to the flag." What kind of cult bullshit is that? Great things don't have to tell you they're great; you'll figure them all out on your own, you don't have to chant and march to find them.

America takes credit for giving you freedom you had anyway. It's like going to a wedding and putting a tag on someone else's box — "That one's for me." You're free anyway. You're born free. You're born absolutely free except for laws of nature where if you get old you die, and if you drink you get drunk, and if you sit on a tack you bleed from the ass. Those are the only laws you're born with, and any government just takes away from those freedoms.

[Beautiful blonde makes her way to a seat in the front.] Come on in. You're free to sit. America gave you the freedom to sit — and give me beaver shots from the skirt. Oh what, you're not a patriot? Fine.

America takes credit for all those freedoms. You can't drink a beer after 2:00 so drink up because I'm going long tonight. You're not that free. You can't put a fucking fishing pole in a fucking fishing hole without a goddamn license. You can't drive down the street without a seatbelt. You can't put a business on your sign without a permit. McDonald's, with just the shit they throw away on an hourly basis, could feed every hungry person in this country, probably the planet, but health laws don't allow it. And if you get sick of all the bullshit, you're not even free to kill yourself in this country. You're not fucking free.

"Well, America gave you the freedom to stand on stage and say what you're saying right now." No, a voicebox gave me the freedom to stand on stage and say what I'm saying. It has nothing to do with America. America doesn't even exist; it's just fucking dirt with lines drawn around it. And as soon as you make that argument, Joe Fucking Shithead Patriot — who's got so many fucking flags on his car window, he can't even see the road, he's driving over pedestrians to show how much he loves America — so his argument is he'll pick out some other country that sucks worse as if that's a defense.

"Oh yeah? Well, you say that but over in Uzbekistan, if you even have a beer, they'll pull out your eye with a hot grapefruit spoon."

So? How does their suck make my suck not suck? That's not an argument. That's like when you're getting fat, you say [pinches love handles] "I'm getting fat" and your really obese friend goes "You think you're fat? I can't even fit behind the wheel of my ice cream truck."

America may be the greatest country in the world but, you know what, that's like being the prettiest Denny's waitress. Just because you're the best doesn't necessarily make you good.

Christianity is stupid

Fucking Jesus country, those fucking Jesus Heads. How many Christians here tonight? [Smattering of applause.] Are you hardcore [says to one guy]? No, not hardcore. You made your own Christianity, didn't you? I'm not bustin' on you, that's what people do. If you'd never — how old are you? 32? — if you'd never heard of the Bible, no one had never talked to you about it, you were just walking through a bookstore today and stumbled across it like a pioneer, a little Lewis & Clark. You were just thumbing through it while taking a shit — you'll read anything while taking a shit. [Head shake from the guy.] Okay, let's say they put it on the back of the Cap'n Crunch box, how about that? How quick would you recognize that as true? Would you go, "Hey, this is exactly what I was lookin' for. Yeah, the fuckin' flood and the Ark. This sounds incredibly true." You'd throw it in the trash, would you not?

That's why they have to pump it into your head when you're still little and you've got a soft spot and you're Santa Claus eligible. They pump it all in your head and then they cork it in there with a whole bunch of fear, and what you do, you go "I'm not all hardcore" and you make your own Christianity. What your brain does is you believe all the parts that don't affect your life at all. "I believe in heaven and Jesus and the Resurrection, yeah, sure." But the parts that affect your instincts — which is your real god if you think about it — your brain grows around that like a club foot. "Oh we have to adapt here. Yeah I believe in the Garden of Eden. Oh what? Premarital sex? I think that was a typo, I think that's open to interpretation. But I believe in Noah, sure. Love thy neighbor, sure, except for that fuckhead up in 3B who plays Beastie Boys till 4 o'clock in the morning. But the Bible was written before Beastie Boys were around so it's open to interpretation."

You don't believe it, you don't. And this is how I know: Every time you see a tragedy — whether it's 9/11 or a bus goes into a lake or fucking Grandma spontaneously combusts, whatever it is — you see people on the news whining "Aaaaauuugggggghhh! It's horrible and it's tragic. Aaaaauuuuuggghh! But at least he's in a better place now. He's with Jesus, aaauuugghh!" Then why are you crying? If with all your faith, with the depth of your soul you believe your loved one is dancing around on a fluffy cloud in an everlasting paradise without a care, happier than pig worms in a baby's stool, why are you crying? You should be ecstatic if you really believe it. You should be calling all your friends on the phone: "Did you hear the great news? Lightning struck my baby. Yeah, he's in a better place. God picked him. I told you he was adorable. God spared him that average 72-year sentence on this shithole planet."

If you really believe that death leads to eternal bliss, then why are you wearing a seat belt? ★

Everybody Wants to Rule the World Except Me
by Jeff Somers

Volume 8

HERE's what I'm up against. Forget the Illuminati, the secret cabals of rich white men oppressing us all. Forget the Saudi Princes funding terrorist attacks. Forget corrupt, abusive cops beating people with their nightsticks, forget racists and muggers and ineffective bleeding-heart liberals and moronic celebrities who think they have political opinions instead of coked-up college dropout bullshit. Forget them all. Here is what I'm up against: I'm up against idiots who can't comprehend how an elevator works.

I work on the 16th floor of a 17-floor building. For those of you who fall into the aforementioned category of people who can't comprehend how an elevator works, this means there is only one floor above mine. At five o'clock, when we're all trying to get home, invariably someone will stroll out to the elevator bank and press both the UP and DOWN buttons. Invariably, the next elevator that arrives indicates UP, and our best case scenario is waiting for it to close its doors and reopen as a DOWN. Our worst case scenario is a quick trip up to the 17th floor and another quick stop at 16 before we can get going. So why do people press *both* the UP and DOWN buttons? Because they think they're getting an elevator faster that way. More specifically, they think the elevators rise up from the lobby preordained as UP or DOWN, and that by cleverly pressing both buttons they are fooling UP elevators into stopping at 16. In truth, of course, the elevators respond to a call, whether up or down. the only thing that determines which way an elevator is going when it arrives is which button is pressed and *which direction the elevator cab is headed*. Since they're almost always rising to our floor, they almost always arrive as UP elevators, which just seems to confirm people's belief about luring UP elevators.

In other words, people are dumb, and I pay the price.

It's a minor thing, of course. Except it costs me time. Not much—an extra ten seconds for a best-case (doors close, indicator changes to DOWN, doors open, doors close again) and maybe a minute in the worst-case (riding up to the 17th floor, going through the door thing, back to 16, door thing *again*). In a complete worst-case scenario, it costs me two hours a year. I don't know about you, but I doubt they'll cure death soon enough to save me, so I don't have any hours to spare. **These damn bastards are stealing my life.**

There are a few possible solutions, depending on your personality, but I think they all fall into two basic categories, which in turn describe general approaches to this absurd life we're all living. the world is always throwing situations like the elevator buttons in our way, and we all instinctively choose to either **Fight** or **Adapt**. Fighters will try to change the behavior that annoys and/or threatens them. Adapters will try to find ways around the problem without trying to change the overall cause. You could look at it in terms of passivity, if you wanted: Fighters are aggressive and Adapters are passive. But a better way to look at it, I think, is in terms of intelligence: Fighters waste time and energy getting things changed to their liking, and fail as often as they succeed. Adapters recognize wasted time when they smell it, and put their energy into finding a shortcut around the problem altogether. Adapters recognize that they weren't put on this Earth to correct the mistakes of others.

Me, I'm an Adapter. My solution to the elevator buttons problem? I leave work ten minutes earlier and avoid everyone else completely. Let the monkeys fight over the buttons, or stand there happy in their belief that they're fooling the elevators. I don't care. I've got two hours of my life back, and if I'm damning future generations to suffer the indignity of double-buttoning on the 16th floor because I couldn't be bothered to change the world, well, bugger them. Save *my* ass, is my motto. If I were living inside a war movie, I'd be whatever character William Holden was playing. Don't know who William Holden is? Bugger *you.*

The easiest way to understand it all, I think, is to put it this way: Fighters fight to have laws changed. They circulate petitions, attend meetings, and write their elected officials. Adapters, on the other hand, let the laws stand and simply find ways of breaking them without getting caught. You can accuse we Adapters of being wimps, or of dooming future generations to repeat our mistakes, and you're probably right. But we have a lot more free time, because instead of being Carry A. Nation and busting up the gin joints, we're just sitting there drinking gin. Or something. Gin makes me mix up my metaphors.

Fighters get all the respect, that's true, but that's because we're all conditioned to love the Fighters because they're playing by the rules, dissipating their energies in useless struggles. Useless? Let's look at a prime example: in 1773 a group of hooligans calling themselves The Sons of Liberty had a little shindig now known as The Boston Tea Party in order to protest George III's policy of taxation without representation. Yahoo for them, it eventually snowballed into the American Revolution and birthed our glorious nation so that we could blow the fuck out of every third-world country in the universe, yay for us. Now we all get to live here in the USA and pay fuck-all taxes. What did the Sons of Liberty do? Nothing, but waste their time. An Adapter, on the other hand, would have paid the lower price for tea that the fucking Tea Act actually resulted in, and would probably have moved quietly to Canada when the revolution broke out.

Fighters, you see, play by the rules in the sense that they make themselves obvious targets and dissipate their energies in campaigns to change the world. That they are occasionally successful is true, as is the fact that some of the Fighters' achievements have been beneficial to me is also true. You can't expect logic like that to penetrate *The Inner Swine*, can you? Because it isn't about changing the world, or helping future generations, bubba. It's about *me*. It's about *my time* and the best way for *me* to use it. Adapters know this: One day, we'll be dead, and no matter how you cut it, the travails of this world will no longer matter much to us, will they? So fuck it. I need to get the most out of the time I have now, and not waste energy on changing the world.

A dangerously narrow-minded and self-interested attitude, to be sure. But you see, the *genius* of this attitude is the fact that the world produces just as many Fighters as ever. You see, we Adapters don't *have* to do any work—the Fighters of the world do it all for us! We grunt around in the slop busy with our selfish errands, and the world gets changed around us anyway. All the Adapters who bought cheap tea and moved to Canada back in 1773 probably moved back in 1790 to enjoy the fruits of democracy. There's always a Fighter somewhere in the crowd, because a) people in general have an inflated sense of their own importance and b) people are dumb enough to think that they're starring in this movie called Life, and it's usually an action movie. Believe me, if I'm sitting having a beer somewhere and I notice that the bar has caught fire, I know I can sit calmly and finish my drink before ambling out into the night, maybe mentioning to the bouncer that the place appears to be on fire as I leave, because I know the place is full of Fighters who will Do Something About It.

Ah well, you all know it's true. By this point in my zine career I've pared it down to the people who agree with me, overtly or secretly, and friends who dare not turn it down, so I doubt I'll get any pissed-off letters explaining to me how wrong I am. ★

Insubordination

May 12, 1985:
What the Corporate Media Didn't Tell You
An Interview with Ramona Africa
by Hans Bennett

Ramona Africa is the sole adult survivor of the May 13, 1985 massacre of 11 members of the MOVE organization. The FBI and the City of Philadelphia dropped a C4 bomb on MOVE's 6221 Osage Avenue home in West Philadelphia. Carrying the young Birdie Africa (the only other survivor) with her, Ramona dodged gunfire and escaped from the fire with permanent scarring from the burns.

After surviving the bombing, she was charged with conspiracy, riot, and multiple counts of simple and aggravated assault. Subsequently Ramona served 7 years in prison. If she had chosen to sever her ties with MOVE, she could have been released far earlier. In the face of this she held true to her revolutionary beliefs and was uncompromising in the face of state terror. Since her release from prison, Ramona has tirelessly worked as the MOVE Minister of Communication on behalf of the MOVE 9, Mumia Abu-Jamal, and all political prisoners and prisoners of war.

A few months ago I visited 6221 Osage Ave. for the first time since I moved to Philadelphia. Upon arrival I was shocked to find "PERMIT PARKING FOR PHILA. POLICE CIVIL AFFAIRS" posted directly in front of the 6221 lot. I later verified that 6221 Osage is now an actual police station. Particularly striking is the presence of Civil Affairs: Philly's political police. As Ramona Africa talks about in the interview Civil Affairs played a key role on May 13 in their role as the official diplomats.

This May, I spoke with Ramona about 6221 today. "Ever since they rebuilt the houses out there, they never intended to sell 6221. They made it a police station with police present around the clock, 24/7." Ramona does feel insulted by the police station there, but says that it "is indicative of this system. On May 13, 1995, councilwoman Jamie Blackwell (whose district includes 6221 Osage Ave.) introduced a resolution to make May 13 'kiss a cop day.' Why May 13 of all possible days? That is the mentality of these people and we don't expect anything different from them."

Things were tense when last Sept. New Jersey Judge Shelly Robbins New reversed an earlier decision granting supervised visits to John Gilbride for his son Zachary Africa who was under the full-time custody of his mother Alberta Africa (a MOVE member).

Because of past psychological and physical abuse, Zachary Africa had told the previous judge that while he loved his father he was afraid to be alone with him, and subsequently only wanted to be with his father if his mother was with him also.

Seeing Judge New's decision as illegitimate, Alberta and MOVE said that they would not hand Zachary over for unsupervised visits and boarded up the windows of their Kingsessing headquarters in West Philadelphia because of the threat of a police assault.

While the Philadelphia PD officially stated that they were giving MOVE their space and did not want any confrontations, their actions showed otherwise. During the nights that I spent with MOVE late at night while they were on 24 hour watch at their front gate, I observed an unusually large number of police cars passing by. Besides this harassment, were two major incidents at this point.

On the night of Sept.11, 2002 the police made an aggressive act in front of the MOVE's Kingsessing home. As a group of MOVE supporters was backing their car out the driveway following their visit, a police car drove up and blocked them (almost causing a collision). The MOVE supporters were suspicious of the police motives and when the cops demanded they leave their car without giving any reason for it, the driver hit the horn to alert MOVE inside the house.

When Ramona Africa and others came out of the house and confronted the police, the cops claimed to not have known that it was the MOVE home. The police claimed that the MOVE supporters' car with Virginia plates fit the profile of a vehicle suspected of kidnapping a young child nearby. During a Sept.20 press conference at MOVE's house I asked Civil Affairs Captain Fisher about the Sept.11 incident and he denied that it ever happened despite the numerous neighbors that witnessed the police cars there that night.

On Sept.13, 4 cops came to the MOVE house to get Zack, even though the court order specified that the first unsupervised visit would be this upcoming Friday (Sept. 20). According to MOVE, the police claimed to have a court order saying that Gilbride would have custody, but when MOVE demanded to see it, they explained that Gilbride himself had it, so they could not show them. This supposed court order

contact: PO Box 30770 | Philadelphia, PA 19104

is also suspect because if he had one, Alberta Africa should have been given one also. However, Alberta and MOVE said they hadn't gotten anything of the sort.

On Sept. 27 Gilbride was shot dead in his car by what looked to be a professional hit. While there was an initial fear that the police would blame MOVE for the murder, the police officially don't suspect MOVE and the murder remains unsolved.

Last month when 7 year-old Zachary Africa and a friend were in Alberta Africa's backyard in Cherry Hill, NJ, they spotted a man wearing all black with dark paint on his face. Given the recent events with Alberta and Zachary Africa, it appeared as if this may have been related. While concerned about who was in their backyard and why, Ramona is unsure about it. "We really don't know whether it was the government, grandparents, or some nut. We just keep a close eye on our kids. That's all we can do."

Hans:*Can you please talk about the weeks leading up to May 13, 1985?*

Ramona: Things were relatively quiet. The biggest thing that happened was on April 29. We heard our dogs barking and upon checking it out, we saw cops out back that were counting the dogs or something. We knew they were up to something sneaky, so we turned on our loudspeaker. Note that we didn't have our speaker on 24/7 like the media attempts to portray.

With the loudspeaker, we let the neighborhood know that there were cops in the back of our house, and we didn't know what they were up to, but we knew it was no good and we didn't trust them. We weren't going to let them sneak in and attack MOVE people without the neighborhood knowing what was going on.

Civil Affairs cops (the official diplomats) like George Draper, Ted Vaughn, and others came to our home that day and knocked on the front door. My sister Theresa Africa and I came out and talked to them at length—with them standing right on the steps of our house for at least a half hour. We explained to them why we turned on the loudspeaker. That's all that happened that day.

Two weeks later, on Saturday, May 11, DA Ed Rendell got officer Ted Vaughn to charge us with terroristic threats, disorderly conduct, and nonsense like that stemming from April 29. Rendell then had the arrest warrants approved by Judge Lynne Abraham (now Philadelphia's DA) who was acting as the emergency judge for that Saturday. Based on the events of April 29, Abraham signed warrants for myself and 3 others.

People need to understand that this incident happened two weeks prior. How in the hell can it be an emergency if it waited 2 weeks? Second, if we were guilty of terroristic threats and officers Vaughn and Draper felt threatened by us, why would they talk to us on our steps for over a half hour. It's nonsense, but that's the excuse they used for the warrants, because they had absolutely nothing else to use.

Ramona (second from left) and other MOVE women protecting their home/HQ during the recent custody battle/standoff with the police … note that windows are boarded up. by Hans Bennett

The City of Philadelphia tells people that there were complaints from neighbors about us. That may very well be true, but they've never been able to verify for us who complained and what they specifically complained about. Even if this is true, you explain to me when this government ever cared about black people's neighborhood complaints. Since when is it such an issue that the FBI & the Justice Department get involved in something like that?

If the government is saying that their solution to a neighborhood dispute is to bomb the neighborhood and burn it down, then there wouldn't be a single neighborhood standing. All neighborhoods have disputes, but they aren't bombed. Look at 8th & Butler here in Philadelphia—a known drug area. The residents of that area have demonstrated, sat out in the middle of the street, and stormed City Council representatives' offices demanding some kind of relief from the drug trafficking. It is so bad that if you pull up at a red light in that area, people will come up to your car to try and sell you drugs. Parents say that they're upset because in the summer they can't even let their kids play outside because they're afraid of a shooting. You don't see any bombings in that neighborhood. You don't see cops en masse coming out to that neighborhood.

In our case, they claim that the bombing was a response to a handful of black people's complaints. Anybody with half a brain cell has to know there's something wrong with that. People also need to understand that when I went to court after the bombing, every charge listed on Rendell & Abraham's May 11 warrant was dismissed. During the pretrial motion, trial judge Michael Stiles was forced to dismiss every single charge. This means that they had no valid reason to even be out there.

They did not dismiss the charges placed on me as a result of what happened AFTER they came out. This is illegal, and an inconsistency because if the police had no valid reason to be out there, that should mean that anything coming after that would also be invalid. They wouldn't drop the other charges because I would have been released. People's emotions were so high at that time after May 13, there not about to put me back out in the streets.

You can see how this was nothing but a setup. Meanwhile, the media sat back and did everything possible to justify what this government did. They had warrants for four adults, but they knew there were many children in the house. On the morning of Sunday, May 12, one of our supporters (Gloria) went to the Italian market for us and took a couple of our children with her. By the time she came back, they had cordoned off the street. But when Gloria pulled her car up, the Civil Affairs cops (including George Draper) looked in the car (seeing Gloria and the chil-

dren) and let them through the barricade to return to MOVE's home.

They let the children back into the house knowing what they were getting ready to do. All that nonsense about looking for every opportunity to remove the children from the situation is a bold-faced lie. They're aim was to kill everybody in that house—particularly the children. According to Police Commissioner Sambor at the time, they saw MOVE children as being as much, if not more of a threat than the adults. So, we understand why they let the children back into the house.

In terms of what led up to May 13, we feel it was simply a matter of the government looking for an excuse to attack MOVE again. For over a year they tried to come up with a plan of action to do it. On Aug.8, 1984 they hundreds of cops out to Osage without actually doing anything. This was just a drill while they were putting together a plan. All of this came out in the Commission that Wilson Goode put together.

Anybody can see that their aim, very simply, was to kill MOVE people—not to arrest anybody. They had overwhelming opportunity to arrest MOVE people if that's what they wanted to do. They knew our schedule as well as we did. They would follow us around when we left the house. I walked the streets by myself and would often stop and speak to the Civil Affairs cops. They could have snatched me up anytime.

Could you please give your personal account about what happened inside 6221 Osage on May 13?

There's unfortunately not a whole lot I can say because I was in the basement with the children the whole time. When it had begun to get dark at around 8 or 9 Sunday night, we saw cops in houses across the street, and we knew they were set to attack us. In response, we took the kids to the basement and after a while down there water started pouring in from the hoses.

Then the tear gas came. They said that they used explosives to blow 3-inch diameter holes in the wall to insert tear gas. But photos show that the whole front of the house was blown off. The police estimate shooting over 10,000 rounds of bullets into the house during the first 90 minutes. They said they used all of the ammunition they had brought and had to get more from the armory. I did hear a lot of gunfire. Then for a pretty long time things were pretty quiet. It was then that they dropped the bomb without any warning.

At first, those of us in the basement didn't realize that the house was on fire because there was so much tear gas that it was hard to recognize smoke. After a while it seemed to be getting hotter and the smoke was thickening and choking us. That's when we started realizing that it was more than just tear gas. Conrad opened the door and we started to yell that we were coming out with the kids. The kids were hollering too. We know they heard us but the instant we were visible in the doorway, they opened fire. You could hear the bullets hitting all around the garage area. They deliberately took aim and shot at us.

I personally tried to get out with some of the kids at least twice before the last time when it was so hot with the flames everywhere. After I escaped with Birdie, they immediately took both of us into custody. I didn't realize how badly I was burned when they threw me onto the ground and handcuffed me.

On the 13 minute police video given to us in court, they were across from us on Osage and you could hear the cops talking in the background. There was a shot where you could see the house fully engulfed in flames and you can hear the cops talking and laughing in the background. You can hear them say: "That's the last time they'll call the commissioner a motherfucker." It shows you their mentality. This wasn't about an arrest.

Ramona at City Hall. by Hans Bennett

In their coverage of the May 13 bombing, the "A&E" television show "American Justice" argued that mayor Goode's physical safety was threatened by a letter signed by you. What did this letter say?

First, as I explained it court, I didn't write that letter. Someone from another chapter probably wrote the letter and signed my name to it, as was usually done because I was the Minister of Communications.

Second, after reading the letter in court after it was entered in as evidence, I didn't see anything threatening Wilson. I did see the tone of the letter being "if you come at us, you can expect us to defend ourselves." This government blames the victim. They are brutal and vicious towards you and then accuse you of being vicious and violent. They're saying that a letter was sent to Goode, but he dropped a bomb on us. That went past words, didn't it?

If we wanted to attack Goode, we knew where he worked every day and could have done it. That's not how we do things and this government knows that. Cops have trampled a 3 week-old MOVE baby to death. Police have beat, stomped, and kicked pregnant MOVE women into miscarriage. They've beaten MOVE men and locked up innocent MOVE people. When did you ever see us go out and try and shoot a cop? Absolutely never. If we didn't do it then why all of a sudden we want to go and attack Goode? It doesn't make any sense.

Showing who Goode was really afraid of, he wrote in his later book (*In Good Faith*) that he didn't come out to 62nd and Osage because police threatened his life and subsequently felt that his life was in danger.

The corporate press often reports that MOVE was shooting guns at the Fire Department as well as the police. What evidence was presented in court in regards to MOVE firing weapons from their house?

I don't recall them presenting anything other than saying that MOVE shot at them with automatic weapon fire and that they heard it. But then they got messed up because after digging through all of the rubble, they couldn't find a single automatic weapon. Then they said they found a handgun and some type of shotgun or something. I've never seen a gun in a MOVE house. Not in the Osage house or any other. That's all I can say about that. After digging through the rubble with those big claws, who knows where that came from? Even if those were our weapons, that couldn't have created automatic weapon fire.

During the later civil trial, two or three firefighters said they never heard or saw MOVE people shooting at them at all. They said they did hear automatic weapon fire but that it was from the police. The fire commissioner tried to say that he didn't fight the fire out of fear of putting firemen in danger. Meanwhile when the whole thing started, he had 4 huge hose on our home for over an hour. If they weren't in danger then, why couldn't they do it later when the house and block was on fire?

By their own admission, they're saying that MOVE gunfire was a response to the use of explosives to blow holes through the walls of our house they. Even if that were true, you're blowing up a house and then you have a problem when someone defends their home?

They will wreck havoc all over the world. They will beat you, kill you, lock you up, shoot at you, bomb you, and do all this crazy stuff to you, but they want to be seen as respectable and righteous. They will say that what they do is in defense of freedom, justice, or national security.

Meanwhile, the right of self defense is lost when cops attack an individual like they did to Amadou Diallo or Abner Louima in New York, or that brother Thomas Jones here in Philadelphia. We're just supposed to accept whatever this government and the kill-crazy, blood-thirsty cops do. You're supposed to accept that as necessary and righteous. In other words, it's acceptable for the government to turn guns on people, but its never acceptable to turn guns on this government. MOVE is saying that the instinct of self-defense is just that: it's instinctive. It's god-given and comes from mother nature. There is not a species alive walking this earth that doesn't defend itself when attacked. Humans are no different.

This government cannot explain how you are wrong to defend yourself. You are wrong if you refuse to defend yourself because that is violent because it endorses and encourages violence. It makes you suicidal. MOVE is not suicidal or masochistic. We do believe in defending ourselves, no question. This government is never going to take that away from us and will never convince us that we are criminal and wrong for that.

What the hell do they say this country was founded on? Every 4th of July these motherfuckers celebrate the so-called "American Revolution." They say that these founding fathers were courageous and brave men who defied legality and went to war against cops called "red coats" and the government of King George. They said "give me liberty or give me death" and went to war. Every day these people are celebrated and applauded in 2nd and 3rd grade history classes and beyond. What makes Nathan Hale a "freedom fighter" for defying legality in favor of

what is right but makes Mumia Abu-Jamal, Leonard Peltier, or Delbert Africa and other MOVE prisoners a "criminal?"

I've heard that Police Commissioner Sambor made an announcement before the May 13 assault saying "Attention MOVE! This is America!" If this was 1776 and he was a British soldier saying to Nathan Hale or Patrick Henry "Attention! This is an English colony and you have to abide by the laws of England," what do you think would have happened to him? He'd be a dead man right about now and the person who killed him would be celebrated as a hero for over 200 years. But he's going to stand in front of our house and say that.

It seems that some are willing to support Mumia, Leonard Peltier, and the MOVE 9 because the evidence available strongly suggests that they are innocent of the crime they are accused of. Unfortunately there seems to be less support for political prisoners and prisoners of war like Ruchell "Cinque" Magee, Assata Shakur, or Russell "Maroon" Shhoats, who were forced to break the law in order to protect themselves from their oppressor.

There is no way in the world that this government (which has the blood of Leonard Peltier's ancestors on their hands) is going to convince us to see him as a murderer. We don't care what happened on the Pine Ridge reservation because it isn't the issue. The very people that dropped a bomb on my family and burned babies alive are going to convince me to see Leonard or Mumia as a murderer?

To make it clear, I do believe that both Leonard and Mumia are innocent, but people are confused and misled by this system. With issues like Mumia, Leonard, or MOVE the government tries to convince people that the issue is whether or not they actually pulled the trigger and killed somebody. Mumia and Leonard are not in prison for the accusation of murder, but rather because of who they are and because they dared to stand up.

If murder was truly the issue it would be applied across the board. If it was about murder, they'd have to charge with murder and imprison those who murdered my family, who murdered Thomas Jones, Amadou Diallo, and Winston Hood back in the 60s. Why aren't they if murder is the true issue? Anytime you don't apply the same principle across the board, you're not talking about equality and justice.

What do you think were the facts presented in the later civil trial that most convinced the jury to decide in your favor?

The point that we made in that civil suit was that first of all this was not an accident that got out of control.

This was a planned murder and wasn't an isolated incident. I had to go to war with the attorneys representing me on this case. I told them that we had to deal with Aug.8, 1978 and the unjust imprisonment of our family because it was the root of our protest prior to May 13.

The lawyers didn't want to deal with it because a police officer had been shot and they didn't want to prejudice the jury by bringing that up. I said "The hell with that! They attacked my family that day. They destroyed the house, the evidence, they know my family is innocent, and that is what we were protesting. They wanted to stop the protest and shut us up permanently. Also, this isn't an isolated incident, but an ongoing problem of police attacking MOVE and killing their babies." I felt that the jury needed to get the clear picture and entire history.

We showed a video of the Aug. 8, 1978 beating of Delbert Africa and the city just went crazy. They did not want that in. When I testified I talked about the history of MOVE with this system and I think the jury didn't have a choice because we made clear that all of the charges justifying the May 11 warrants had been dismissed.

There was nothing the city could say to justify the assault. That jury did not want to find in my favor. Besides an asian man and a black woman on the jury, the rest were white suburbanites. It took them about 5 days to come to a verdict. They were in there battling. In fact, a white man got discharged during the deliberations. He just couldn't take it. We know they didn't want to find in my favor because they just ordered police commissioner Sambor and fire commissioner Richmond to each pay me one dollar a week for 11 years. That was their penalty. The jury decided the City of Philadelphia had to pay me $500,000. Especially after paying my legal fees, that wasn't much money. A woman got a one million dollar award for spilling hot coffee on herself at McDonald's

To add insult to injury, the judge comes back after the jury arrived at their verdict and overrules them in regards to Sambor and Richmond (granting them immunity). The judge never expected the jury to find Sambor and Richmond liable. He was willing to take the chance of finding the city liable. The City of Philadelphia is a faceless entity. They had already given Wilson Goode and many others in the city immunity.

This judge was an old white man. He didn't relate to me but rather to Sambor and Richmond and he never expected the jury to find them individually liable, but they did. In justifying his move, the judge said that he believed Commissioner Sambor's statement that had never given the order to let the fire burn.

Is there anything else you'd like to add?

People had better wake up for their own protection, because where this government is heading and what its involving itself in is very dangerous and a threat to all of us. People need to wake up and start taking charge of their own lives and make their own decisions because that's the only way all of this insanity can be stopped. Those running this country are completely out of control. Taking control isn't easy. It takes a lot of commitment and hard work, but when you look at the alternative there is no choice and that's' the bottom line. ★

kiss machine

Jamming the Trigger
by Camilla Gibb

We play a game she and I. She calls me Elmer and I call her Fudd and we sit under the dilapidated roof of my family's farmhouse in the kitchen with its mildewed linoleum floor. She watches with mock terror as I grip the rifle between my legs, caressing its barrel, cocking and uncocking, awakening our senses, our futures, with the comfort of the gun's quick click/ping.

Are you going to shoot me in the balls? she always asks. I'm going to blow them right off, I reply, sever those sacs, ugly turkey twaddle that they are. Then I raise my rifle and point at the target between her legs and she shrieks: shoot! And I shoot, I always shoot, but the gun isn't loaded, never is.

What did I tell you about playing with my gun! my dad shouts when he comes in from the fields and finds raspberry jam on the trigger. You're going to end up shooting yourself one of these days. I'm only twelve years old, you see, not old enough to be holding a rifle, but I can hardly say: Daddy, Emma wants me to point it at her. Every time she comes over after school, it's the only game she likes to play.

I never object when Emma insists on playing, so I know I am at least partially to blame. But how can I say no? It's the only time Emma smiles and she doesn't have much to smile about. Her parents are pagans – which means they're the only people in the area who don't go to church, so on Sundays she's lonely. She walks back and forth in front of the church waiting for me because I'm her best friend – her only friend, really.

One Sunday last summer, a guy on a motorbike came past and whacked her on the back of the head with a hammer. She'd gone face first into the ground and he dragged her like that into the cemetery, and then raped her behind the crypt of the only wealthy family in town. Everyone was at church, including me. There she was dying with her face in the dirt while we sang a stupid hymn.

Of course, everybody in town whispers: now that's what you get for being a pagan. Like they blame her; blame her parents. I, for one, blame the wealthy. If that crypt hadn't been there, there wouldn't have been a crime.

So when she asks me to shoot her, shoot her in the balls, what else am I supposed to do? It's the only time she smiles and she doesn't have much to smile about. It's a strange game, I know that, but Dad tells me I'm an odd duck, so I think of it as a game that the odd duck plays when the real Gwen is somewhere else. Like asleep, or on a camping trip or on a midnight train to some stupid other place. I pretend she's away most days after school when Emma and I are playing.

But it gets boring after a while, this game of pretending to shoot Emma in the balls, so one day I say, Why don't you shoot me today for a change? 'Cause you're a girl, she says. But so are you. Not any more, I'm not. Ahh, what are you talking about? I got balls don't I? The ones you're going to shoot off. Seriously, Emma, what are you talking about? Just shoot me, she says. Ok, ok, I give in, raising the gun. ★

contact: PO Box 108 Station P | Toronto, ON M5S 2S8 Canada | kissmachine.org

Hostage

by Deirdre Hanna

"If this were played upon a stage now, I could condemn it as an improbable fiction."
-William Shakespeare, *Twelfth Night*, Act 3, Scene 4

He crouches in the alcove by the Church of the Redeemer. Later, when she tries to envision exactly how he was poised, she thinks of panthers, but there is nothing particularly sleek about the pale man with the dark, tangled beard and navy blue parka.

She assumes he is a jogger trying to find a discrete spot to stretch but, peering anxiously south to see if the 8:16 p.m. bus is coming, she catches sight of him moving smoothly in her peripheral vision. He does not seem bothered by leg cramps.

A light drizzle makes the road just wet enough (no traction) for the streetlights to glow where they reflect off the pavement. It's weirdly quiet and bitterly cold for mid-November. Even the movie theatre around the corner feels deserted.

When the man starts towards her she just assumes he's resuming his (apocryphal) run. She pays more attention to the lone white car slowly turning north onto the street than to the quiet creature. There's no bus coming, so she starts to look at her Cartier watch, utterly beat from a long day at work during a draining pregnancy.

Then comes the shove. Hard. From behind. Directly into the path of the oncoming white car.

Somewhere at the brain stem level she comprehends that now that she's down on the ground, and the quickest way out of the car's path is to roll back towards the pusher through the curbside puddles and then grab (grab!) the pole at the bus stop. If she's holding into it, arms locked, it won't be easy to push her back into the street.

The car's driver steers wide while the prone woman rolls. When she gets to the curb she grasps the light standard and notices three things: the car has cautiously pulled to the curb half a block beyond her; she can hear the assailant running north, towards the Four Seasons hotel; and her Coach bag is still on the road, marked with a tire track.

"Help!" she calls a few times while pulling herself up, embracing the pole. "Please help me!" It's as if her life depends upon not letting go, but she can't be heard by the car's driver. The windows remain resolutely shut. The assailant emerges from the shadows to approach the car and the windows open a crack as he speaks softly to the driver. Then he darts back to the shelter of the deserted Renaissance Plaza. The white car's windows close again and the driver turns onto Cumberland, leaving the pregnant woman (doubly vulnerable) feeling very much alone.

There's still no bus coming, so she makes a break to run south along Avenue to Bloor, frantic to get away because she's certain the stranger will try to attack her again. She's sobbing and shaking and covered in mud, and her would-be white knight has already turned his back on her. Fighting her nausea so she can run faster, she hears footsteps following (hadn't they stopped?), but then suddenly the sounds change. The jaguar retreats. A southbound taxi driver calls to her: "Can I help you? Lady, are you okay? Can I help?"

Mute with shock, she crosses six lanes of surreally absent traffic to climb onto the taxi's ripped vinyl seat behind a retractable bulletproof glass barrier. "Is that your purse?" the cabbie asks, then he pulls a U-turn and opens his door so he can pick it up from the street.

"Lock the car," she whispers, then, "Please take me home." It takes a while before she can remember her address. Her cell phone – her safety talisman – is crushed. She can't call 911. Bewildered, she watches its LCD morph into an inkblot.

By the time the cops get to her house she's changed to dry clothes but is still trembling. If she can identify her assailant, the police tell her, they'll stand a good chance of prosecuting because the driver of the white car (a witness!) was a Very Famous Lawyer.

"He called it in right away," they tell her. And then drove away, she add silently to herself, fighting another wave of nausea. She visualizes the trademark pinstripe suit the driver wears during his frequent media appearances.

"Why didn't you remain at the scene?" the police ask. She doesn't know how to respond.

Later, when she calls the Very Famous Lawyer to thank him for not hitting her, she mentions that he knows her family, and that her unborn baby is fine. It's only months later, when she learns the case got lost somewhere in the shuffle between two precincts, that something the failed white knight told her comes flooding back as relevant:

"I didn't want to pick you up," he said, "because I thought it was a domestic." ★

Kitchen Sink (volume 1; issue 3)

Deeper Into Middle Earth:
Lord of the Rings and the Race Question
by Arme Johnson

"All were slain save those who fled to die, or to drown in the red foam of the River. Few ever came eastward to Morgul or to Mordor; and to the land of the Haradrim came only a tale from far off: a rumour of the wrath and terror of Gondor."
-from *Return of the King*, by JRR Tolkien, found at the head of a website called War Now and several weblogs supporting war in the Middle East.

In the post-politically correct, post-affirmative action, post-feminist, post-post world we live in, where Maxim rules the newsstands and it's considered reasonable to hold Middle Easterners in solitary confinement for two months, seeing society through the lens of race or sex seems archaic or even regressive. When Shaquille O'Neal, the mountainous bully of basketball's Los Angeles Lakers, mocked Chinese star Yao Ming by parroting a Chinese accent and faking kung fu movies on national television, many pundits and Shaq himself rolled their eyes in exasperation and argued that he was just funning; as if joking is such a noble and blameless endeavor that one should never besmirch it with analysis, or imply that humor could do harm.

It is in this climate one has to take a deep breath before implying that entertainment as well made and satisfying as the *Lord of the Rings* trilogy has dallied with racism. In anticipation of the films, online forums burned with defense of Tolkien's books and their racially divided Middle Earth. The stunning thing is that, though the films preserve and even enhance the books' divisions, and arrive in a time of intense prejudice against Middle Easterners (even the second film's title, *Two Towers*, is like a conspiracy nut's dream come true), nary a peep has emerged from the critical mainstream about a *mise en scene* where dark skin equals evil and Aryans are the highest order of life. Are critics so cowed by the threat of being labeled PC that they dare not comment? Or have we been so conditioned to accept the associations of black and white that we don't notice when the divisions border on the fascistic?

One of the few voices to speak to *LOTR*'s problematic nature has been Dr. Stephen Shapiro, an American expert in cultural studies currently residing in England. His rather judicious criticism of the marked racial themes in the books was greeted with incredulity and dismay. In an interview for *The Scotsman*, in which he lays out his argument that Tolkien was reacting to the influx of colonial immigrants and a fear of foreigners overrunning England, Shapiro points out a core issue with *LOTR* which can be said to apply to most science fiction and fantasy movies of the last 30 years.

"Tolkien wrote the *Lord of the Rings* because he wanted to recreate a mythology for the English that had been destroyed by foreign invasion. He felt organic English culture had been destroyed by the Normans. There is the notion that foreigners destroy culture and there was also a fantasy that there was a solid homogeneous English culture there to begin with, which was not the case because there were Celts and Vikings and a host of other groups."

Why is it that whenever a film attempts to resurrect mythology, to create modern legends and archetypes through alternate worlds, the future/past it imagines seldom seems to include the majority of the world that's not white, or the complexity and diversity of originating cultures? What's called "Earth" or a "Federation" in sci-fi and "A Time Long Ago" in fantasy inevitably ends up looking like America without minorities or England in the Middle Ages. Tolkien's books may have set a standard, but in everything from *Star Wars* to *Legend* to *The Mummy*, young Aryan men are the ultimate heroes, and characters/species with overt ethnicity are at best sleazy or untrustworthy comic relief; at worst, they are villains.

One could make the argument that this is how mythology is created; that it always reflects the history and desires of the writer and his imagined culture, and this is what gives the work its resonance. On the other hand, a few notable exceptions point to the possibilities of diversity being married to legend making. The most obvious is, of course, *Star Trek*. Ignoring the increasingly diverse casts as the series morphed over time, with women and African Americans as captains and various alien species on the side of right, the original show's cast of the late '60s still stands as more reflective of the world-as-it-is than most stories created since. The essential places in the cast for an African-American woman, a Japanese-American man, an alien (Spock) and even a Russian (an ethnicity certainly as frightening and foreign as any during the Cold War) made the *Enterprise*'s encounters with

contact: 5245 College Ave. #301 | Oakland, CA 94618 | kitchensinkmag.com

Otherness fraught with a complexity that never dampened the show's popularity or mythic resonance.

The reason cinema's legends and Tolkien's choices matter is that they are consciously-created archetypes aimed for the role of legend, whereas most myths have grown directly out of the oral tradition of a culture and become mythology over time. While Tolkien's England may well have been predominantly white, certainly the crumbling English empire included many races, and his predilection for casting dark-skinned people from the mysterious South and East as the legions of evil is insulting to the peoples that England subjugated for decades. It was also conscious. Check out this passage from *Two Towers*, as Smeagol/Gollum (who fits the description of comic relief/untrustworthiness, with his broken English and alien features) describes an oncoming army of Haradrim from the South:

> Dark faces. We have not seen Men like these before, no, Smeagol has not. They are fierce. They have black eyes, and long black hair, and gold rings in their ears; yes, lots of beautiful gold. And some have red paint on their cheeks, and red cloaks; and they have round shields, yellow and black with big spikes. Not nice; very cruel wicked men they look. Now, is it really possible that the similarity of this description (and even the name of their race, which rings of a generic Middle-Eastern soldier) is accidental? While Tolkien hated it when real-world analysis was applied to his work, the racial makeup of his world is unavoidably linked to the world in which he wrote. As these two quotes—the first from the noble and wise Faramir, the second from protagonist Frodo—make clear, Tolkien was aware that the evil of the Haradrim and Easterlings was associated with their racial differences from our heroes:

And they made a truce with the proud peoples of the North, who often had assailed us, men of fierce value, but our kin from afar off, unlike the wild Easterlings, or the cruel Haradrim.

illustration by Jonas Diego

This was no assault upon the Dark Lord by the men of Gondor, risen like avenging ghosts from the graves of valour long passed away. These were men of other race, out of the wide East-lands, gathering to the summons of their Over-lord.

The second sentence of Frodo's quote directly contrasts the "valour" of the "avenging ghosts" with a reference to race, as if race corresponded directly to values. Faramir, too, points out that the peoples of the North, though warlike, were still kin and of "fierce value," unlike the apparently disastrously swarthy Easterlings. Because Tolkien created a world where the sympathetic characters spoke lines like these—de-spite all their sententious sound of mythmaking, they were not passed down as a sort of cultural stream-of-consciousness—he must be held responsible for the Fellowship's racial idealogy.

Now, imagine you are Peter Jackson, confronted with some questionable passages and a possible fire-storm in this supposedly more racially sensitive era. How do you adapt admittedly wonderful stories that you are completely devoted to recreating faithfully without confronting issues of race? On the *LOTR* film website, Jackson anticipates any controversy by stat-ing that looking too closely at "a story that is essen-tially 50 years old is a little inappropriate," that Tolk-ien was "horrified at modern analogies being placed on his work," and that because Tolkien included—in a work of several thousand pages based on a terror of foreignness and miscegenation—a single passage where Samwise the Hobbit muses on the humanity of a dead Haradrim, he could not have been racist.

First of all, D.W. Griffith's *Birth of a Nation* is over 50 years old, but does that mean someone should recreate its Ku Klux Klan heroism word for word as a ripping good yarn? The idea of something being older and therefore sacrosanct was dismissed long ago. Secondly, as to Tolkien being "horrified" at people paying attention to his work in ways that he didn't intend—tough shit. If there's a section of Hades for writers, he can bitch to Shakespeare. And, as for Samwise's speech about how the dead soldier at his feet may have had a family and his own thoughts and dreams, it's really about the Hobbit's humanity, isn't it? How much more telling would it have been to have a single sentence, a word even, in the entire trilogy that showed the Orcs, Southrons, Uruk-Hai, Variags or Haradrim thinking about such things? OK, so you're creating a mythology. Is there any real rea-son why the good Humans, or the Hobbits for that matter, can't include people of more than one color or racial characteristic?

If you grant that the work was written 50 years ago, and reflects its time and the prejudices of a cranky old academic who wrote an otherwise satisfying tale, fine. Then what's Jackson's excuse? Not only has he done nothing with the benefit of hindsight or analysis to ameliorate the text, there are many parts where he enhances potentially problematic aspects. Take the Haradrim, for instance. While Tolkien's description leaves little doubt that the soldiers are Arabic/Indian in nature, nowhere in Gollum's or anyone's descrip-tion do the soldiers don black eyeliner and mujha-deen-like scarves around the bottoms of their faces. These may seem like small details, but it makes you wonder why Jackson didn't do more to defuse an as-sociation he was fully aware of by de-emphasizing their parallels to the Middle East.

Jackson's vision of the Uruk-Hai is equally troubling. Described by Tolkien as "swart," or dark-skinned, not much more detail is given in the book about these ferocious creatures except that they were bred from Orcs and Goblins. Not only does Jackson make them emerge from their muddy wombs with dreadlock-like hair—locks that alternate for the rest of the movies between dreads and a Pacific Islander-looking tumble of curls—but he takes their emblem of the white hand from its place on the helmet, where Tolkien describes it, and puts it in white grease paint on the Uruk-hai's faces. The resulting image is dis-turbingly reminiscent of Australian aborigines or Afri-can warriors. And what little humanity they are given in the book—they do in fact speak quite fluently—is reduced to screaming and barbaric bellowing.

While much has been made of Jackson's faith-fulness to the books, here and in other places he has insinuated his own agenda. His depiction of the elves is suffused with a nostalgic sadness. These aristo-cratic Aryans are the purest of races, and once wield-ed great power, but now they fade into the "great ocean" of history and legend. This obvious elegy to whiteness and the European aristocracy, and their sense of order in a chaotic world, is hardly hidden in Jackson's version. There's an astoundingly visceral thrill at the beginning of the first film, where teem-ing, chaotic, ugly, dark masses of Orcs lurch for-ward into war and meet the gleaming, golden rows of elves who respond with a gasp-inducingly precise and synchronized swing of their weapons. This vi-sion of civilization, of perfect cleanliness and purity turning into a buzzsaw for the teeming legions of confusion and filth, is a frighteningly uplifting and charged appeal to fascism that still resonates long after the film is over. You can't help but feel terrified by and yet attracted to the elves and their orderly violence.

Just in case you missed the point, Jackson brings the elves back in the battle for Helm's Deep in *Two Towers*. Again, this is not in the original book, so the returning image of their precise movements and ee-rily blond blankness serves only to emphasize the dif-ference between good and evil, since the Humans are dirty and scraggly enough to be confused with the bad guys.

The movies are overhung with gloom and danger, countered by the urgency of acting on clearly-defined principles: a rallying call to unify a society. Even Tolkien allowed more ambiguity and less hurry. Certainly those clamoring for violence and a war divided along cultural lines would be assured by the way Jackson handles the Ents in *Two Towers*. In the book, after meeting up with Treebeard and alerting him to the encroaching wars, the Hobbits Merry and Pippin wait quietly with an Ent named Quickbeam until the Ent Council slowly comes to a decision to declare war. In the movie, it isn't until Merry makes an impassioned and teary speech about acting urgently to save their friends, about not standing aside because this is their war too, that the Ents become warlike. Though this scene may have been intended as shorthand on the way to adapting a very wordy trilogy, Jackson's solution is rife with associations. It's very hard not to feel that Merry's speech is meant to tap into our impatience with slow-deliberating but good-hearted peoples, with kindly Ent-ellectuals who talk too much while the world burns around them. While Jackson certainly couldn't have anticipated 9/11 (the films were begun years ago), or a world deadlocked about war in Iraq, this speech still resonated across a Western culture that was already facing a wave of terrorism and Islamic fundamentalism.

It seems unlikely that Peter Jackson is fascist, racist or even socially conservative. The fact that he felt compelled to answer accusations of racism before they arrived shows that the subject at least concerned him. And, certainly, he amplifies those points in the book that delineate a war between uncontrollable industry and the forces of nature, a decidedly liberal theme. But his films have typically delved into what are probably his own personal nightmares, and the resulting atmosphere of dread and horror gives *LOTR* much of its potency. Unfortunately, when you combine that skill at uncovering universal terrors with Tolkien's mythmaking, you get a dangerous combination. His work taps into our primal instincts, and its reliance on the old standards of dark vs. light and the bestial vs. civilization, makes its entry into the war on terrorism and a world in the grip of racial profiling a disturbing one.

Assuming, on the other hand, that Peter Jackson didn't make all these changes to reflect some kind of unconscious agenda, and was merely a conduit for Tolkien's themes, is he blameless? In recreating Tolkien's world, Jackson delivers a film with the kind of epic grandeur and special effects wizardry not seen since the original *Star Wars*. The first film in particular is truly cinematic mythmaking of the highest order. So why quibble? Perhaps because one always has to be vigilant, to ask what it is in oneself that resonates so stirringly to Jackson's powerful drums. The Nuremberg rallies were an awesome spectacle as well, and Leni Reifenstahl's filmic record of them was stunning. *Birth of a Nation* is one of the greatest films ever made. In todays explosive climate, it seems dangerous to wave aside that little voice in the back of our heads because we're so desperate for satisfying entertainment and righteous warriors to lead us from the dark. That's how all the storms have come throughout modern history, as a lancing light through the murk of confusion, that suddenly turns to a torrent which washes everything away. ★

Kitchen Sink (volume 1; issue 4)

Where Have All the Girls Gone? India's Abortion Dilemma
by Anuradha Sengupta

A seven-month-old baby girl's father leaves her with a stranger in a hospital when he goes to the bathroom. The child had been coughing for some days and had been brought to the hospital for a checkup. The father never returns. Another girl is found abandoned at a garbage dump and rescued by the police ("We had to fight off the dogs and crows to get to her," quotes a report in the English daily, *The Times of India*). A mother swaps her baby girl for a boy in a hospital in a southern metro city. A leading English-language alternative health magazine carries an ad: Male or female child? You can choose the sex of your child yourself.

India's female population is larger than the combined total population of Canada, the United States and the Russian Federation, according to the United Nations report, *Women in India: How Free, How Equal?*. Yet, 20 to 25 million Indian women are "missing" — that is, they are not born, or they do not live.

There are two ways this happens. In poor families, the girl child might be killed immediately after she is born, by the dais or midwives who deliver her. But go up the class and money rung a bit and infanticide would be replaced by feticide. The moment an ultrasound screen shows the genitalia of a baby girl, the fetus' fate is sealed, it is aborted. Though official figures do not support the claim, the Indian Medical Association estimates that every year at least five million females are killed at birth or aborted as fetuses.

In India, the right to abortion is not under siege as it is in the United States. In 1971, a year and a half before Roe vs. Wade legalized abortion in America, the Indian Parliament gave women the right to abortion. Though the law allows abortion only under certain circumstances, they are loosely defined and can be broadly interpreted. One such circumstance, the most frequently cited excuse, is failure of contraception. The Indian government passed the pro-choice law without much debate or opposition because it was desperate to control the country's burgeoning population, and saw this as a viable tool.

Right to Choose in the Wrong Hands
But what could be interpreted as a move to give women the right to choose is just the opposite. The right to abortion is used most often by the men in a patriarchal society to get rid of unwanted girl children. More often than not, the women have no say in the matter.

Feticide, or sex selective abortion, began in India after the invention and importation of prenatal diagnostic techniques, such as ultrasound in the '70s. What was meant to be a breakthrough for preventing infant mortality became the answer to the prayers of a male-child-hungry nation. New Delhi had the first ultrasound machines, but the technology spread rapidly to other parts of the country. The tests came to be known as sex determination tests, or SD tests. A leading daily, The Indian Express, reported in 1980 that most people didn't even know that ultrasound was used for detecting defects in the fetus. Ads were found all over — in railway stations, on buses, in newspapers — "Pay Rs 500 now (about $10) and save Rs 5 lakh later (about $10,000)." The latter amount, a reference to a hefty dowry that parents of a daughter must pay the groom.

"One can still excuse the poor, for back-breaking poverty drives them to it," says Satish Agnihotri, a consultant with UNICEF in Calcutta. "A son means more hands on the field, but a daughter means dowry. But what about the people with money? How does one excuse them?" Most marriages in India are still arranged by families, and a man who does not marry for love learns he can marry for possessions. The dowry system, outlawed in the early '80s, has degenerated into extortion that goes on long after marriage. For a man and his family, a woman becomes the ticket to a few imported watches, a stereo, a refrigerator, a motorbike or a car through the system of dowry. A dowry, once a way for a father to endow a Hindu daughter with material goods when she could not inherit property, has evolved into a reward paid to a man and his family to take a woman off her parents' hands. "The value of a woman goes down every time

contact: 5245 College Ave. #301 | Oakland, CA 94618 | kitchensinkmag.com

the value of gold goes up," says women's activist Kaberi Sen.

The practice of dowry — and sex selection — is prevalent as much among the rich as the poor. "If you see the latest census data, you will find that female feticide is growing among the moneyed people — we have seen that the richer you become, the more your household consumer expenditure, the more masculine is the sex ratio," Agnihotri says.

Redefining Right-to-Lifers

When a series of media exposes uncovered the female feticide trend, there was shock all around. Yet nothing was done, no doctors were hauled up, no one went to prison. But by then, women's groups across the country had put a ban on prenatal diagnosis techniques at the top of their agenda. After years of sustained campaigning, a law was passed in 1994 banning prenatal sex selection through ultrasound and other post-conception sex determination techniques. "Intent of the act was to stop the declining female child sex ratio; it didn't matter at which stage sex-determination came," notes Dr. Sabu M. George, who has campaigned against female feticide in the country for the last 16 years and is on the panel that filed the successful court petition. George says it is Indian society's inherently patriarchal and pro-male attitude that has led to a "devaluation" of women, a lack of respect and worth.

The ban on ultrasound did not serve its purpose — sex selection centers only went underground. A doctor from Sirsa (where media reports stated that at least 200 abortions per week were taking place) declared that the ban would only result in doctors hiking their fees, "and as a result the poor will suffer." The 2001 census revealed a highly skewed sex ratio: 933 women for every 1,000 men. The juvenile sex ratio (among children younger than six years) was even more worrying. For every 1,000 boys in this age group, the number of girls dropped from 945 in 1991 to 927 in 2001. What seems like a fairly small drop is amplified by the country's more than one-billion-person population, second in size only to China.

Women's groups and activists in India are now lobbying hard to get legislation passed that will ban pre-conception sex selection methods in the country. "Technology has, however, always been a step ahead of the law and the need to legislate on pre-conception sex selection techniques is now being debated," George says.

"Laws will never achieve anything," says Rupa Bajwa, a 20-something journalist based in Calcutta. Bajwa is originally from Punjab, one of the worst affected areas, and is herself a survivor of female feticide. The third in a line of three daughters, her paternal grandmother told her mother to abort after an ultrasound. But her mother refused. "I was fortunate that I had a mother who had a mind of her own. In our society, we are never really taught to respect women. Unless we do that, no amount of laws will help." ★

illustration by Donna Barr

Home and Security
by Gavin Grant

With thousands of like-minded others, I went to the big peace rally in New York City on February 15th, 2003. It was a cold day, and my wife and I walked up Third Avenue from 32nd to 68th Street before we could cut over to First Avenue and join the rally. Which was really a slow march, but since the city government wouldn't give us a permit to march, let's call it a rally.

What do we want?
So many things.
When do want them?
It doesn't seem possible, but now, please.

...March 5th, 2003, Local News: Writer and editor Gavin J. Grant, 33, (picture) of Northampton, Massachusetts is believed to be one of hundreds of detainees held after police and other government agencies moved in to calm a noisy and potentially-violent peace rally in New York City's Washington Square Park....

I joined the United for Peace and Justice email list for information on future rallies. I forwarded their email about a march and vigil on the fifth of March to my wife. She had to pick up some freelance work in New York and readily agreed to go.

Tell me what a democracy looks like.
From here, a dictatorship.
This is what a democracy looks like.
This march, or this war? It's hard to tell.

...March 7th, 2003, Email: Gavin, Dad here. Got a call from INS (IRS?) saying you had been held (under Patriotic act?) after rally and asking re: marriage and so on. Confirm ok by you to send these? Love, dad and mum. xx....

The march and candlelight vigil on fifth of March was as depressing as the February 15th rally. Thousands of people gathered outside Senator Hilary Clinton's office and marched to Senator Chuck Schumer's office to protest their voting to send the USA into war with Iraq. We marched down Third Ave. to 42nd Street and then snaked over to Fifth, blocking crosstown traffic. We marched to Washington Square Park and were closely watched by the Fifth Avenue business owners — some of whom seemed to dither between a desire to join us and a fear of the crowd. But we were no mob. People drummed and danced, sang the usual songs, held or wore signs that were as funny and direct as ever ("The only Bush I trust is my own" was more popular this time), yet, will this stop a war? Hundred of police seemed to think we might start a Battle of Seattle ourselves. Which leads to thoughts of whether we might place some of these police in the White House.

...March 8th, 2003, National News: Detained immigrant Gavin Grant's website (Internet Archive link) has been taken down by the federal government under suspicions of terrorist links. Grant, a freelance writer who has written for alternative publications such as The Urban Pantheist, Weird Times, and Xerography Debt, recently published altered transcripts of two of President Bush's remarks on Iraq on his website. Citing freedom of speech and linking to satirical websites such as The Onion, Grant simply switched the President's name with Saddam Hussein's in two transcripts. The first transcript made it appear that Hussein was about to attack the USA with 3,000 cruise missiles -- with no differentiation of civilian and military targets. The second transcript, however, was perhaps even more threatening and, given the present Orange Alert, is likely the reason Grant was arrested. Grant altered President Bush's remarks on the possibilities of an internal coup in Iraq and changed them to suggest that generals and others in the US Armed Forces might find themselves well rewarded if they initiated an internal revolt. The White House announced there would be a press conference concerning the latest detainees at 2 PM today and referred all questions to John Ashcroft's office....

We, The People, Don't Want This War!
Shame Bush hasn't noticed.

March 15: The thing is, I haven't been arrested. I'm not even in hiding. This morning I sanded the ice in my driveway and talked to Jeff, our contractor, about building some bookshelves in a room upstairs. When

I opened my email there were 250+ emails -- mostly from people I didn't know. 90% were supportive, but some were just vitriolic. I haven't even posted my articles yet, they were just ideas I was playing with. I was going to contact a lawyer friend and another guy I know who ran a satirical website to get some advice before I posted. The lines keep moving and I wanted to make sure I wasn't going to cross any of the dangerous ones.

...March 12, 2003, <u>NYPD Spokesman</u>: We can confirm arrests of a number of individuals participating in an anti-government rally in Washington Square Park on the evening of March 5th. These individuals are no longer in our jurisdiction. They are being held under the auspices of the Domestic Security Enhancement Act of 2003 in an undisclosed location....

I don't like singing and chanting with the other marchers. I think walking quietly is just as important. That way we don't all look as if we're being carried away in an ecstatic trance. Other people jangled their keys as they walked. I wondered if it was just an impulse to be rhythmic or if they had read Ursula K. Le Guin's story about a revolution, "Unlocking the Air"?

<u>Drop Bush, not bombs.</u>
Or at least his lapdog, Blair.

At the end of the February 15th rally when the closely-herded thousands of us were leaving, I went to walk around the outside edge of a phone box. A policeman stopped me and told me I had to stay on the sidewalk. Cold, frustrated by this abject stupidity and niggardliness, I objected.
"That," and I pointed to the two feet of sidewalk between the phone box and the street, "is the sidewalk." The policeman declared it was not, and another policeman moved closer to the first in case I was trouble. I repeated that the space between the phone and the road was, in fact, sidewalk. The policeman, putting his hand on his billyclub, repeated his determination that it was not. I held my hands up in the air to show I wasn't about to start anything, could not stop myself from calling him a fascist, and left. I wondered how near to arrest I'd been.

...September 5, 2003, <u>National News</u>: Detainees from the March 5th peace march in New York have now been held for one hundred and eighty days without access to family, legal aid, or media. The Department of Homeland Security refuses to release the number of detainees or any identifying information. Twenty-three of the detained have since been stripped of their citizenship and deported to their countries of origin. Mothers of the Disappeared, a new New York City-based organization claims that the detainees are being tortured and tried in secret courts. White House spokesman Jim Morrell refused to comment on what he called "pure fabulation."....

The US government declared the war in Iraq over in May 2003. The ongoing reports of killings in Iraq remind me of growing up in the U.K. War was never formally declared in Northern Ireland, but the headlines were often about bombings, murders, and shootings. The peace process in Ireland is one thing that fills me with hope. Perhaps the past can be let go -- <u>not</u> forgotten -- and a new future can be chosen based on peace and negotiation rather than on the acts of a randomly chosen period one, two, or three hundred years ago.

...March 5, 2004, <u>National News</u>: The one-year anniversary of last year's national peace rally and the accompanying series of arrests was marked today by rallies, countrywide student sit-ins, and the third masked Black Bloc flashmob appearance (click for exclusive <u>video</u>) in New York City this week. Although a number of the detainees are known to be serving prison terms, the Department of Homeland Security resolutely refuses to release the original number of marchers detained, or any identifying information. Mothers of the Disappeared claim the detainees have been moved to the US military base in Guantanamo Bay and that, citing Amnesty International interviews with ex-prisoners from the Afghanistan war of 2001, the conditions in Guantanamo are an abuse of the detainees human rights. White House spokesman Jim Morrell refused to comment on what he called "pure fabulation."....

I never carry my green card with me. I know the number, but I don't want to lose it if my wallet were stolen. So if I were arrested my identity cards would be my New York driver's license with my old address on it, credit cards, and membership cards for the library, Pleasant Street Video, AAA, and Amnesty International. I look in the mirror and I'm not sure who's there. There's a man with lines around his eyes, and a somewhat blank expression. What does he want? When does he want it? Not this president. Not this future. ★

Leeking Ink

Stupid Things I've Done Lately
by Davida Gypsy Breier

I've done some really stupid things lately. I don't think I'm usually this mindless and dense, but here's proof otherwise…

GOING POSTAL

I had written Andy a letter on my train ride to work, but didn't have an envelope in my bag (my bag is my traveling office). When I got to DC I used one from my stash of work stationary, stamped it and sent it on its way to Portland. A week or so later the letter was back on my desk…opened. I had forgotten the apartment number and it was returned…to the hands of my petty, *Seinfeld*-obsessed "director." He smirked about it. The letter had been rather personal and worse yet, confessed to/gloated about leaving a work event several hours early a few weeks before.

SUB-CONSCIOUS LUDDITE?

I was working on two freelance projects at home. Without a shred of forethought, I got up from the computer, walked into my bedroom and decided that *that* moment would be a good time to take the air conditioner out of the window. I took it out all right. The window was sticking because of the high humidity and stormy weather. I had one hand on the AC trying to balance it and the other pounding the window. It finally sprang upward, causing my upper body to surge forward and push the AC out the second story window. I ran downstairs to make sure none of the dogs were outside when it fell. They weren't. I went into my mother's room to explain the crash. She stood there at the door looking at the now mutilated AC and turned to me and said, "It landed in a pile of diarrhea you know."

OIL AND WATER

I know the danger of having lip balm in my pants pocket, but I got home from work near midnight and just threw the pants in the wash without thinking. I had to go out and buy Patrick new pants for work that weekend.

SELF-POISONING: "ALL-NATURAL" CAN KILL I

I decided I would try and take better care of myself and eat a healthy breakfast routinely. I found a new, self-proclaimed, "healthy" cereal that I liked. It took nearly 6 weeks for me to realize that all the cracked and unprocessed wheat in the cereal was causing my stomach agonies.

NEVER A BORROWER BE

My minivan had died a few weeks earlier and my boss needed me to work one Saturday. I picked his van up and was to use it for the photo shoot and give it back to him when he got home Monday. Well, Saturday evening rolled around and I needed to go take care of my friend's cats while she was away. Using the van wouldn't hurt, would it? On the way back I decided to stop by the grocery store, which was where the van started making a terrible noise. I was afraid to drive it and I couldn't get in touch with him, so I parked it and left about 10 messages explaining what happened and begging forgiveness for using the van without asking. It had thrown a spark plug and had nothing to do with me driving it, but having just watched my own minivan pass away I wasn't sure.

1ST DEGREE IDIOT

Patrick came to see me at lunch on my first day of work and we went to get hot drinks. I wasn't feeling well and ordered hot tea, watching the woman heat the water with an espresso spout. It was far too hot to drink, so I thought, "Oh, I'll just put some ice in it." I put the open cup under the ice chute and pushed. The water that splashed out of the cup was hot enough to cause blisters on the top of my hand.

SELF POISONING: "ALL-NATURAL" CAN KILL II

I had been sick for nearly a week. I left work early and stopped and got what I thought would help: nice "hippy-dippy" herbal cough syrup (by Tom's of Maine). I got the nighttime formula and took some as soon as I got home. I didn't get sleepy…in fact I felt a little peppy. That peppiness would quickly transform into an inability to sleep and perpetual anxiety, only I was too sick and stupid to realize it was the cough syrup causing the problem. After three days I went to the doctor who said my heart was racing and that it was likely the cough medicine. I was utterly exhausted by that point. She also said I probably had mono.

DOMESTIC SELF-ABUSE

Christmas night I fell victim to a violent bout of gastroenteritis (the stomach flu). In the middle of the night, on yet another desperate flight to the bathroom to throw up, I ran face first into the wall. It began to bruise and swell immediately. At the hospital a few days later I would be asked if anyone had hit or threatened me…just me.

contact: PO Box 963 | Havre de Grace, MD 21078 | leekinginc.com

Letters from a Bicycle

letters from a bicycle
#1

by Five

Dear Raechel,

i've always liked laughs and yours was one of the best i've ever heard. Free and loud. You were always willing to talk and check in with people. You actually cared how people were doing and would seek them out, especially if you thought that for some reason they were having a bad day. You really were one of those people who got along with everyone.

In the smoker's alley, you'd ask "can i have a cigarette?" and i'd say "no." you'd just smile and say "thanks," in a way that would actually make me feel good.

You came with Kate and i once when we skipped class. We trudged through the snow on the field at the middle school, toward the Conoco station to eat cheap junk food and smoke cigarettes. i didn't think that you and Kate would get along but i ended up just listening to the two of you talk the whole time.

i remember the look on your face when my name was called over the intercom a few weeks later. The office had finally caught on to all of my truancies. It was

contact: c/o IPRC | 917 SW Oak St. #218 | Portland, OR 97205

that motherly look, Like - you fucked up - but mixed with a little sideways smirk. i fucking hated Mr. Heathman's drawing class. He'd refuse to grade a drawing if he thought it was "too evil" because he was a dogmatic jerk, so i'd ditch and sit with you in the commons while you graded papers for the teacher assistant period you had.

 i told you about what my mom said about sending me to military school. and you just rolled your eyes. "Yeah right, don't sweat it, just don't do it again," at least not for a while." i laughed.

After x-mas break our class schedule changed and i saw you less and less. The occasional session during lunch time, breif conversations during passing period. You always asked for a hug and that was a really special thing to me. Not many people did that and out of those who did, few were genuine about it.

It's hard to write this all down. How could i ever really capture what happened and how it felt. My hand will freeze, i'll stare at nothing and get zapped back eight years nearly to the day.

i still come really close to losing it every time i hear "Tears in Heaven" by Eric Clapton, they played it at your funeral, right after Tara sang. i couldn't really figure out why she sang at your funeral. i didn't think you two were ever friends..

A few lines into her song, it looked like someone slapped her across the face. She stopped singing and put the mic down.

She left the alter, but the piano player kept going. For some reason i thought to my-self - "it serves her right." and i know that's a wicked, wicked thought.

That week was the first that i ever had the overwhelming feeling that i didn't know what to do with myself. i explained to my mother, who looked at me with worried eyes, that i felt helpless. Mom would know what to do.

Your favorite color was purple. My mom owned a quilting supply store at the time, so she gave me a bunch of purple fabric to make ribbons out of. I passed them out at school to everyone who wanted one, with a tiny gold safety pin. The purple ribbons were in memory of you and the three others. i still have my little green backpack with the purple rec-tangle sewn to it.

What were you doing in that van? Everyone knew that Nate and Ronald were friends, but it didn't really seem like you and Tammy were. or you and Nate and Ronald. Maybe it was a random thing, like you were all hanging out on main street and decided to go for a ride. Maybe you were all at a party that i still don't know about. The cops said there was no alcohol involved.

They said you died on the way to the hospital in the ambulance. The rumors said that somebody's body was bent in half the wrong way. There were dark stains on the road for a long time. The bark that came off the trees never came back while i still lived in that wicked little town.

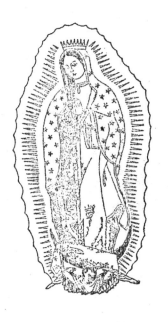

i hope it didn't hurt. i
hope you weren't scared. i hope
it was fast and short.
i hope that there was at least
one moment that evening that you
felt alive, or free, or young, or
all of these things.
i hope that you didn't feel
alone.
   i still miss you.

Love, five

I love my job ...
by Jamez Terry

12-11-02

I love my job. I do. But this past week it hasn't always been easy to remember that. I wouldn't even say it's been a bad week, all told - there have just been some particularly rough bits...

THURSDAY

It snowed. And snowed and snowed. I'm not sure how much we got altogether - 4 inches? Six? Nothing enormous, but a heck of a lot more than DC was ready to handle. Everything closed - schools, businesses, governments - but not Domino's.

Now, snow is one of my favorite things. I love the way it looks, especially on trees. I love the way it tastes and the way that it somehow makes it okay for adults to stand with their tongues sticking out at the sky. I love how it crunches under my feet and balls up in my hands. (No, I'm not a fan of gloves.) And then there's that surreal pseudo-silence that seems to take over the world whenever it snows. Snow even has its own special smell...

contact: 111 W Archer Pl. I Denver, CO 80223

[So I'm gonna do something that, as a
non-TV-owner, I never do - make a TV reference. There's a WB show called The Gilmore
Girls, and it's my mom's favorite. Mine
too, I guess. One of the main characters,
Lorelai, loves snow more than anything.
She can always smell the first snow coming,
and it's celebrated with great joy, very
little sleep, and midnight donuts. So
yeah...]

(For these people, like me, who grew
up under a rock ...That, a TV)

Anyway, what I don't love is driving in
the snow in/around DC. Plowing and such
takes <u>forever</u>, and people forget how to
drive at the first sight of anything white.
Thus, there are not only wrecks all over
the place, there are generally also ridiculous amounts of abandoned cars along
the highways. I mean, what do they do
- get out and walk??

"Oh no, what if my car dies? I
better start hiking now, just in case..."

But regardless of bad drivers, impossible side streets, and all the fun I could have been having in the snow, by 11:30 I was ready to start delivering boxes of steaming, cheesy goodness to all the people who wouldn't dare brave the roads themselves... (Damn, now that was a run-on sentence!)

Pretty early in the day, I had to drop some pizzas on Livinston Terrace, a place where I go all the time. It's a pretty substantial cluster of apartments, and this delivery was going to the very back building. The main driveway, a steep uphill, had thick snow still, but one of the residents was out, spreading sand, and it wasn't too bad.

At the top of the hill, I had to turn left into the appropriate parking lot. Looking at how deep the groundcover was, I hesitated and almost parked where I was. But walking wasn't what I wanted to do either, so I drove in, carefully staying to the center path, on which at least one car seemed to have made it out.

And then I was where I needed to be. And that's when I made my fatal mistake.

You see, I just recently acquired my current car. The only car I'd ever had before was a Caprice, a REAR WHEEL DRIVE. Alas, the new car is a front wheel drive. Of course that's fine, as long as I remember it, but I'm used to throwing my front wheels wherever I want and having the back ones to pull me out. So that's what I did - right into a big snowpile - SHIT!

But regardless of bad drivers, impossible
side streets, and all the fun I could
have been having in the snow, by 11:30
I was ready to start delivering boxes
of steaming, cheesy goodness to all the
people who wouldn't dare brave the roads
themselves... (Damn, now that was a run-
on sentence!)

Pretty early in the day, I had to drop
some pizzas on Livinston Terrace, a place
where I go all the time. It's a pretty
substantial cluster of apartments, and
this delivery was going to the very back
building. The main driveway, a steep
uphill, had thick snow still, but one
of the residents was out, spreading sand,
and it wasn't too bad.

At the top of the hill, I had to turn
left into the appropriate parking lot.
Looking at how deep the groundcover was,
I hesitated and almost parked where I
was. But walking wasn't what I wanted
to do either, so I drove in, carefully
staying to the center path, on which at
least one car seemed to have made it out.

And then I was where I needed to be.
And that's when I made my fatal mistake.

You see, I just recently acquired my
current car. The only car I'd ever had
before was a Caprice, a REAR WHEEL DRIVE.
Alas, the new car is a front wheel drive.
Of course that's fine, as long as I remember it, but I'm used to throwing my front
wheels wherever I want and having the
back ones to pull me out. So that's what
I did - right into a big snowpile - SHIT!

Or not. So much for my brilliant plan...

The kids still wanted to push, so I figured what the hell. None of them were older than 10, but at least 8 of them gathered at the front bumper and pushed their hardest. Not the slightest movement.

I decided to try digging around the wheels and quickly had many eager assistants. ("I'll go look for a shovel." "Want me to get my dad?" "Can I dig too?" "Maybe I'll dig around the back wheels.") The snow was really largely ice and hand-digging was most ineffective.

Another kid kept insisting that if I packed snow into my tailpipe, it would solve the problem. Somehow, I didn't think so.

One of the girls asked how old I was and volunteered that she thought I was much younger. "I thought you was, like, 13 and just had a car or something." What??

Meanwhile, there was a grown man who had been watching this whole escapade from a distance. I'd been debating asking for his help, but figured that he knew what was up. If he wanted to help, he'd offer. Besides, I felt pretty silly. Not to mention that, as a faggy little white boy, I don't necessarily expect warm welcomes around here.

So, for whatever reason, he decided to come over as I was trying to dig. He appraised the situation, kicked at the snow some, adjusted my cardboard and offered to try pushing. Along with a handful of snowsuited helpers, he got the car rocking, but not rolling.

A little bit earlier, a pseudo-fight had broken out between two little boys. Somewhere in the scuffle, a girl had gotten hit. And then life had gone on. Now, all of a sudden, a youngish man in overalls came stalking across the lot looking pissed and scary as hell. He went up to one boy and started yelling, "If you EVER touch my daughter again..."

didn't touch the kid - just scared the crap out of him. Then he turned to go back home, thus passing my car for the second time, and the hard lines in his face softened considerably. "Need some help?"

That's about all I heard him say and he definitely never smiled, but he added his efforts to pushing and I was out in no time. My profuse thanks seemed to be ignored, but I could tell they were hearing me.

And I remembered that I _am_ part of this community, faggy white boy or not, and that people can tell. It's days like that, the hard ones, the tiring ones, that help to restore my faith in people. In the end, I have to admit, I was glad to have been stuck...

Nomy Lamm: Interview with a Punk Princess

by Rocío Carlos

Nomy Lamm's website (www.nomylamm.com) calls her a "Fat ass, Bad ass, Jew, Dyke, Amputee." Her new show *Effigy* is the result of ten years of body image activism. Nomy became very visible in the early 1990's during the peak of the artistic and political phenomenon of Riot Grrrl, when she began writing to empower herself and her various identities in terms of size, sexuality, and physical ability through the medium of the punk rock counterculture. *Effigy* is a sort of electro-pop opera combining visual images, theater, and synth-pop music, not to mention very distinct characters and personalities. Nomy herself is a princess, a cheerleader, a victim of western medicine gone wrong, and a veiled bride all in the same two hours. Her cast of hot chubby back-up dancers, baton twirlers, and a punk Chicana rapper make this a truly multimedia, if not multi-tasking experience. I met with Nomy the day after *Effigy* opened in L.A. to talk about art, colonization, and body image today.

Rocío Carlos: This issue is about body image politics. After many years of doing this kind of activism, what do you have to say about body image and standards today, in the U.S. and globally?

Nomy Lamm: Well it's definitely a form of control, a tool of consumerism. We live in a consumerist culture that has really specific ways that we're supposed to act and be in the world and I feel like it's this huge distraction for people. If you think that there is something wrong with you and that you have to change somehow in order to be loved and have a good life, then that's what you're going to focus on instead of trying to detangle all these –

Like get health care, or decent wages –

Or even just being *listened* to by your friends or your family. Like if adolescent girls could stop having the conversation of "I'm so fat…," they could talk about real problems that they're having. As long as we have these intense value judgments around fat, we can't look at our actual experiences and say "this is the way that I can operate in the world because I have a thin body," or "I have to work a little bit harder in the world because I have a fat body" or whatever. And it keeps fat people silent. The beauty standards are developed by such a specific group of people.

Tell me a little bit more about the colonization of our bodies by this standard. How do we de-colonize?

There's just so much to deal with in this world, even just thinking about how we live on colonized *land*. I mean what we see around us is not right for this land. There is not a normal way to function in this society, because our society is totally fucked up, and the only way you could feel like it's okay is to have a lot of fucking money, which most people don't.

I saw this woman speak once and she said that everyday that she wakes up she knows that she is on colonized land. That white people have the privilege of not being aware of that, or only thinking about it when it's convenient, and that she wanted everyone to think about that everyday when they wake up. I was really impacted by that. I think it takes a certain amount of figuring out the system, and then figuring out how to bring our personal truths into the world in order to be able to survive.

It's really hard to grow up in a fat body or later get fat and not feel intense shame around that. Making your own body invisible in the world is a really hard thing, all of your energy gets focused into it. I've been doing fat activism work for like ten years and still it's there, everyday. Growing up I had a fake leg, I was fat, and I was on diets all the time. I was embarrassed about my body all the time and didn't want people to see it. I was getting shit from my parents for being lazy or not exercising enough, but at the same time I had nowhere to put that energy, nowhere to really connect with my body. It took a lot of years of treating my body like shit and not knowing what was good for me. And meanwhile I was doing all this political work about loving your body and still treating myself this way because I didn't know how to take care of myself. I quit smoking about a year ago. I've started doing yoga. Preparing for this show has been a really intense process for me physically because it's very demanding – especially vocally – and now I'm okay. I have to take care of myself enough and understand myself enough to be able to do this thing that I love.

There's not a lot of encouragement for that, for fat people, or people with disabilities, to work with our bodies and our talents and our abilities. You know, there's certain things that I can't do, and there's certain things that I can do that nobody else can do. I think it's really cool to watch my dancers and be like "you're wearing hot pants!" They're so cute and so hot and it makes me very happy to have these other fat girls on the stage who are going through the same process with it. That can affect the people who see it.

There are those people who still call that objectification rather than empowerment. How do you respond to that?

You can't just write off sexuality. Sexuality has a lot of different elements. I think that it's about a certain person or industry that is controlling that objectification and the ways that people are compensated or aware or exploited that makes it a tricky feminist issue. But in this context, there are a bunch of queer people presenting queer art. The queer community is just really open sexually in a lot of ways to a lot of different things and it's not about, "I'm doing this because I saw on TV that this is what makes a person sexy." It's more like, "there are a lot of different ways to express your sexuality and here is one of them."

Are there any mainstream role models that you are like, wow she's fat and proud and still getting work, like Cameron Manheim?

I think people who work within the system are important. But then it's like, will there ever be a fat celebrity who doesn't get thin? Cameron seems pretty down, but there are so many different people who –

Missy Elliot

Yeah! Missy Elliot. I mean, I have no idea why her body changed and that's not for me to judge. I have a lot of friends who've been fat and changed not because they were hating themselves and dieting but because their bodies changed, and that's what happens sometimes.

It's a big let down, especially for young girls who invest in this role model as someone who doesn't give in to the standard. It gives them strength, and then when they do get thin, it "proves" that fat people can't succeed or be happy.

Yeah like Carnie Wilson –

Who had her stomach stapled.

It doesn't make sense to me because I remember when she was fat and she would have these talk shows like, "how fat women can be sexy," and then two years later she's talking about how great it is and how happy she is [now that she is thin].

I think that my work works best through underground networks, with people connecting to it and finding it rather than being fed it. I personally don't want to live a life that is in that [mainstream] realm, I don't want that kind of attention or that kind of pressure. I feel like just being a person and being visible is subversive in itself, but the more exposure you have, the more vulnerable you are to people's judgments and opinions too. I recently got this really fucked up email from somebody that said: "You're kidding yourself if you think you're beautiful. Most people don't think you are. In fact you're totally ugly and disgusting, you look like a fetus that should've been aborted and lived for too long. Why don't you do everyone a favor and kill yourself." Why would somebody waste their time writing that? I thought about all these different responses I could have. And it's actually been empowering to tell that story at shows, where the audience gets upset about it. Here is somebody else freaking out about it when I couldn't. That was really cathartic. My existence is my own and it doesn't matter what anybody else thinks about me.

How long have you been working on Effigy*?*

I started writing the songs right after I finished working on *The Transfused*, so that was almost three years ago. From *The Transfused*, I got a little bit of money and bought a drum machine and that was when I started working on programming stuff and writing these kinds of pop songs. I moved to Chicago in the fall so it's been a really different process since I haven't had the people around me to sit down and work on it with, it's been all through email. Jenna and Courtney – my dancers – they sent me an audition video, and I would send them instructions on the computer. I'd be like "O.K., beat seven, put your head up!" I had at one point flown a friend out to Chicago to help develop the album as a script. I had another solo CD that came out about five years ago and I never really promoted it, but for this one I really wanted to. I worked really hard on it. But when I thought about touring I was like, "I don't want to just go out by myself and sing in rock clubs!" – not that that's bad. And actually we are ending up doing a lot of shows in rock clubs and that's been a lot of fun. But I just think of things really theatrically and I was like, this is what I want to wear and this is how I want to come across. I feel that having back-up dancers makes it so much more than just ME performing this stuff by myself, especially because I don't have a band. And this time my sister is on tour with me!

After 10 years of this activism – doing it, living it – are you ever seduced by the monster of the standard?

It's really hard when your body doesn't look like anything you see around you to keep up that stamina. But this is me and that's awesome. I'm not going to hide myself or live in the world in a way that makes me feel like I'm not a part of it. I'm fucking here, so I'm going to work it! ★

PowerPoof Boys
by Matt Fagan

contact: 1573 N. Milwaukee Ave. | PMB 464 | Chicago, IL 60622
geocities.com/meniscusenterprises

LuLuLand

Do They Still Wear Eye Patches?
by Amy Adoyzie

Kien was fucking pissed when we first met. We struggled together as study buddies in our liberal arts math course at the community college. His anger wasn't directed at math, or anyone in particular for that matter. He just had a rotten disposition that never bothered me because he just scowled a lot, which was pretty harmless. I thought perhaps it was because he was some trashy-romance-novel-bad-boy who could only express passion through crazy monkey sex.

I was wrong, he was more of a socio-political textbook.

For his first years in college, everything Kien did was a political act, dating and love were not excluded. Apparently, our short-lived romantic relationship was tantamount to giving the finger to "the man." I thought we were just making out.

It didn't become a nuisance until he prohibited The Weakerthans from being within earshot because of their song "Wellington's Wednesday." John K. Samson sings, "Oh, you've got green eyes. Oh, you've got blue eyes. Oh, you've got gray eyes…"

"What about my brown-eyed sistas?" He asked.

I just rolled my slanty brown eyes and sighed. The Weakerthans ban was finally lifted when I informed him that JKS had not even written those words. "It's actually a line from a New Order song."

He paused for a moment before sheepishly saying, "Yeah well, the 80's were notorious for hating on Asians." He blamed all of the cocaine.

The militant ethnic pride phase cooled considerably after he realized that he was sucking the fun out of everything. Even Willy Wonka was not free from his criticisms.

"Why was it that only white kids found golden tickets? Shoo, my whole family shared a bed for the first years of my life *and* kids called me Charlie all the time. It shoulda been my yellow ass burping bubbles."

He was completely serious too.

But I can't blame him for finally embracing his Viethood. Kien spent much of his early life desperately assimilating, suppressing any notions of being "that other kid." He hated history class and recoiled into himself whenever the Vietnam War became the study topic. The way all the other students would instinctively turn to him when they mentioned that little Southeast Asian country always made his stomach sour.

Then he discovered empowerment, the delirious drug fed to culturally starving college students with no grocery budget.

It prompted him to take regular trips back to his parents' house. Hungry for his mother's phó. Hungry to learn *his* history. The history that he tried so hard not to acknowledge for 18 years.

Even after we stopped "seeing each other," we stayed close because he couldn't stand being around anyone else and I just had general anxiety about meeting new people and stayed closed to ones I already knew. After his trips home, he'd repeat to me what he had just learned. He'd call again later the same night to tell me all the details he left out the first time.

He learned about how much his mother misses the beaches of Vietnam. She used to take baby Kien on day trips to the beach town of Nha Trang, lounging in the sand while sipping tapioca drinks. He learned about the refugee boat ride in 1979 that he almost didn't survive at six months. His mother, suffering from chronic motion sickness, strapped his fever-ridden body to her back as she dry-heaved at the ocean during the entire three-day trek to Thailand, before being flown to America. He learned that his fever wasn't the only thing that could have killed him. His dad ominously told him about the threat of modern-day pirates.

We call it the "Pirate Clause," a provision where Kien's allowed to be a moron because his family was almost-maybe attacked by some sea-faring thugs. The Pirate Clause is usually his defense when it comes to neurotic relationship antics.

"My family didn't risk a pirate attack so that I'd be stuck with a girl who said to me, 'All of my five senses feel, except for the one in my chest.' Ain't got time for emo crybaby shit. Total pirate bait!"

"My family didn't risk a pirate attack so that I would date a filthy woman. The girl had literal bed bugs. How fucking third-world is that?"

(He even pulled out the Clause on me a few times.)

"My family didn't risk a pirate attack so that I would pay $7 to go see the Rocky and Bullwinkle movie. That's like a whole days wage in my home country."

Touché.

Kien's not so pissed anymore now that he picked that chip off the floor and firmly adhered it to his shoulder. ★

contact: PO Box 356 | Van Nuys, CA 91408-0356

MamaPhiles:
a mama zine collaboration

Mamaphiles

Birth of a Movement: Mama Zines
by China Martens

If you ask me, the fastest growing genre in zinedom today is zines made by mothers. In 2002, mama made zines caught on like a wild fire. And it is still blazing - no end in sight!

Generally, the concept of making a zine is a very catching one. It is a simple but - oh so "ding" light bulbs going off in your head - profound idea. Just the same way a bunch of monkeys learn to develop a new tool or the way a certain doodling style spreads all around an Elementary School, our social movement has spread this method of self expression—like a happy case of the cooties—right and left. First came the printing press. Then came cheap copier machines. Then came Zines in the baby carriage.

Before the printing press each book was made uniquely by hand. It is amazing to think of the labor and penmanship that monks would put into copying a bible. Then to think of the reproduction of the printing press! Books were still a rare treasure of the elite. It was still very laborious to produce them - being it rag picking to make paper, walnut crushing to make ink, or getting a license from the elite powers that it could even be printed at all.

That, however, is the dusty past. Books were widely available by my generation. Paperbacks were in the supermarket and novels by the likes of William Burroughs and Henry Miller (who fought a 27 year long battle with censorship, won in 1961, before Tropic of Cancer could be printed in the USA) were widely available on all the library shelves.

If anything, our media was flooded, and if not by the elite, it was dominated by the concept of stardom. Only some can make it to the top. What hope does one have to make a break through and get published? It is many children's dreams, which many parents try to crush and prepare their children to make a living in the "real world". We learn to read in school, that knowledge is power - yet it seems only a task to be controlled and graded. What about the thoughts that are contained within the written word? Somehow the fire of meaning is lost within the mandatory reading.

Before the zerox machine, people sometimes made little books and comics for the amusement of their friends and families. But no one thought of these homemade things as any more than a singular nature. It was with the advent of cheap reproduction available to the masses, that we could share these personal creations with each other. Photocopying gave the in-

dividual sole creative control with no censor nor permission needed.

Before zines we had underground newspapers. Before that we had other forms of radical press. Zines are just one of the current incarnations. But they are the incarnation of my generation. I broke onto the "scene" in the early to mid 80's where zines were flourishing, hand in hand with the subculture that transformed my way of looking at the world and what I thought was possible.

It was not until I became a mother (in 1988), however, that I made my first zine. As a subculture mother, I was a minority group. I felt isolated, disenfranchised, and oppressed. I wanted to build community and empowerment in the same way that the anarcho-punk rock scene and counterculture experience had shown me that all things were possible. There was constant discussion of anti-ageism, anti-sexism, anti-prejudice, animal rights, gay rights, class war, social justice - surely parenting issues could be brought to the table with the same gravity?

I have seen a lot of changes in the 20 years that I have been aware of zines and reading them. In the 80's, the first wave of punk parents began - and the first publication that I saw was called Punk Parent - which I got in the anarchist daycare room in SF in 1989. I met other mothers and also met Amy of Nausea (a famous NYC crust band). She was the first punk rock mother I saw, as some have told me, I was the first mother in the Baltimore scene that they saw. Like wow, punks can have kids. You don't have to turn into someone else to become a mother. We are still raising our consciences as mothers, to figure out what our role is. While so many groups of oppressed minorities have blossomed, our development has sometimes lagged behind. As a group we are often isolated and separated.

This is why Zines call out especially to mothers. Between facing sleep deprival and a role that means 24 hours a day 7 days a week - you can not believe how precious free time is to mothers. Often we did not have a clue what we were getting into. Our society does not encourage the ages to mingle nor is set up to include youth in the lives of the child free. We often do not have role models in our mothers, for the generation gap is too big—we want our lives to be different. Things have actually changed a lot in the

contact: PO Box 4803 | Baltimore MD 21211

last few generations, yet so many questions have been left unanswered as to how one can be a mother and a feminist, be a mother and a _____ (you fill in the blank) and survive in this society.

Zines give mothers a voice in a way that is historically unique. Zines can be held between tasks and are forgiving of bad punctuation and the writing style called "anyway-you-can-or-not-at-all".

I did not see many zines put out by mothers in the 80's and early 90's. My peers often did not choose to have children or delayed having children into their late twenties or thirties - while I had my daughter when I was 21. Slowly this trend has caught up and we can no longer deny that there are parents among us; that there is a wide window of rebels who are "grown up" as much as we try to stretch out our youth.

I have definitely been here for a part of zine history, although I don't comprehend its history in full. We hear of some names more than others, and that is not history the way I would write it. Of course our personal influences might come from a zine that only 50 or 100 other people have ever read. In zines, Quality counts over Quantity and the smallest fish can have the same impact as the biggest. That is the beauty of it. There is something for everyone and there is a great deal of mental stimulation and freshness out there.

Why do we, as mothers, start a zine?

Because there was nothing out there like what we wanted to create. Because we needed an art form that could exist alongside with motherhood. Because we saw others doing it and said "I can do that too". Because we were inspired by other voices to find our own voice. Because we found the kind of stories that we enjoyed reading, that we would like to write. Be-

cause motherhood presented us with new inspiration and new challenges we needed to write about. Because motherhood radicalized us. Because we were radicals who became mothers. To find others like ourselves and to share information and support. Because we had written zines when we were in high school and continued making zines as we got older. Because we express ourselves through writing, had worked on newsletters before, and when we found out about the concept of what a zine is—it expanded our options as a writer to know we could self publish.

At one point, I did not see any real life representation of motherhood as I knew it in the independent or mainstream media. Things still are not ideal in this country. Injustice and Oppression are everywhere. But the radical mother is conscience raising. She need not be Anything, but herself. There is no mold. A movement is taking place, gently building steam. Witness Mamaphonic.com. It is a website for writing mothers. In the zine thread, I can not keep up with all the zines that are coming out. Homeschoolers, Activists, Pagans, Punks, Midwives, Latinas, Women of Color, Lesbians, Office Workers, Stay-at-home moms, Teen moms, Nerdy moms, Free thinkers, the mom next door... they are all out there with their zines. Sometimes afraid - as mothers are often afraid to speak the truth of their lives, their down failings, struggles and experiences - fearing their problems are personal failures. But encouraged by the community, by seeing others speak out, the truth of their lives. For mama zines are very fertile right now. Which means the individual woman has more options at her fingertips. And the population as a whole will benefit, as it always does, when a minority group adds its flavor to the general consciousness of society. ★

Mama Sez No War!

MAMA SEZ NO WAR

writings, photos and experiences
by mothers against the war

april 2003

A Mother's Thoughts
by Sarah Goodyear

My son turns one year old on March 18th. I'm going to bake a carrot cake, and decorate it with a bunny drawn in icing.

Somewhere in Baghdad, there is another woman who will be marking her child's first birthday that day. I doubt that she will be baking a cake, or wrapping presents, in the days leading up to this milestone. Because she must know, as do I, that March 18th is likely to have another meaning this year. It could well be the first day of the American war on her nation. The first day of a military action the Bush administration has chosen to call Shock and Awe. It sounds to me like a video game I would not allow my son to play, when he gets older.

So my counterpart in Baghdad, whether she supports Saddam Hussein or is eager for his overthrow, whether she dreams of coming to America or would gladly see us wiped off the map, will be preparing for March 18th in another way. I can see her in my mind's eye, going about her business as calmly as she can. Her son on her hip or clinging to her skirts--at this age, they still don't want to be out of arms for long--she will be gathering together what food she can find. She will be buying candles, or kerosene for lamps. Electricity is spotty in Iraq anyway, and power plants will be among the first targets. The 1,000-pound Tomahawk missiles will surely come screaming in at night. They always do. She knows that from the last time.

Perhaps this Iraqi mother--let's call her Salma--will be leaving her home for the countryside and the hope of safety, locking the front door in what she knows is a futile gesture against the forces that are about to be unleashed on her city. Wondering if she will ever see the inside of that place again, ever again return to those familiar objects, cook a meal in her kitchen, welcome her husband into their bed. She will have to leave some of the baby's things behind, but she will be careful to bring the toy he likes best.

Or perhaps she has nowhere else to go, and she is planning where she will sit with her child when the bombs start falling in the dark. How she will comfort him.

I am planning my cake. Unlike most of the people in Iraq, I have access to more food than I need. There is no reason for me to stint on sugar, except that I don't want Nathaniel to develop too much of a taste for it.

No reason for me to leave nuts out of the recipe, except that I am worried about an allergic reaction. No reason for me to cut a smaller slice for myself, except that I, like so many American women, am trying to lose a little weight.

In Iraq, for many years women have had to worry about how to get enough calories, rather than how to cut them. While I was making trips to the Ben & Jerry's down the street every night of my pregnancy, while I was joking that my son was being made out of the steak I consumed two or three times a week at a local restaurant, while I was taking my expensive prenatal vitamins, I imagine that Salma was trying to find enough to eat.

Since the United Nations voted in 2000 to remove the cap on oil sales for Iraq's oil-for-food program, the government food ration has increased, from 1,090 calories per day in 1991 to 2,215 calories a day. And yet for a pregnant woman that is not enough. Salma's husband and other members of her family likely urged her to take some of their share, for the baby's sake. It may have been difficult for her to accept; she knew her husband needed his strength in his search for work. He has been unemployed now for months, his university degree no good in a shriveled economy.

Maybe Salma managed to get enough to eat, so her baby was born healthy, like mine. I like to think so. It would not be something she would take for granted. In 1998, 24 percent of Iraqi babies were born underweight; that was a major contributing factor to an infant mortality rate that soared in the 1990s. Between 1995 and 1999, 105 of every 1,000 children in Iraq died before their fifth birthday.

Things have improved, but hunger is still a reality for the children of Iraq. In Baghdad, where Salma lives, a child's chances are better than in rural areas. If she is educated, as I am, her son's hope for decent nutrition is better still. And yet her education will not be able to protect her son from her nation's polluted and contaminated water supply.

Who is to blame? One could point a finger at the United States and other western nations that have imposed strict sanctions on Iraq since the 1991 Gulf War. Or one could blame Saddam Hussein, for running the brutal, war-seeking dictatorship that prompted those sanctions.

contact: PO Box 20388 | Tompkins Square Station | New York, NY 10009

But when you're trying to feed a child, or protect a child from falling bombs, blame is beside the point. Blame will not help a one-year-old child understand why there is not bread for his supper. It will not help him sleep in the middle of a missile attack. It will not give him parents who are not afraid.

I, too, am afraid of the day the bombs start falling, even though I do not let this stop me from planning my cake. I live in New York City. We have been told--as if we needed to be told--that we will be on the front lines of any war against Iraq. That we can expect terrorist attacks. My situation is the same as Salma's. Whether I like this president or not (I don't), whether I believe in this war or not (I don't), I will be in the line of fire. True, terrorists openly target people like me, while our military says it will do its best to avoid killing people like Salma. I doubt that offers her much comfort, and it will offer none at all for her baby.

The other night, I was out of the house without Nathaniel. My partner had kindly offered me the opportunity to go eat in a local restaurant with a book and myself alone, and I took it. I was walking home, a few doors down from my house, when I heard an explosion. I felt a puff of air on my face--a percussion wave. I started running to the place where my baby was. On either side of me, windows flew open and my neighbors poked their heads into the night. "I think it's OK," I yelled up to them. "It sounded big but small, if you know what I mean."

I was right. On the street up ahead, a manhole cover had blown off, a routine hazard of spring, when underground wiring is corroded by melting snow and salt. No one was hurt. Big but small.

My neighbors knew what I meant because so many of us had heard what big--really big--sounds like. I was sitting at my dining-room table drinking tea when I heard it. It sounded like a dump truck going over a big pothole, except that it didn't. I looked at the clock, because I knew something bad had happened, and for some reason I wanted to know what time it was. My clock said 9:01. It was the second plane hitting. I still don't know why I didn't hear the first.

That day, three months pregnant, I went to the top floor of my house and stood outside the room that was to be my son's nursery and I saw the towers burning. I had so much looked forward to showing him those towers, the promise of them, from his bedroom window. Now, when he is old enough, I will have to explain their memory instead.

I have often thought that Nathaniel protected me that day. If I hadn't been pregnant, I would have rushed down to the promenade on the Brooklyn waterfront. I would have seen the collapse in person. I am glad I did not see that.

Now that he is outside of me, it is I who must protect him. I must create a safe space for him wherever he is and whatever is happening. This is something Salma and I are both worrying about how to do, every day. My chances look better than hers.

Long before the government issued us an advisory about plastic sheeting and duct tape, I was thinking about my basement. It is spacious and dry. It could be quite comfortable, in a pinch, and easily sealed off. But every time I think of sitting down there with Nathaniel, I remember another story I read.

It was about a Kurdish woman who was in a village gassed by Iraqi troops in 1988. She went with her two-year-old child into a basement to escape the poison in the air. She took him to her breast, thinking that he would be safer if he were nursing. It is an instinct all nursing mothers can understand. What comes from our breasts is good and nourishing and meant especially for our babies. They are almost inevitably comforted by it, and we are comforted too.

What that nursing Kurdish mother didn't know was that the gas Hussein's troops were using was heavier than air. It sank. It filled the basement where she had her baby at her bosom. The child died first; then she died, still holding him to her, still holding him tight.

I am wary of basements. Perhaps Salma is, too.

I wish I could talk to her--the real woman behind my imaginary construct. I wish our children could sit on a rug fighting over toys together. I wish I could tell her how terrible I feel in my helplessness to stop this war. We would understand one another, I am sure of it, even if not completely. We both live in the world of women.

I used to not believe in this world. I used to be adamant in my belief that women and men were essentially the same. That has changed. The change began when I was pregnant. When I went into labor, it deepened. I looked around me at all the other people who weren't in labor and I thought, the only people I am truly connected to at this moment of pain and fear and animal determination are other women who are trying to bring their babies into the world safely.

And right now, as I wait for this war to begin, as I get ready to bake my son's birthday cake, I feel that perhaps I am only truly connected to other women who are trying to keep their children in this world safely. Women like Salma.

The only problem is, Salma and I cannot live in the world of women without also living in the world of men. Some would call it the real world. I'm not so sure. ★

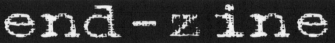

the sense of place

by the mediageek

You might have noticed in this little zine several references to Champaign-Urbana, IL, the place where it was conceived, produced, and the 'burg where all contributing writers happen to live (right now). That these crazy twin cities infuse this zine isn't accidental. In fact, at least for mediageek, it's unavoidable.

I've talked to people who are just itching to move to somewhere better, somewhere cooler, where there's more of a scene, where there's more action. More bands, better clubs, bookstores, hip cafes, alternative weeklies and art. If only they could just get there, then they'd be ready to bust out with plans and projects.

Sure, maybe. But what was it like in one of these cool places, maybe Portland, OR or Austin, TX, before they were happening?

My point is that it all had to start somewhere. At some point one person got it in her head that she was going to get up and make that thing she just had to make. She made a zine, started a band, painted a mural or wheatpasted a screed on a post. Then someone else said:

"hey, that kicks ass. I can do that."

And so on.

Then there was a scene, and that made it worth being there.

As much as I've spent years trying to deny it for myself, place infuses what we do. More significantly, what we do infuses the place. It's hard for me to think of my mediageek endeavors detached from the place where they were born.

If I hadn't been stuck in grad school in what seemed to be farm towns isolated in nowhere Central Illinois, then I wouldn't have found my favorite community radio station, WEFT – a station foolish enough not only to let an overconfident 22 year-old on the air, but to even elect him as chair of their programming committee. I wouldn't have gotten a taste of real

contact: PO Box 2102 | Champaign, IL 61825-2102 | mediageek.org

community media, where old time country music coexists with underground rap and death metal.

This dose of truly independent grassroots communication was utterly intoxicating and I couldn't kick it. As cliché as it sounds, it changed my life.

Now, I could have ended up at some other community radio station, like WORT in Madison, WI or KGNU in Boulder, CO, and the story might be the same. I'm not claiming that WEFT and Champaign are so exceptional, except for me--I landed here, not there.

What really made it for me was having people around me to share it with. Like minded folks and misfits who just aren't willing to swallow what the mainstream feeds us.

Yet, I completely understand that for a lot of people the place where they are is not so comfortable or happy. Hey, I know that Champaign-Urbana is that miserable place for a lot of people who feely they are stuck here. But there's also a part of me that thinks they're not quite so happy because they haven't found that place for them within the place.

I think those of us who dare to believe we can create media are part of the force that makes a place worth being in. We're the individuals who come together to create a scene.

Compared to Portland, Austin or Madison, Champaign-Urbana is pretty far off the cool map *(and I probably wouldn't mind being in those other cities, either... they're pretty nice, too).* And yet in my ten years here I've watched a slow explosion of culture bursting from independent media. Starting with the seeds community radio, these little prairie towns have grown one of the largest Independent Media Centers, a vibrant local music scene and a very new blossom of independent publications. All 100 miles in any direction from a major city to suckle from.

It happened here because somebody started it here.

So my parting shot for this zine is another exhortation to go out and make something, but to also make it where you are. You might love your hometown, or you might hate it, and have no power to leave. In either case, sharing a little bit of yourself—or the source of your enmity—might make it better.

If you're afraid of ridicule or retribution, make it anonymous. Put it out there in the dead of night wearing a black hooded sweatshirt.

Don't cede your place to the suffocation of the mainstream. Don't surrender to those who make you hate your place.

In the morning when you pass by that stack of pamphlets, the flyer or stencil, you'll know that it's something you made, and that sometime in the day it will affect somebody else. That person might say, "Hey, I can do that."

Then it's out of your hands. Then it might just get interesting.

Merge

Backpacking
and Other Abuses of the Natural World

I had been backpacking before with people who actually know what they're doing. Freeze-dried food, three season lightweight hollowfill sleeping bag, MRI backpacker's white gas stove, hurricane matches, insulite, flashlight, goretex raingear, hat, sunglasses, suntan lotion, maps, compass, gaiters and more. It was with some confidence that I arranged my pack, making sure the appropriate items were quickly accessible.

The four of us met at my place Friday evening, my place being the old rundown two-story junker I rented for $110 a month. The landlord – an attorney and very nice guy – reimbursed me for the paint and supplies I bought to repaint the inside of the house with. As the months went by and he never came to check on things, I decided to personalize the place a bit. I painted one whole wall with a posterized version of Frank Zappa's face, wearing that black derby from his Hot Rats album, circa 1970. I projected the image onto the wall, drew it out lightly in pencil, stylizing shapes and simplifying things into smooth, high-contrast shapes. Then I painted it in with flat wall paint using my special brush lettering brushes. It was a huge and dominant image in that room, like the giant stone Toltec heads watching you from the jungles of Mexico.

After painting the refrigerator flat blue I stepped into the paint in my old tennis shoes by accident. So I took them off, rolled the bottoms with blue and pressed them onto the living room wall like giant rubber stamps, making a path up the wall, then across the ceiling to the far side of the room. Well that seemed pointless, leading nowhere until I remembered a friend's painting. So I painted the tennis shoes blue and screwed them onto the ceiling at the end of the 'trail.' It felt like an invisible person was standing upside down in the room, looking at a blank wall.

Then I got the idea of painting a full moon on that wall. Using the same blue paint (thinking of my landlord's expense) I did a reverse image of the moon, painting the wall blue but leaving all the light parts of the moon the off-white of the original wall. It turned out to be quite realistic and dramatic, being around six feet wide. Now the prints and tennis shoes made sense, a phantom traveler entranced by a full moon.

With these images tricking out the living room, the remaining wall seemed naked, begging to be included and upgraded. On it I painted a floor-to-ceiling version of a stone stela from the ruined jungle Mayan city of Copan in Honduras. It is a marker of some kind, being carved deeply with hieroglyphics, kings and patterns. The stone pieces like this one are set upright in the plazas for all to see, like historical markers. Mine was painted with flat pale colors, a pastel sentinel.

That completed the living room, so to finish painting the place I added the image of that mound-builders serpent from the Ohio landscape onto the lower panel of the front door. They were all nice additions I felt, adding value to the place provided the next renters were also Frank Zappa fans.

We all met at my house, loading up my old 1964 Chevelle Malibu 4-door grandma-mobile with packs, boots, cooler and all. It was fun having an old junker car for awhile. You never felt the need to wash or wax it. By the time I had to replace it for my own safety, it was more of a garbage barge than a car. The only nice thing about it was the chrome foot gas pedal I added to dress it up a bit. When I put an ad in the paper to sell it, it read: 1964 Chevelle, runs, just washed. $125 firm.

On our way out of town we stopped at the liquor store to pick up something to sip sitting around a nice fire in the mountains. On the road a bottle of tequila somehow got opened and was being passed around the back seat. Soon a harmonica was being played loudly from that direction. As the tequila flowed, the blues flowed out of that harp in shrieks and blasts even Robert Johnson would wince at. This was impromptu, stand-up harp. At some point during the drive I realized I was in the back seat too. This next part gets foggy and jerky, like watching a film that is being eaten by the projector but still getting glimpses of it. It was dark out now. The headlights lit up the morose old dirt road we were now on. It had to be the wrong trailhead, it was too overgrown and rutted. I was driving again now. We couldn't tell where we were, looking at the map and bumping up the road very slowly. I looked back just in time to see the harmonica player's feet going out the window. I didn't think too much about it since we were barely moving. Next I remember someone jumping on the trunk, then onto the roof, jumping onto the hood where he then jumped off in front of the car laughing with a circuitous visage that was an embarrassment to the surrounding woods. This happened again and again until one attempt when I heard him slip on the roof and fall with a shudder, legs sprawling. A wall of puke flowed down over the windshield. No kidding, on this warm beautiful clear summer night. The wipers were a rudimentary help, clearing little more than the realization that things were unraveling here.

We attempted to turn around on that narrow road. I backed into a tree, wrenching and jamming a back passenger door that was somehow left open by someone. I was being warned loudly about the open door but I couldn't hear them above all the other screaming going on in those profoundly shamed woods. The lacerated back door would no longer close. So we acquiesced to this fools paradise. Stopping in the road, realizing it was abandoned and no one would be using it tonight, we gave up until morning when clearer heads might figure out how to turn around. We set up camp right there in the thicket. Later, with a nice fire crackling in the dry woods, our wantonly harmonica bluesman busied himself by running amuck through the black woods at full speed in bare feet. Think about this. You can hardly stumble three feet into the dark pathless woods in your boots to pee. Imagine running barefoot. I know you think I am just being entertaining, but I assure you this all happened. This barefooted interminable seeker was not just risking his own life by running through the woods. He began running through the campfire too. From out of the foreboding unknown he would dash into the fire spraying sparks all over us and the dry tinder and be gone into the dark again. We yelled at him unrestrained to knock it off, but with the strength of a perditious crazed beast he would be back again in our midst to pounce relentlessly on the fire. The Mythic Harp-Playing Crazed Beast of the Rockies. Since this forlorn activity didn't kill him right then and there, he eventually settled down to tearing into his backpack for something apparently at the very bottom as he threw everything he grabbed over his shoulder into the bushes.

Next morning it seemed as though all the abuses, curses and unnatural acts perpetrated in these woods the previous night had returned as a bad-ass sax screaming in my head. The Beast was busying himself by gathering his things from the bushes, picking up what looked like Christmas decorations laid out by loathsome inebrious cretins. It was just dumb and embarrassing now. The rest of the trip was strangely uneventful, nursing wounds and denying the throb in our heads. That was the only time someone fell out of my car while I was driving it. ★

Modern Arizona

Wassup Mamma Luke?
-or-
"If You Don't Like the War Travis, then move to France so they can Call You LeTravis."
by Joe Unseen as told by Travis

A few days after the war started, I dropped in on Travis and he told me about how he had spent his St. Patrick's Day down in NYC. You might remember that St. Patrick's Day 2003 was the so called deadline that Governor Bush placed on Iraq or war would start. The NYC St. Patty's Day parade would go on as scheduled, as it had every other year. There was an increased "terror alert" as they are called, so there were National Guard Troops placed throughout the city and tons of extra police were on duty as well.

Travis went down to the city with a group of friends to drink and celebrate, but their group became split up in a drunken confusion on a crowded street. Travis and his friend James walked through an open door only to have that door slam behind them! They found themselves locked inside a vacant building that was under renovation. Blasted and confused they wondered about looking for an exit. Almost an hour passed and everywhere they tried to exit was blocked. They eventually found their way onto some construction scaffolding outside the building where they could see people bellow on the sidewalk. They called out for help and were met with shouts of, "What are you doing in there?" "Help us, we can't get out!" they responded. A man working at a nearby eatery then pulled out a cell-phone to call the police. In no time, what seemed to be a battalion of cops converged on this building. They talked Travis and James into climbing over a tall chain link fence with anti-intrusion spikes on the top, to get them out, only to place them under arrest!

You see, across the street from this building, was the United Nations and in front of the UN was a huge Anti-War rally. The police simply assumed that Travis and James were protestors who were trespassing "War Protestors? We're not with them!" "Tell it to the MAN downtown son!" was the exchange. The two guys were then taken away in handcuffs, right in front of thousands of protestors who all took notice and some ran up to ask, "Are you okay? Are you okay?" and "Solidarity Brothers!" Travis screamed back, "Fuck Off! Leave me alone!" A journalist ran up and tried to get his name, "What? I'm not telling you my name!"

They were then taken downtown to Central Booking were they spent the next 22 hours in a grumy, grimy holding cell with a fresh harvest of New York City criminals. It was St. Patrick's Day so almost everyone was drunk. The cops brought in a huge Hispanic bruiser who referred to all the police as C/O's and then took off his shirt revealing a huge body covered in Christian Cross and Jesus tattoos. "I should have shot those pigs who grabbed me!" he slurred aggressively. Travis noticed a scar from an old stab wound on the man's back and couldn't help but stare at it. For a lack of anywhere else to sleep they slept on the dirty floor. The huge Hispanic guy chose to sleep inches away from James and began to get night shivers. He would twitch and whimper out loud like a pit-bull having a nightmare. James' eyes were white with fear. "I think he's laying on part of my jacket!"

They were eventually taken from the holding cell and questioned by police who asked them the hard, deep probing questions about their criminal activity, like "What kind of music do you listen to?" and "Do you support or oppose the war?" Travis told me that he had already spent so much time in the holding cell he was ready to tell them whatever they wanted to hear just to get out. "Um…I'm for the war." And the officer said, "Good, because if you answered otherwise you'd be right back in there!" A cop asked Travis if he was a user of Marijuana. Travis went into a long diatribe about how Marijuana was a drug of hippies and protesters and he would never use Marijuana because it makes you stupid. The cop sat patiently listening to Travis make his proclamations and when he was done, the cop pulled out Travis's confiscated pack of cigarettes and pulled from it an empty Marijuana bag. The smile on T's face dropped as did his head. They were eventually released without being charged with any crime. ★

contact: PO Box 494 | Brewster, NY 10509

james
by jeep

jail, what is it good for? or

j★a★M★e★s*
by jeep

As James* loves to recount to everyone, I met him in Key West, Florida. I was on vacation with my family at Christmas in 2001. And we ran into each other one night after I had snuck out late to go see a drag show. It was a funny, un-glam show, real nasty and unpretentious. I was sidled up on the bar and he was behind me. He was from Houston too which was a good conversation starter. He lived on Yellowstone in South Union. The fact that I knew that street and told him I lived five minutes from there clearly set me apart. He was surprised, I think, with my knowledge of the neighborhood. We had a bond. And so many things have grown from there.

Once we were back in Houston we started a little rhythm, talking on the phone, going to arty movies and eventually hanging out with his crew of rowdy Black and Latino same-gender-loving guys. There were more than a few Sunday night and holiday barbecues with bud, ribs, mac 'n' cheese, pick-up trucks, Li'l Kim-my-pussy-my-crack, and drama. James and I became friends.

A couple days after new years 2003, while I was talking to a friend, the call waiting clicked. I flashed over, and it was one of those pre-recorded lady voices from the Harris County Jail. I assumed it was a call for a previous person who had my phone number. I think one Sandra Gomez, one Juan

Gonzalez, and a whole bunch of other folks had this number before I got it, cuz I receive calls for them all the time. So I assumed the jail call was not for me and flashed back to the other line. In a few seconds, the call waiting clicked again and this time I accepted the collect charge. It was James.

* Pseudonym.

contact: PO Box 414 | Berkeley, CA 94701

I found out then that there was a lot I didn't know about my friend. It turns out James had been on parole since the early nineties when he served four years in a Texas state prison 30 miles west of San Antonio for robbing a friend who owed him a lot of money and wouldn't pay him back. We talked real briefly on the phone that first time; he sounded shockingly upbeat. I said I would come visit him real soon.

When I went to the jail a few days later, I visited him on the eighth floor. I came to find out the floor is reserved for child molesters, rapists, and other sexual offenders who wear purple bracelets for i.d. and the self-identified homosexuals and transsexuals in yellow bracelets. The lumping-together of all peoples with deviant sexualities seemed so eighteenth century Europe, so Foucaultian, so mindlessly categorical. But in the bad light, the no windows and the funky stank, it all seemed a little too unfortunate to theorize about. There were all kinds of queers up there. A lot of couples shouting to each other through the glass, conversations about longing and missing and other mundane details; they were shouting since the little speaker hole didn't work at all. We too had to yell out our words through the glass.

I strained to hear what James said. He told me how he was looking at another period of years in jail for a parole violation. He was supposed to stay in his aunt's house on Yellowstone, but, because his aunt was on drugs and making life pretty hard for him, he moved out of there to stay with friends. Well, when the parole officer came to check on him, his aunt turned him in. James told me he hoped he didn't get sent real far away this time. He wants his friends and family to be able to visit. At least, the gay guys on the floor with him seemed to make jail a little more bearable.

That same week I visited James, three other friends of mine got sent to jail too. One black girl in a "domestic dispute" that if she were white and moneyed never would have even involved the police much less a stay in jail. She is in court now fighting an expensive battle to keep the misdemeanor off her record. Another Chicana who was sent to jail for not paying traffic tickets. And one twenty-something gay whiteboy who got chased by a mob out of his trailer park after a sixteen-year old boy he was sleeping with cried foul play.

And as I started talking to people, most of my friends have been in jail at some point or another in their lives. Without a doubt my class and race privileges protect me. It scares me how the government can more easily lock up young people (mainly working class and of color), than invest in education or in art or other social services that give people resources to control their own destiny. How somehow investing in a system that humiliates, isolates, and degrades people will "scare people straight." How WE refuse to invest in empowerment and education to let people really have control over their own lives.

As I left the eighth floor of the jail, moving in the slow packed elevator, I wondered how James would hold up. I thought about one story he told me. That on Friday and Saturday nights, the eighth floor is packed with queers (mainly of color, mainly young) all dressed up about to go out clubbing. Folk stop by to visit their friends before heading out. I looked at one gay guy going down in the elevator with me. I had seen him visiting a guy in jail. They were blowing kisses through the glass. And I wondered how many people I see at gay bars, in Key West, in Houston, how many young folks at hip hop shows, how many kids everywhere have been through this same ritual of incarceration and visiting. Too damn many, I thought. Too damn many, I think still.

I worry about what these experiences of punishment, fear, and containment do to us, to how we speak with each other and treat each other, to how we think about our lives. Our worlds can shrink so small, our visions so narrow. I know these experiences drive people apart, make us scared and hungry to a point where it becomes even more difficult to truly communicate. And if we can't talk to each other or love each other, than we can't even start to make the revolution we truly need.

I write James letters as often as I can. It's hard to really talk through all of the glass and the walls and the injustice of it all. James says he is getting depressed now more often, and I worry about him, about what all of this will do to him. So this story is really one more way to learn to communicate through the barriers that conspire to keep us from hearing each other.

Yes, operator, I'll take the collect call.

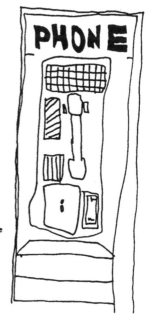

mutate zine #7

Tearom Confidential: Part 1 and 2
by Milo

Part 1

I work next to the cruiseist men's room on campus. For years growing up in Milwaukee, I had heard about all the places men went to have sex with each other. Juneau and Estabrook Parks, BA Beach (yes, Victoria, the Great Place by a Great Lake used to have a nude beach), the third floor lav in Gimble's department store, and the bathrooms at the university.

Now, I'm a product of the newkweer generation of the 1990's. I've been 'out' for years in any number of ways. I've never felt shame in my sexuality, and fortunately have usually been able to find playmates whenever I wanted. Most of the time these meetings would happen in more traditional settings – class, at a dance club, or through the introductions of friends. As a result I don't totally understand the art, artifice, and politics of cruising public spaces to get off.

In the tearoom I'm speaking of, the stalls are graffiti covered with all manner of crap. The usual four letter words, aspersions being cast on people's mothers and girlfriends, and the question that I often find haunting me – "Does anybody come here just to shit any more?" The rest of the graf consists of notes and signs that men use the place to either meet up or to get off. There are charts in a couple of the stalls done in three column style. The header reads: Age | Size | Date/time.

Under that, there is a list of presumably people who have or want to hook up there. I'm not entirely sure what goes on at those hookups. I'm guessing that it's a lot of mutual masturbation, and maybe the occasional blowjob.

At the end of the row, the wall between the first and second stall has a little hole in it. The stall structure is made from granite, or something that resembles it. The hole came from an obvious move of the TP dispensers. It's not big enough to be a glory hole in any real way, but it's probably big enough to watch someone through it.

I guess my biggest fear is that the guys who feel like getting it on in the lav will get busted. Part of the urban mythology around cruising sex always included people getting ticketed or arrested. At the Uni,

the campus cops are notorious for entrapping guys in just such a situation. Even the newspaper on campus publishes it in the crime report. Usually it shows up as "Indecent Exposure" or "Lewd Behavior".

I often get nervous when using the facilities of the tearoom for their intended purpose. On the one hand I'm fascinated by the concept, and sincerely want to see what goes on. I like sex in it's multitudinous forms, and this certainly qualifies. On the other, I'm a little freaked out at the thought of getting busted, maybe more by my co-werkers than the cops. I also am not into totally anonymous sex these days. I like talking with my partners a little first. I guess I'll just keep my eyes and ears open, and enjoy this bathroom for all its amenities, but only utilize some of them.

Part 2

As I was doing research for the Tearoom Confidential article, I decided that I needed to know more about cruising bathrooms and having public sex. I got a bunch of pointers and the inside scoop from an anonamous stranger online and am just printing the transcript as a point of interest.

> *hi*
> *hi*
<str8shooter> hi
> *so, what else?*
<str8shooter> ever gotten sucked in a bathroom
> *no, but i tossed in a video arcade a couple of times...*
<str8shooter> are you gay or bi?
> *bi. have a BF and GF*
<str8shooter> cool
<str8shooter> what state r u in?
> *WI, but i lived in NoCal for 19 mo.*
<str8shooter> I see...
<str8shooter> I am a tearoom expert
> *w00t!*
> *then you're the guy i want to talk to*
<str8shooter> ask your questions
> *well, i work next to this tearoom that has all the graf-*

fiti signifiers on the walls, but to the best of my knowledge i've never seen any live action

> usually i just do my thing and leave

<str8shooter> people who visit tearooms spend hours sometimes to hook up

<str8shooter> there are two ways

> typically, do cruisers stand next to each other at the urinals?

> ok

<str8shooter> if the urinals have no "fag guard" between the urinals that is a good start, the best is the 1 long trough type of urinal\

<str8shooter> but stalls can be used if this is not avail

<str8shooter> usually the cocksucker sits in the last stall, furthest from the door

> well, these stalls have a 'leave age, size, time date' notation

<str8shooter> they tap their foot to indicate they are in the program

> so that's not a myth... cool

<str8shooter> leaving a note on stall wall rarely works...

<str8shooter> but back to the urinal

> ok

<str8shooter> you see the urinal is the best because you get a good look at what is most important, DICK

> hehe... but there's no playspace there

<str8shooter> oh yes there is, the best fun is had there

> how so?

<str8shooter> well you see once two guys make contact (this is done without saying a word) you hang out jerking each other off at the urinals between other people coming in & out

> ahh...

> is there any etiquette for afters?

> or is it just zip up and leave?

<str8shooter> I went into a rest room once & believe it or not, there was this guy..let me back up, it had the kind of urinals that go all the way to the floor, anyway, this guy was standing in the urinal, squattin

> taking a shit?

<str8shooter> sucking off any guy who stood at "his" urinal

> wow!

<str8shooter> there was actually a small line at one point

> hehe I'll bet

> so, anything else i should know?

<str8shooter> usually urinal action is mostly mutual jack off allthough....

<str8shooter> sometimes one will nod towards a stall where there are some procedures

<str8shooter> there are 2 ways to get sucked in a stall

<str8shooter> u there?

> ok.

> yeah...

> the lav doesn't have gloryholes

<str8shooter> ok well obviously no one wants to go to jail so there are some precautions

<str8shooter> not gloryhole listen...

> g'head

<str8shooter> once urinal hook up is made & decision to go in stall has happened there are 2
    ways 2 do this

<str8shooter> the first

<str8shooter> the cocksucker goes in stall first, climbs on the toilet seat & squats. the guy who needs service then goes in & takes out dick.

<str8shooter> that way if someone looks under stall they see one pair of legs pointed at toilet as if guy is pissing

> ok... then the suckee just looks like he's peein'

> hehe

<str8shooter> the second is better

<str8shooter> obviously you can't pee that long & there is no water tinkle sound

> right

<str8shooter> And this is the real inside scoop I'm giving you here kid

> hehe... i'm all ears

> (well, not ALL ears ;))

<str8shooter> the cocksuker has an empty shopping bag with him. he sits on the bowl, with his pants down like he is taking a shit & the guy who needs service STANDS IN THE BAG

> that's awesome...

<str8shooter> this is popular in shopping malls

> paper or plastic?

> or shopping...

<str8shooter> if you get a bag from an expensive store in the mall, even mall security will leave you alone as you are now a "good customer"

> nice

<str8shooter> bag type don't matter, so long as it's logical that you were shopping and now you are taking a shit

> nice

> ok... i need to run off to class.

<str8shooter> paper grocery bags work GREAT (1 per foot) if there is a nearby supermarket

> you've been SUPER helpful

<str8shooter> try this stuff out later

> i will.

<str8shooter> ok cool

<str8shooter> later

> my zine can be found at http://www.mutatezine.com

<str8shooter> I'll check it out!

> next time in in LA i'll look for you at the urinal :) ★

OFF-Line

OFF-Line

A Chouston-Manor Onesico Publication
Issue # 23 • Winter 2004

Scandalous Disclosures Issue Contents

THE WRITER'S BLOCK
• Phil Berrigan: A family with class•Vincent.......................3
LIFE ON THE LIQUIDATOR
• Chalk it up to learning•Diary...................................
• Work discussion: FDTA: Disclosing Dubious Tax..............42
Amendment..............................
PIXELBILGA.........................
• Jittery • Claire...............................
READERS' FORUM
• Letters and reviews•Issues...................

FDTA: Facilitating Dubious Tax Avoidance

by Vincent J. Romano

Who really enjoys handing over a large chunk of their earnings each year to the government? I certainly don't, and my conscience won't condone it—so I don't pay. Most U.S. corporations share this aversion to paying taxes, if not my anarchopacifist motives for doing so. How ironic and painful was it, then, that my first job out of college, in the year I began my principled tax resistance, was as an administrative assistant at the FDTA, a non-profit organization in White Plains, New York, that existed to educate wealthy corporations in how to legally sidestep their tax bills?

If many for-profit corporation names are alien in their sound and questionable in their spelling—Rite-Aid, Amoco, DynCorp—the joke in the non-profit world is that nearly every organization's name forms a meaningless acronym. The FDTA did one better by being an organization whose name is acronyms within an acronym—FSC/DISC Tax Association. Those stretch out to stand for "Foreign Sales Corporation" and "Domestic/International Sales Corporation," two similar entities set up by multinational corporations that are, in essence, "paper companies."

The rules for these business confections required little more than a list of names to constitute the board of directors for the FSC (pronounced "fisk") that would meet annually. The papers are filed in a FSC-friendly area, such as Guam or the U.S. Virgin Islands, and poof—a corporate mogwai has spawned a little FSC gremlin. The profits are re-routed and the U.S. taxes avoided.

The complicated rules for incorporating a FSC required specialized education for corporate tax attorneys and accountants. The FDTA came into existence to meet this need, spreading the word to corporations from coast to coast that these subsidiary entities, with the blessing of the Internal Revenue Service, allow their parent corporations to chop a healthy 15 to 30 percent off their tax bill.

The FDTA called this promoting "tax compliance," which sounded to me like a code for corporations wanting to pay the barest minimum of tax necessary to avoid IRS tax audits. "FSCs are not tax shelters," FDTA literature insists. "Rather, they are recognized, legitimate tax incentives for exporters built into the tax law."

I don't pay federal taxes as a principle of anarchism, opposing the coercion involved in seizing people's income against their will. I object especially to the government's use of the money, more than half of which goes to pay past, present and future wars. I'd rather give my tax money to organizations doing work for peace and justice in the United States and abroad. However, expecting corporations to share these motives is like expecting a pimp to establish after-school programs for the neighborhood children.

I graduated college with dreams of finding a place with the perfect non-profit agency doing work to save the world. I was open to anything: writing for a magazine, helping the homeless get back on their feet, advocating against the nation's military addiction. After being home for three weeks, my bills were mounting, my saved cash was almost tapped and I was still jobless.

So I decided to upend my daily pattern of seeking work amid open-ended leisure in the most extreme way possible: I'd suck up the overnight shift at the local 24-hour CVS drugstore. Taking the 10:00 p.m. to 7:00 a.m. schedule would pay me $7 an hour, $2 more than the hourly wage for day workers, and I would be a proud member of the working class. That seemed far more romantic than whoring myself to a brokerage firm—some slick dude in a suit pestered me outside a White Plains job fair to learn the ropes as an investment banker, and I had to beat him off me with my résumé portfolio.

I adjusted to my new avocation as a cash register jockey and stock monkey. The store security guard laughed as I nodded off at the checkout counter and had to snatch a breath of fresh air outside to stay conscious on the first night. Fellow clerks would leave for their "lunch" break and return two hours later, presumably after a refreshing snooze. I tried to find fulfillment in filling the racks of Bubbalicious and M&Ms.

Then my mother told me that a company in her office building in nearby Purchase needed someone to cover their employees' vacation time, and they would pay $10 an hour. It sounded like corporate schlep work, but it would be a $3 raise—and during the daytime—so I asked her to let them know I was interested and available. I figured I could do that for a few weeks and put aside some money, then say I'd found another opportunity when it came along and bolt. How ideal!

The interview, a stage for self-exposure that always resulted in part of me leaking into the clothes I wore, was as easygoing as the greased chute into hell when I learned I was the only applicant. The office manager, Natalie, a tall, wiry woman in her late 30s with a teased beehive hairdo, told me FDTA was a small non-profit that provided tax advice for exporters. The data entry and administrative tasks would be boring, she warned. "That's OK," I assured her, "I don't expect the job to be a circus."

My transition to a grubby corporate sell-out was complete. All that remained was to inform my boss at CVS. He was more upset than most people are when they learn I am leaving. Over just two weeks I had established a reputation for reliability, and apparently the mutual exploitation had been even better for him than it was for me.

In fact, he was so angry, he threatened to blacklist me from CVS so that I could never work for the company again. I somehow managed to feign a contrite and mournful expression. The other employees cackled when I told them, and encouraged me: "Go out and get yours. I wish I could leave here too!"

My first day at FDTA, in the summer of 1996, was anxiety-riddled. I asked a lot of questions and tried to absorb the procedures quickly. I'd be inputting data on the computer, sending faxes and helping to archive old documents. My co-workers in the mornings were Karen and Lynne; Natalie and Diane came in for the afternoons, and Bob Ross, the boss, was in all day—except for the next few Thursdays and Fridays, when he would be away at FDTA conferences around the country. Got that?

I felt my bile rise right away as I witnessed an office squabble. Natalie complained to Bob about the quality of Lynne's work. I detected a clear tone of sucking up, a good girl versus bad girl duplicity that revealed the morass of shifty politics I had to avoid here. As Natalie was my immediate supervisor, it was an augury of rough times ahead.

As for Lynne, a plump woman in her late 40s who let her red hair fall to her shoulders, I took an instant dislike to her when she learned I graduated from the College of the Holy Cross in Worcester, Massachusetts. "I recently passed Worcester on the highway," she said about a trip she took that summer. "I had to get off there to find a restroom, and it was awful! What a filthy city! That's where you went to school?"

I relished every chance I got to leave my artificially beautiful campus on the hill, from which point the College overlooked Worcester—especially when I visited the run-down corners of that "filthy city" to bring food to the homeless. Lynne, a resident of the wealthy, insular enclave of nearby Rye Brook, made sure that her housekeeper kept her world free of the unclean lifestyle to which the inhabitants of Worcester and other common folk were accustomed.

I was struck by her candor, which extended to the job at hand. Seeking clarity about the organization's mission, I asked her, "So, the conferences that FDTA puts on aim to teach corporations how to use all the legal means available to pay the least amount of taxes possible?"

"Exactly," she laughed. "We really have no idea what we're doing with this tax stuff! It's all over our heads. What's important is the teamwork, the organizational aspect, getting all the meetings together."

It seemed I was the only one in the vicinity who felt that that might be in any way problematic. I knew in 1996 that U.S. corporations were paying the smallest percentage of taxes collected by the U.S. government in the country's history—less than 10 percent of the total, down from 33 percent in the 1940s. (In contrast, individuals paid more than 75 percent of the total tax collected, and the tax rate on wealthy individuals had fallen from 91 percent in 1959 to 39.6 percent.)

It was clear that through my office tasks, I would be working not for the little guy, but for the already privileged to become more so—because when corporations skirt taxes, that money is added into their profit margins and doesn't trickle down to regular folks. If anything, it goes to fatten executive compensation packages.

The greatest irony was that the FDTA itself didn't pay a dime to the government—because it was a 501(c)3-class organization, created for "educational purposes." With Bob Ross living well in Scarsdale, New York, one of the country's richest communities, and driving a Mercedes-Benz, the FDTA's "not-for-profit" status plainly did not extend to all of its staff.

Yet are there no positive aspects to the FSC? As an incentive to exporters, the thinking goes, they contribute to a strong U.S. economy. White-collar executives who launder corporate income in Caribbean tax havens, but have never laundered their own shirts in a washing machine, expect people to believe this spin—if they ever hear about the FSC at all. Manufacturers don't need an incentive to export. Foreign markets present limitless opportunities for profit after companies have saturated the United States with their products.

On one occasion, a FSC operator from the U.S. Virgin Islands, one of the preferred offshore locations for the phantom headquarters of a foreign sales corporation, called the office and induced me into a fugue state. "You should photocopy this article in today's Wall Street Journal," he advised, "about Microsoft suing the IRS for millions in back taxes that could have been applicable to FSC exemptions."

I got Bob's copy of the newspaper and he continued. "You see at the end of the piece, where it notes that the company could save $200 million in five years through the FSC?"

I did. "That's not what we want people and Congress to think about!" this shell game barker exclaimed. I felt my mind slipping into a lecture hall, where I once heard noted foreign policy critic Noam Chomsky address just this kind of bait and switch. "The article should talk about how many jobs the FSC would be creating!"

Worrying about Congress rethinking the FSC law was not unreasonable, since the rest of the world doesn't view these tax breaks in a positive light either. For all of its sanctimonious pronunciations of the wonders of free trade, the U.S. practice of condoning FSCs serves the opposite end. By allowing corporations to pocket more money to reinvest in their business, it confers an uncompetitive advantage over other multinationals without such subsidies. But what is questionable economic policy to some is a way to easy money for others.

Bob Ross founded FDTA, the only organization specifically devoted to FSCs and DISCs, in 1984 to take advantage of the Reagan administration's boon to the corporate tax code in his Tax Reform Act. He built his business over a decade and offered an increasing array of seminars and conferences for corporate executives at luxury hotels in major cities around the country.

One of my duties was to type survey responses evaluating FDTA conferences into one summary document. Bob would then kick back in his leather swivel chair to peruse the critiques and review the average ratings given by attendees of his meetings. It was common to find him with his feet up, gazing out the window and contemplating the big picture—or his next vacation in Russia.

Bob Ross was no relation to the painter of the same name, who had a popular instructional program on public television that showed aspiring artists how to paint "happy little trees." With Bob Ross at FDTA, it was all about happy little tax conferences.

Bob himself was chipper most of the time—and why shouldn't he be? He hobnobbed with the likes of George Steinbrenner and Miss America at invitation-only events in New York City. If the weather was above 50 degrees, he was out the door and hitting the golf links.

On only one occasion did I observe events outside Bob's control upset his unflappable demeanor. The morning of April 1, White Plains had a heavy snowfall, and the FSC/DISC Tax Association wasn't fully up and running until 11:00 a.m.—not because we had a snow delay like the local schools, but because of an April Fool.

After I got to the office, Lynne locked the door and put up a sign: "FDTA closed due to snow."

Bob laughed at the joke when he arrived, then cut off his mirth as a thought occurred to him. "Has anyone seen Diane?" he asked. "I thought I saw her walking from the building."

Lynne, Karen and I exchanged looks. Could she really have bought it?

Suddenly, the little gas we all got from the gag became as painful as someone passing gas in a tight space. Bob fell into a spastic fit about irresponsibility and valuable nonproductive time lost. He paced throughout the office, muttering; Lynne tried to smooth things over by offering to pick up Diane when she got home and ferry her back to White Plains.

Diane lived 45 minutes away, so—in this, the era before cell phones that made you locatable and on call anywhere at any time—it wasn't until 10:00 a.m. that we heard from her. I took the call and explained what happened.

"That asshole," she spat into my ear. Diane hadn't come into the office because she'd left her keys at home, she said, and she didn't bother to knock because of the sign.

When she arrived, Bob already had returned to placidity. Like a bemused Shakespeare overseeing the motley players in his production, he laughed at the "comedy of errors," but Diane still glowered like a deceived King Lear, and Lynne pulled her Fool's cap over her eyes, hiding in her office.

A variety of reasons convinced me in college to avoid employment in the corporate world. Amoral business goals and practices were one; the inhumane treatment of employees in a hierarchical environment was another. I found what I wasn't looking for at the FDTA, and Diane embodied the worst characteristics of a cruel supervisor.

The youngest person after me at FDTA, in her mid-30s, Diane was a striking brunette who invariably wore pressed dark-colored suits and walked with confidence. She made it clear almost every day that she didn't like me. I wasn't the only object of her scorn, but seemed to be like an irritating pimple on the point of her nose that she just couldn't keep from picking.

For instance, Diane took issue with the snacks I added to our orders of Staples office supplies. Everyone munched on the pretzels and peppermints that came with the boxes of three-ring binders and file folders, but it was an unauthorized use of company funds, she said. Later I overheard Diane suggesting to Natalie that Bob leave petty cash in the office so that the girls could order out to lunch once in awhile.

Natalie wasn't averse to joining the persecution. Bob asked me to mail the payments for FDTA's bills, and when Natalie came into the office and discovered this, she exploded. "I don't want you doing that! You don't know my procedure," she asserted. Of course, I was only doing what the head man requested—and it didn't seem too difficult to put checks into envelopes—but she groused that she'd "talk to Bob about it."

Diane also took exception to anything outside the routine, yelling at me once when she learned I'd revised the conference database to reflect a registration substitution, a detail I'd handled before with no problem. Now I'd managed to step on her toes somehow, and Diane seethed, "If you ever touch one of my conference registrations again, I'll kill you." The other women laughed. Lynne was no longer the one in the doghouse, so there was no exhortation about the value of teamwork this time.

I should have drawn the line there and got in her face: "Excuse me? Who the hell do you think you are? I didn't do anything incorrectly. Even if I did, you have no right to speak to me that way. Don't you ever say that to me again!" But I just walked away and gave her another incentive to be a bully.

My plan to make FDTA another brief stop on the employment line derailed in slow motion. Watching the progression of my life was like seeing grisly news coverage of train cars jumping the tracks one by one: Friends who talked casually about sharing an apartment with me in Boston bailed from the plans. I realized I hadn't saved nearly enough cash to get an apartment of my own, which might require a security deposit, the first and last month's rent and a hefty finder's fee for a real estate agent. My résumés to media watchdogs, residential assistance programs and activist organizations were disappearing into a black hole. It was going to take some time before I could extricate myself from this mess—no doubt the intention of the system that makes higher education and the necessities of life so expensive.

In the meantime, I learned more about the nature of the business—and the justifiable paranoia that surrounded those in the know. A Q&A section in an FDTA newsletter admitted, "In this age of antagonism to 'corporate welfare,' we have to continue to lobby for FSCs, as they could come under attack at any time."

Some of the players didn't know where the cash grabs should stop, such as one of the speakers for the FDTA conference on big-ticket leasing. Instead of lecturing on the tax advantages of contracting the use of airplanes and other large-cost items, he had to be replaced at the last minute. He couldn't make the event because he was on trial for embezzling money from Chase Bank.

The FDTA annual conference program boasted topics including "How U.S. multinationals in Mexico can use maquiladoras to cut down on manufacturing expenses." The North American Free Trade Agreement already was a blueprint for labor exploitation, encouraging U.S. corporations to relocate their assembly plants to the practically unregulated maquiladora zone in northern Mexico. There they could pay their workers four dollars a day instead of union wages in the United States. Now these same businesses could fatten their profit margins yet again by paying a tax division to fill out some paperwork—an interesting method of job creation indeed.

One day I took a call from a man who introduced himself as being with KPFK, the independent, progressive Pacifica Network's radio station in Los Angeles. He inquired about the FDTA's international tax conference, entitled "Reducing the worldwide corporate tax rate," in L.A. that week, and asked for an interview.

"Why?" I asked. "Aren't you public radio?"

"Don't you think we might be able to help your business?" he countered.

"Not if you're serving the audience you're supposed to be informing!" I laughed.

I passed the call to Bob. Either KPFK was being clever and sneaky to do a little exposé on corporate welfare, or the radio station had sold out and was pandering for business support. The crisis that arose the next year at Pacifica radio, in which the stations' management banned "controversial" and insubordinate programmers, and the network's board of directors sought to raise funds from foundations and corporate sponsors, suggests which alternative was the case.

Once Lynne asked me to photocopy an article for her files. The lead paragraph lamented, "Henry David Thoreau urged people to 'Simplify, simplify.' His words would have gone unheeded among the majority of cross-border leasing participants," he argued, because the complex finance structures involved had attracted the unwanted attention of the IRS, leading to regulations, taxes, and the loss of profit. To see Thoreau, who in the 19th century was a pioneer of principled tax resistance with his opposition to the Mexican War, being used to augment a call for better corporate tax evasion, was about as surreal a moment as they come—but all in a day's work at the FDTA.

As soon as the teacher walked out of the classroom, the girls got to fighting. Bob left for the day at 12:30, and Natalie took the opportunity to grill Lynne about various days she didn't come to work. "You're behind in making up the time," Natalie charged.

Lynne protested vigorously, but Natalie only increased her hostility and patronized Lynne all the more. "You know, you really make it difficult for others to work with you. I'm installing a new payroll system," Natalie declared, with the clear implication that she would have solid proof the next time some discrepancy arose with Lynne's hours—and nail her.

Suddenly a model of professionalism, Lynne responded calmly and carefully. Natalie's continued frothing at the mouth, however, goaded Lynne to abandon what had been a model of restraint and raise her voice.

"Don't you ever use that tone with me!" Natalie spat.

"Well, listen to yourself!"

"No, I don't think so," Natalie huffed, clearly pleased that she now had a fresh offense to report to Bob, regardless of whether she was right or wrong about the hours in question.

The hot topic the next day was the letter of resignation Lynne left on Bob's swivel chair. "I can't work in this environment," it began.

Karen, a part-time administrator, said I could easily do the work Lynne managed, and Bob confirmed this: "You're the man now, Vincent!" There were no tears shed for another expendable worker.

"What is this about a difficult working environment?" Bob asked Natalie, attempting a modicum of impartiality in his usual unruffled comportment. "She says you 'accosted' her and treated her 'like a child.'"

Natalie proffered her familiar ingratiating tone, wheedling like a student insisting she wasn't talking—she was just borrowing a pen, is all. "Bah-ob, you know me better than that!"

It was like a run-down smoke alarm battery to me, but washed over Bob like a string quartet. "Well, I think it was very unprofessional of her to just walk out when she is in the middle of working two meetings," Bob glowered. "She didn't even consult with me first! Well, she can go—but she has to finish what she started." Bob dialed Lynne's home to issue his judgment, and she said she'd come in the next day—when Natalie was out of the office.

A number of people who called the office thought I was Bob. "Wow, you really sound like him!" they'd exclaim. One told me confidentially, "Over here we call him 'Whispering Bob,'" and did a dead-on raspy-voiced impression that called up an image of someone flashing the inside of a trench coat and trying to sell you a watch on the subway.

In November, when Bob was planning a move to an office building in White Plains, he looked into getting his own photocopy machine. A representative of a copier company came to make a pitch and sold Bob on the model, but Bob angled for a lower price tag. "Do you give any breaks to struggling young companies?" he inquired. When that line didn't hook anything, the sales rep and I tried to contain our laughter as Bob persisted: "Some of the more reputable copier companies, I've heard, allow for some freebies."

Definitely a cheapskate with expenses, Bob could also be generous when occasions warranted. Although he cast me among the 45 million Americans who didn't have health insurance—I certainly could not afford it on the wage he paid me—he did give a Christmas bonus and a summer bonus, both unanticipated rewards. "I guess no one ever filled you in on the procedures," Natalie said each time she handed me the check.

True to form, Natalie informed me that I was invited to the office Christmas lunch party two hours beforehand. Bob took us to Mulino's, a swank place with more lights hung on the trees outside it than in the rest of the city. Gaudy decorations of Nutcracker soldiers and frolicking elves crowded a window that looked out to a bubbling fountain. The nearly three-hour meal featured discussion of each staff person's family and plans, and Bob showcasing photographs from his recent trip to Vietnam. Before the tip, the bill came to $280 for the six of us.

A month later, I noticed a postcard Bob had sent to the office from Vietnam, which the women hadn't shared with me at the time. He wrote, "Most people here work with their hands and seem very happy, even though they have very little. We have a lot to learn about the simple life."

That day, Bob had a beautiful, expensive-looking rug delivered to the office—"To cover up the spots on my carpet," he explained. I had never noticed any spots.

I grew absolutely sick of the job, sick of contributing to the corporate incest. I was splitting my time between non-profit organizations, working for the robber barons on the one hand and volunteering for the local peace and justice organization, WESPAC, the Westchester People's Action Coalition. At their office, just a few blocks from the FDTA, I'd just seen a video documenting the U.S. government's drive to expel Hopi and Navajo Indians from their reservation to further the mining operations of the Peabody Coal Company. All the owners of this rapacious interest—Bechtel, Fluor, Hansen plc—I had recently added to the FDTA database. I wouldn't be surprised in the least if Enron was another FDTA client. Even Lucasfilm Ltd. called, wanting brochures to show them the way to keep as much of the truckloads of money they were earning on the Star Wars re-releases as they could.

So I was determined to do as little work as possible while getting away with as much as possible. It didn't seem to make sense that I should get carpal tunnel at the computer keyboard if the women in the office took every opportunity they could to gossip, talk about soap operas and make personal calls on company time.

I thought it might inspire a few double-takes if I inserted another word into the middle of my typical telephone greeting: "Hello, Tax Evaders Association. Can I help you?" That would throw some people off. I abandoned the idea of adding Cookie Monster to the database so he could receive brochures as well—that was a little too obvious.

Alone one Friday afternoon, I tried to follow in the footsteps of 1960s radical Abbie Hoffman by welcoming the WESPAC director to the office. I made him acquainted with the copier, the stamp machine and the snacks, which fueled our joint education campaign about the dangers of the local nuclear power plant. At least the FDTA got to contribute to something socially responsible.

I came to the office after hours to photocopy hundreds of leaflets for local protest actions I was helping to organize. However, this slacker's selfishness outweighed his shrewdness: I also made a long-distance call that showed up on the phone bill. Natalie tried to track down the culprit by dialing the number; luckily, my friend's mother had the presence of mind to admit nothing, and I did the same, so blame fell upon the cleaning people.

It was still an issue two months later. Bob called me away from data entry to sit in his office for a chat. "You know, Natalie paid the phone bill and noticed that telephone number someone dialed from here," he said. "That brought it up in my mind again. Now, I'm not saying that anyone did it...but you wouldn't have been here on a Friday night, would you?"

I looked at him as if he was crazy.

He harumphed and muttered about taking keys away if it happened again.

I left and hoped that would finally be the last I heard of that disaster.

I knew damn well who made that call. Tell him the truth? Please—I didn't see the women coming clean about the charges they added to the bill for their surreptitious calls. The man threw money away on all kinds of frivolity, and didn't compensate his employees nearly enough, but if he felt someone stole from him—what, 10, 13 dollars?—he was incensed.

I fantasized about just walking off the job and out of my house, embracing homelessness throughout the warm summer. Maybe I could find some work that would pay just enough for food and my student loan bills—someplace that would actually want me to work for them, not some clonable drone; someplace where I could contribute to helping someone in need somewhere, go home and then call it a good day.

I reported for duty the next day. Bob told me my work was helping to bring a lot of business, and announced he was giving me a raise of one dollar an hour. The offer came without forewarning, and I accepted the money.

The months passed and I was still showing up every day at 9:00. In March, before Bob left to hit the ski slopes of Colorado, he summoned his staff into his office. This was unusual—although there were only six of us, we were atomized by office walls and cubicle dividers, and we never gathered for staff meetings. Whenever Bob wanted to communicate something, he'd make the rounds, so this suggested a big, smelly shoe was about to drop.

"Well, you know we've been thinking of hiring someone," he began. "But we didn't find the right person. So I wondered if maybe we weren't getting enough out of the people we already have."

Of course, the boss himself is one of those people, but he was about to take his third vacation already this year. No ominous pause was necessary to communicate that the other foot coming down was encased in a heavy ski boot.

"Now," he continued, "Diane is overworked, and she's not utilizing all of her creative capacity, doing too much administrative stuff. Since Karen's been here longer, let's give some of that to her. And Vincent can do some of the things Karen does now."

Diane radiated a serene sense of victory.

"Sure, Bob," Karen agreed.

"No problem by me," I added.

"But now, Vincent, we've never really discussed your future with us," Bob resumed.

Gulp. My expression suggested a neutrality rivaling Switzerland's.

"You were looking for a job, and now it seems you're not. But are you here to stay? Because we can give you more challenging tasks."

Bob leaned back and cast his eyes to the ceiling. "There's all sorts of reasons someone might choose to work a job," he waxed philosophically. "It's easy, convenient, pays well—but we don't want rationalizations, we want someone who likes what they do, whose heart is in the job."

I nodded. I felt the women's eyes—Diane's and Natalie's in particular—boring into me, ascertaining my position, waiting either for the lie that would forswear my nature and tether me bodily to the plow, or the truth that would give them the opportunity to pounce. I shifted in my seat, feeling the flames these she-devils stoked singe my pants, as they silently implored the Great Satan to turn up the heat, it was chilly in here.

"Now, I'm excited about coming to work. I'd enjoy this work even if I made half of what I make now!" Bob proclaimed. Easy for him to say—he was pulling in a bit more than $11 an hour.

Bob leaned forward, his feet hitting the floor with a thud. "So, Vincent—what's your story?"

I felt like I was George Costanza in the presence of Seinfeld's version of George Steinbrenner. The gauntlet had been thrown, oh yes, but a careful response could yet be a feint that would keep me alive in the match.

"I'm more than willing," I said in measured phrases, "to take on additional administrative tasks. I've helped Karen with them in the past, so they shouldn't pose a problem."

"OK, then," Bob announced. "We'll try this for a couple of months. If it works out, maybe we'll pay you a little extra and not get another person, who we'd waste a lot of time training on the job. Let's go with the people we know for awhile." It sounded like a sound, exploitative business plan to me.

"But there's no guarantee of employment," he warned. And on that note, he adjourned the meeting. He fell for my lunge, and I took his thrust with grace and a minimal loss of blood. So parry on I would.

It wasn't that he wanted me to do more that irked me. It was that I was doing all that he had asked me to do—mainly data entry—and now he was reorganizing my responsibilities and having the gall to make me feel insecure about it.

I hadn't returned to my desk for five minutes before Diane collared me. "Oh, I know Bob didn't give you a chance to talk. He's like that; he gets off on tangents," she chirped, as if she was sharing a cute little observation with me. No kidding, I thought, that's what I was counting on.

Then her face darkened; flirtation over. "So what is it? It's OK if you're not interested in the job, but we need to know."

Playing the content employee was fine for Bob, but I couldn't see giving her that satisfaction. I stared right back at her and replied, "I can't see myself here too much longer," trying to indicate with my tone that she was a principle reason.

"OK!" she smiled, and bounced off. I couldn't help feeling like that admission was going to hurt me somehow.

If you do something like this ever again, that's it—you're outta here, I don't care!" Diane raged. She was angry this time because she'd found a diskette in the supply cabinet that wasn't blank. I'd forgotten to reformat a few diskettes I'd used the previous day after trying to make a backup copy of the database for Bob's laptop PC.

So instead of facing her down, I approached Bob and demanded that he compel her to cease speaking to me that way. Bob gave me a lecture on priorities instead. "I know it's tough working for more than one person, but you have to be more thorough," he insisted.

Only Lynne, who had returned to work but was not long out of the doghouse herself, offered sympathy. "Diane doesn't know how to talk to people," she said. "We've all had to deal with it."

One day, Karen broke the copy machine. She closed its cover on a book, and it shattered the glass. "Oh, well," she shrugged. "Accidents happen."

"You know if I did it, Diane would have lynched me," I joked.

Karen laughed and agreed.

Some time later, Diane took it upon herself to inform me that I could not take my one-week vacation when I wanted, during the third week of August, even though I'd reserved it two months in advance. "I don't want to be alone in the afternoons," she said. The way the schedule was set, that would only be the case on Monday and Friday that week. Still, that was enough to justify scuttling my travel plans. For someone who enjoyed my presence like a good case of head lice, this was a particularly venal and suspiciously low blow.

On another occasion, I was heavily involved in a project and finally came to a stopping point at 1:30. When I returned from my one-hour lunch, Diane went on one more power trip. "How come you just disregard what I say? You take your lunch at 12:00 or at 1:00—don't make me tell you again."

It was clear she didn't want to be the one answering phone calls, if just for a half-hour. Of course, she had no compunction about leaving at 2:00 for her lunch and leaving me alone for an hour. Oh, well—accidents happen: I forgot to work for that period.

At last, after a year of looking high and low for a match, I was thrilled to be offered an excellent internship with an international peace organization at its U.S. headquarters, not far from White Plains. I submitted my notice to leave FDTA four weeks in advance. Even though this news was a dream come true, I couldn't help but get heart palpitations like I do nearly every time I have to speak in public or become the focus of attention.

In declaring my imminent departure, I sweat through my shirt in my usual physiological freak-out, as I did during my interview before coming to the FDTA. As usual, Bob received the information with blasé equanimity. "Well, people move on," he said. "You certainly have helped in a lot of ways around here." And that was that!

To her credit, Natalie took the opportunity to apologize for some of her irrational behavior of the past year, such as the incident in which she castigated me for mailing the bills. "I eventually figured out: 'Don't kill the messenger, go to the source!'" she winked. Ha, ha.

Diane, on the other hand, couldn't usher me out fast enough. Admittedly, I left myself open to an easy attack when a package of office supplies I'd ordered before my vacation arrived while I was away. Diane approached me five minutes after I'd arrived on the Friday before my last day, holding a pair of audiocassette tapes. "What are these?" she asked.

I had been adding a few tapes to each Staples order for a month or so, recording "Democracy Now!", a terrific hour-long news and views radio program, each morning on my portable radio as a favor for a friend who missed the show after moving from the area. I knew the gig was up, and I was all but out the door, so I felt unencumbered in confessing. My factual, guilt-free explanation probably wasn't the mode of disclosure she wanted to hear from me.

"You know, you think you're such a do-gooder, and think you've got everybody fooled," she condemned me, spittle escaping her lips. "But you're really a hypocrite, a thief and a liar."

I didn't confirm or deny her assessment. I just stood impassively. I had a few choice words for her as well, but I wasn't going to say them. Even with nothing to lose, it wasn't worth it to me to sink to her level.

"How can you justify it?" she asked.

It wasn't a good moment to offer some education on how generations of political radicals viewed nickeling and diming corporations for good causes. My feelings about her hypocrisy would only escalate the battle, and as much as I disliked her, at that moment I wasn't in the mood for a confrontation. "I didn't think much of it," I decided to say, "because it was petty." You know, like the petty cash you use to order lunches?

"It doesn't matter that it's petty—it's still thievery," she judged. "Well, we all know about it now, and now I have the hard evidence in my hand."

So? I thought. What do I care?

"We all know you made that phone call in January, too."

I said nothing.

"AND you're still buying those snacks I told you not to!"

This was too much. "Come on, Diane, everybody eats those snacks!"

"No, we eat the popcorn and the pretzels, but not the nuts," she maintained.

I felt my ground in the conversation begin to slip, as we plainly were beginning to teeter on the edge of the absurd.

"You know, Bob is deeply hurt by this," she continued, "and he started poor—he had nothing. Yes, he's wealthy now, but he had to work for everything he got. He may decide to press charges for petty larceny, or he may just dock your pay, but you're not getting paid for today—so get your things and go home," she commanded. "I don't trust you and can't work with you alone."

I mocked her response to the situation. "What, do you think I'm going to sit around all afternoon calling Staples and ordering snacks and tapes all day? It was $10 worth of stuff every two weeks!"

"No, I can't trust you, I can't baby-sit you," she repeated.

It wasn't a hardship to walk out at 9:15 on that beautiful summer day.

The next Monday, I met with Bob. I was steeled for a big flare-up, but, as in most situations, he was a pussycat. "I think Diane went a little overboard last Friday," he said in his soft tones. I think she goes overboard every time she's talked to me for the past year, I thought.

"I'm a little disappointed," Bob allowed, "but it was a small mistake, not a serious thing. You've done many more good things in the past year for us. I'm not going to hold it on your record." No questions asked.

"I want to forget about it," he said, "but I just want you to pay back what you owe to the company. Because we're not a big company, like IBM, where everybody's doing it and the losses are just factored in. We're like a family here."

That last bit almost knocked me out of my chair. It sure felt like a family to me—the kind of family where the parental figures order you around and expect you to jump, where the abusive older sister tells you you're worthless, where everyone gossips but no one listens, where everyone knows their place but no one knows what they're doing.

"Now, if you want to get some personal things because it's easier or you've got a better deal, fine," he continued. "Just tell someone. But if you feel reluctant to tell someone, you've got to wonder, maybe it isn't right to do. But I think other companies would handle this situation in the same way. I don't think it's a matter of not trusting you to work on your own. I just think you should pay back what you owe," he repeated.

I'd been rethinking the situation since the weekend. What did those cassettes cost—$50? That's a generous estimate. How much does health insurance cost? Maybe employer payments would be $100 a month? Maybe $200? I felt like telling Bob, for the 14 months I've worked here, subtract the tapes (and the snacks, don't forget them) and maybe he owes me $1,350. And that's a lowball calculation.

Being so aggressive is not my style, perhaps to my detriment. I simply said, "The job I'm going to next offers full health and dental insurance."

"I didn't know you wanted health coverage," Bob said.

I looked at him incredulously. "How could you think I wouldn't want it? The other full-time workers in the office have it."

It was an unassailable point. And so we never arranged how I would repay "the family."

"You know, we're going to miss you," Bob declared. "We're having a luncheon for you on Thursday."

I blinked. That was going to be far worse than anything I could have faced in this conversation! On the other hand, it would be a pleasure as Diane ate crow next to the liar, thief and hypocrite as he was honored on his next-to-last day.

However, when it came down, the luncheon also passed smoothly—perhaps because Diane was "out sick" that day. The other women tried to give me an exit interview over Chinese food. Natalie led the interrogation: "So, what did you think of working here? Tell us in two sentences, and no four-letter words!"

It would have been a great time to offer my anti-corporate philosophy, but I skirted the issue by noting how I'd developed skills in talking on the phone and learned how to juggle tasks and prioritize.

"I'm still not clear on what it is this other place you're moving on to does," Lynne admitted. "Then again, I'm still not sure what this place does."

Two months before Bill Clinton left office, he approved an act of Congress that changed the status of the FSC law. Responding to objections from European Union nations—including the likelihood of an official complaint with the World Trade Organization

(WTO) that would force a dismantling of the FSC as an obstacle to free trade—the act abolished the FSC. However, it also replaced it with a new Extraterritorial Income (ETI) tax write-off that awards corporations the same 15 to 30 percent benefit.

With its name now obsolete, in May of 2002 the FDTA became CITE—the Council for International Tax Education, an alias it had used as an alter-ego in marketing certain conferences that weren't specifically related to FSCs. As CITE, it continues to promote the new ETI exemption as part of a broader mission of corporate tax education.

Of course, the ETI is hardly any different from the FSC. If anything, it makes procedures vastly simpler by cutting out the middlemen—if a phantom board of directors running an "offshore" subsidiary can be said to be that. Now corporations can get the savings directly though their tax returns.

In essence, Clinton followed a pattern he had established with the U.S. Army School of the Americas. He responded to protesters calling for its closing, because of its notorious record of training soldiers from Latin America who would return to their home countries and commit human rights abuses, by closing the school—and then re-opening it a month later under a new name, the WHISC (Western Hemispheric Institute for Security Cooperation).

The bait-and-switch fooled none of the SOA protesters, and it certainly didn't dampen European protest of U.S. subsidies to its corporations. The future of the ETI—and CITE itself—is uncertain, and CITE's literature reflects a sense of mournful urgency: "The Republicans want the WTO dispute resolved and do not appear adverse to terminating the legislation. This would be a good time for corporate executives to contact their Congresspeople and let them know how the ETI legislation helps them to compete overseas." ★

Pick Your Poison

You Can't Spell Teamwork without "Me? Work?"
by Nate Gangelhoff

ONCE A WEEK at the Super America we would gather in the break room for a "team meeting", a boring ritual with the typical monologues of "Someone's been stealing this" "customers are mad about this" blah blah blah. Twenty minutes of trying desperately not to laugh, basically.

Greg's meetings were usually about sales, profits, promotions and so forth. I think he actually thought we gave a flying fuck about how much cappuccino the company was selling, that we would feel a swell of pride to hear we had increased the amount by 3% the month prior. I guess maybe it made him proud, so he had to tell somebody. The people in the outside world could care less about the things he had accomplished as Store Manager; society did not look upon his position as one of honor, prestige or significance. So when he had us as a trapped audience back there in the break room, he'd list the achievements, go through his ideas, and hope that maybe one of us would care. "I actually took a pay cut for this position" he explained at one point to illustrate his sense of commitment to the job, and our apparent lack. "Before, I was paid by the hour as an assistant manager and I was making 40,000 DOLLARS A YEAR" he continued, pausing for dramatic effect. This was even less impressive when you factored in that he was working 80 hours a week and on the verge of a complete breakdown.

Jen's meetings were far more pessimistic. We would not be told that our daily register countdowns were looking better; we would be scolded that floors needed to be mopped more often, and people really, really had to stop wearing blue jeans.

I didn't want to hear it. Even more so than Greg's meetings, I would zone out her voice and let my eyes scan the room, examining the circle of "teammates", my comrades in the cashiering world. As Jen droned on about correct shelving techniques, I made a vow to learn more about my fellow employees: that would kill time better than keeping up with celebrity fashion via People magazine as I had been doing.

It was a revolving cast of delinquents staffed there at the Super America, whose only thing in common was that we all possessed the necessary prerequisite of being able to write our name on an application. This "You're not going to kill anybody while you're working… right?" hiring strategy lead to some interesting characters at your side tearing off lottery tickets. Mostly high schoolers, but you had your share of weird older employees.

The meager pay forced a good percentage of these workers into falling back on second jobs, most of which seemed vastly superior and made me wonder why they even bothered with the Super America in the first place.

Karl was a lifeguard; all he would do was get stoned and lay around the beach. If you ever chided him on his laid-back duties, he'd get defensive and say "I save lives, man"

JJ worked full-time at the SA but yet sold enough coke on the side to get by easily without the added 40 hours of cashiering. I didn't understand his motivation. It couldn't have been a trick to explain to his parents where the money was coming from, unless they were really fucking stupid. The rest of us gas station attendants were not buying brand new cars and gold chains and shit.

My constant cashiering companion Jessica also had a second job, as a model for Ambercrombie and Fitch, where she made $600 dollars an hour or something ridiculous for the occasional photo shoot.

"God damn! Then what are you doing working here?!" I asked in disbelief

She laughed. "Oh, I don't know, I don't really like modeling anymore."

"What's so bad about it? I mean, this job fucking bites" I waved my hand around the store, catching a glare from a customer "But if I was getting 600 bucks an hour, I'd be here bright and early, with a smile"

"The hours are long" she explained "You have to stand still for, like, a really long time and then if you move just a tiny little bit, they make you start all over and put the make-up on again and stuff" She shrugged "I just got sick of it"

"I guess…." I said, as she left to go scrub down the bathrooms.

But most stunning of all was Jerianne, who I learned one day was receiving $20,000 every two weeks due to her family owning a large portion of a local casino. Seemed like an obvious question, but I had to wonder "WHY THE FUCK ARE YOU WORKING IN A FUCKING GAS STATION?!" I never asked her, though. It probably had something to do with not wanting to feel spoiled, not taking everything for granted. Maybe she even got a bit of satisfaction from a hard day's work. Me, I'd be trav-

contact: PO Box 8995 | Minneapolis, MN 55408 | pickyourpoison.net eling the world, never working a second for a goal I didn't care about.

What was wrong with me? All these other kids were doing the same thing as me, and it didn't seem to put *them* in a ravenous, vehement rage. They were working two jobs, even, and still dealt with the gas station as a duty, the seven dollars and twenty five cents a perfectly fair trade for an hour of their time. What the fuck, I thought. Seriously, what the fuck. ★

Taking the Law into Your Own Hands
by Nate Gangelhoff

After getting "downsized", or "thrown on the street in the name of higher profit margins" from the shampoo factory, I scored a temp job at a massive law office downtown. Not a big fan of the law. But, I figured it would be interesting to see it from the other side, to watch laws get crafted rather than see them in action. Besides, it was a food company so I assumed I wouldn't have to take part in anything sketchy. Had it been the office of some smug lawyer who tried to put potheads behind bars I would have passed on the opportunity, but I figured nothing too shady could be going on here.

That assumption would prove to be wrong, but at first it was just tedious busy-work, filing and typing and all the typical office grunt-labor, which I was fine with, all things considered. The place wasn't as serious and staid as I had envisioned it. I had been almost expecting them to tell me to arrive in a suit and tie, but yet I was able to easily employ my "erosion of the dress code" technique (Like this: You get told to garb yourself in the dreaded "business casual" attire. A lot of people blindly obey this and show up in a paycheck's worth of bland clothing, but it doesn't have to be that way. First day, you wear a pair of khakis, a white t-shirt, and a pair of tennis shoes. You're already testing the waters by avoiding the dress shoes. And, you don't tuck in your shirt, because tucking in your shirt is stupid. After a week, try a pair of blue jeans and see how that goes over. Odds are, you'll be fine. Then maybe a t-shirt that's got some sort of design or slogan on it. Pretty soon you'll be able to dress as you would normally, and your co-workers will either no longer notice, or just view you as "that loveable wacky temp with the Budweiser t-shirt". Of course, this doesn't work with every office job, but you'd be surprised at how often it does. I had one job where I ended up wearing these ridiculous jeans with gaping holes in the knees to work every day, and it was great, I didn't feel nearly as awkward or stifled as I usually do in those sort of jobs. When walking through the hallways past management, I'd just drape my leather jacket in front of me so they couldn't see the holes, and everything was a-ok. Hell yeah! Give it a try)

So ANYWAY, the gig was alright at first. It was going to a be a brief assignment; I was only filling in while they screened applicants to take on the full-time position. It was strange—watching nervous suited individuals come in and sweat through lengthy interviews for a position I had been handed without lifting a finger.

One of my tasks was to file away the resumes of these prospective employees. Of course, I read through them and was shocked to see that most of them had gone to school specifically for the position I was now holding. Two years of school for this? What, is the first year devoted to answering phones, and the second to opening file cabinets? The job seemed pretty damn easy to me. You didn't even need to know any legal jargon; as long as you were capable of manning a keyboard, you'd be ok.

And yet none of them were getting hired! "Not what we're looking for" one of the lawyers sighed. "Wish we could keep you on, Nate!" he added with a chuckle. I had to give the temp agency credit: if I had applied for this same exact position directly, I wouldn't have stood a chance—I would've been laughed out the door and probably somehow sued for incompetence by bored attorneys. But with the agency's name and the term "Temp" attached to me, I carried a certain air of legitimacy and was accepted.

This arrangement of watching obviously more qualified individuals being turned down was somewhat amusing in its weirdness for awhile, but soon enough the dark underbelly of the profession revealed itself. One day as I surfed the internet, I heard two lawyers talking. "Alright, here's the situation. Some guy ate a party pizza with metal shavings in it." "Shit" "Yeah, I guess it tore his intestines up pretty bad." he let out a sigh "We gotta take care of this before it gets out" He spoke in annoyed tones, as if it was the pizza eater's own fault. I wondered if they'd throw the guy some money to shut him up, or if they would employ some legal tactic to shift blame and avoid responsibility. That would suck, laying in a hospital bed with a shredded stomach, finding out the multinational company that fucked you over is trying to squirm out of it. The lawyer's frank talk of "publicity" and "profits" rather than "intense pain" and "lacerated stomach lining" lead me to believe they were concerned with nothing but the bottom line. Bleeding consumers be damned.

It got worse. The trademark lawyer gave me an assignment one day as I stared vacantly into space, doing the "zone out" all temp workers know. The company had a contest every year, and my assignment was to make sure no one else was using the contest's name. The thing was, it was a very common phrase that they just happened to own the copyright to. So, it seemed rather absurd to try to keep the phrase to themselves. I mean, if I copyright "Garage Sale", does that mean people are going to have to come up with something else when they try to peddle their shit on a Sunday afternoon? Nevertheless, she tried to explain the logic to me. (DISCLAIMER: Here's the fucked up part--- if I were to mention the company's name and what the contest was, even though this zine has a relatively low circulation, I am positive it would eventually fall into their hands and I'd get a nasty legal letter. I worked with these lawyers-- I know how nutty they can be. I guess it would be sort of funny and fun to reprint the legal warnings and stuff, but all things considered I'd like to avoid it so I will make up names: The company is Food-Co, and the contest was the BBQ. This will work fine, because the actual contest name was just as familiar and common as BBQ, so the absurdity of it should be clear.)

"OK, here's the deal" she explained. "We have a BBQ contest every year, where people compete, get judged, and the winner gets a million dollars"

"Yeah, I've heard of that"

"So, we obviously trademarked the name, and we therefore own the rights to the term 'BBQ'. It's an important and powerful trademark. When other people use it, it loses the connection to us and becomes less powerful" Noting my blank stare, she continued "Well, here's a perfect example: Rollerblade. The company Rollerblade came out with rollerblades and were very successful, but they did not protect their brand name. Now, 'rollerblade' is just a generic term, and the company is not distinguished. We need to make sure the same thing doesn't happen with BBQ" I felt like pointing out that BBQ was ALREADY a generic term to people, but didn't bother. "Um, OK so what do I do?" I asked, not liking where I thought this might be heading.

She opened a folder and put in on my desk. It was stuffed with newspaper clippings. "We hire a firm that goes through newspapers and pulls out anything with the word BBQ in it, and then sends the clippings to us. What I need you to do is look up the address for any of the companies or organizations found to be using the phrase. What we do is send them a Cease and Desist letter letting them know we own the rights to BBQ and they need to stop using it. If they continue, we pursue legal action." You gotta be fucking kidding me you goddamn lunatic I didn't say. "So, just find the addresses, and then mail this letter to them with a copy of the newspaper article as well"

I opened up the folder after she left and looked through it. The first clipping was from a tiny local pa-

per called "The Lakeville Gazette" or something, littered with city council notes and wedding announcements and so forth. How did they FIND this shit? The clipping was in regards to a notice for "The Lakeville Public Library BBQ to Raise Money For Kids With Cancer" Alright, that's it. I resolved right there, no way was I going to do this. I could take no part in saying "Sorry kid, I know you're ravaged with leukemia, but we have a brand-name to maintain!" I resolved to throw the envelopes in the trash next to the mail bin when I left that day. The lawyer would just have to assume that none of the tiny companies and local communities bothered responding.

Pretending to look busy, I leafed through the rest of the folder, which was all pretty much the same, mostly tiny local papers announcing a local BBQ that would likely be attended by a couple dozen people. It was unbelievable this huge corporation was bothering to go after them. What were they thinking? What confusion could possibly arise from other people's usage of the phrase? "Waitaminute, Doug—YOU'RE having a BBQ in your backyard? I thought that was a Food-Co thing!"

Whoever had the job before me had sent out a bunch of the letters already, and put the responses in the folder. There were some pretty good ones. One guy wrote "Thank you for the letter. We have been doing our local BBQ every year for about ten years now. People get together, eat good food, give out prizes and have a fun time. I never realized that we have been hurting your brand name this whole time, and I would like to offer my sincere apologies. I realize your sales must be in the toilet because of us. We immediately cancelled this years BBQ after getting your letter and all sat at home, praying the profits of Food-co were safe. Recently my wife mentioned the word BBQ while we were in the kitchen of my home and I whispered "Shh! FoodCo might be listening!"

I was glad the assignment was a brief one; the tricky legal shenanigans I was witness to were making me feel shitty working there. Again it amazed me what sort of things people allow to happen when they place profit as the only thing of value. Any of these people would normally look at the party pizza incident as completely the pizza maker's fault, and the BBQ debacle as being absurd—but since it was their company on the defense, logic was heaved out the 34th floor window. ★

Rated Rookie

Anatomy of an Infestation
by Joshua Bernstein

It's harder to say when it began, but it's easier to say when I went crazy. For two years I resided in a cigar-shaped apartment in Queens. Bedrooms anchored either end of the roughly 700 square feet. I shared this dwelling with two roommates, Aaron and Steve. The living quarters were cramped yet doable. Only when guests crashed did space become a concern; claustrophobia equals craziness. So maybe you can see why, when my apartment hosted more than 10,000 unwelcome guests, my grip on sanity slid down a bug-slick slope.

The cockroaches were benign my first year and a half at the apartment. The space was newly remodeled—fresh sheetrock, fresh paint, functioning refrigerator. And the apartment stayed spotless thanks to Aaron's Windex and Ajax obsessions. An occasional pinkie-sized cockroach scuttled across the kitchen, but rubber-soled shoes were a nice deterrent. Besides, I thought of the insect emissaries as a Jell-O mold, NYC's way of greeting me. Welcome to New York, motherfucker; we'll be here long after your rent stabilization expires.

But like cigarettes' slow encroachment on lungs, the cockroaches' shift toward pestilence was so infinitesimal I failed to register appropriate concern. I ignored warning signs like a caffeine-deprived truck driver. For example: Needing a glass of water at 3 a.m., I'd stroll to the kitchen and flip on the lights. Blargh! A half-dozen cockroaches would scuttle across the kitchen toward darkness. All sleepy-eyed and barefoot, I'd wait for the cockroaches to hide before filling my glass from the tap. That's okay, my pretties, Uncle Josh just needs a sip of water. Then you can play with his leftover tortellini.

There were exceptions to my half-assed blind ignorance. If a cockroach made an egregious pass across the living room or invaded my bathtub, SPLAT. Those were sacred grounds. For the most part (and I assume full culpability for the ensuing predicament) I permitted the cockroaches to run across the kitchen and trashcan. Shit, no sense letting that dumpling on the floor go to waste.

Of course, the free-range roaches eventually wandered into off-limits territory. Steve's room. The kitchen cabinets. My vegetable crisper. When I found cockroaches lounging inside my wok—Mecca in the kitchen—I realized my lax parental attitude had been abused.

Our apartment was far from filthy. Twice a week I scrub-a-dub-dubbed the bathroom with bleach. Aaron fell in love with Formula 409. Steve kept clean if you ignored his Mt. McKinley of dirty clothes. Still, an apartment building's fatal flaw is that cleanliness is only as good as your neighbors'. Apartments share walls. Bugs live in walls. If one neighbor neglects to clean up after dinner, what's to stop the bugs from meandering next door to survey our leftovers? Nothing, especially when one has a hygienically slack Mexican family as neighbors.

Inhabiting the apartment was a rotating cast of dozens, ranging from a large-breasted 16-year-old daughter and a prostitute-styled mom to an 80-year-old who spat on the stairwell. Though we rarely exchanged words, I still despised the family. Their Chihuahua yipped at all the wrong times. They stored their out-dated dishwasher and wood-paneled TV in the stairwell for upward of five months. Combine that with the fetid garbage bags they stored in the hallway and, well, you could see whom the cockroaches loved so sweet.

Because I'd rather allow a relationship to fizzle than experience confrontation, I bought roach traps filled with poisonous granules. "These will murder the cockroaches real good," said the swarthy bodega owner. I arranged the traps around the apartment and waited. Three days later—nothing. Poison was Popeye's spinach; instead of dying a painful death, the bugs mutated to index-finger lengths. I even found several inch-long cockroaches in my wok making what appeared to be cockroach love. I dumped the paramours onto the ground and smooshed them.

"Aren't you gonna to clean up the guts, Josh?" Steve asked, pointing to the flattened carcasses.

"No way, man," I said. "I'm going to leave their bodies right there as a warning. Don't fuck with me, motherfuckers!"

I smiled. Steve took a few steps back. And then I went to bed and slept a good sleep.

When I awoke, I walked to the kitchen to visit my victims. Egad! The remains had vamoosed. I consulted my roommates to check if they'd moved the carcasses, but no such luck. Other cockroaches, I suppose, had snuck into the kitchen and rescued their brethren as if they were fallen POWs. Was my apartment becoming a Queens Vietnam? Could I win this war? It was time to go on the offensive.

I operated under darkness. When the clock struck Cinderella twelve I'd tiptoe into the kitchen with a rolled up Time in hand. I'd flip on the lights. Dive to the floor. Sight my targets. Splat. Splat. Splat. Crunch. Moving the trashcan revealed more enemies. Crunch. Death from above. I'd climb onto the table. Roaches on walls became brown abstract art. I'd drop back to the floor. Fill corners with roach spray. And then I'd turn off the light. Leave the kitchen. Wait five minutes. Repeat. Wash. Rinse. Kill. Roaches may withstand a nuclear winter, but they smooshed real good beneath a double-issue of Time.

And so it went. I killed roaches every night. I went to bed and killed roaches in my dreams. I inhaled more than the recommended daily allowance of bug spray. I re-upped my magazine subscription. But no matter how many roaches I slaughtered, 10 more returned.

"When I went to go grab a glass from the cabinet last night, Josh, I found a roach family chillin' in my Bud glass," Steve said one morning.

"They were in my coffee cup," Aaron added.

The infestation was nearing critical mass. Every situation has a breaking point, a moment where Twisted Sister's "We're Not Gonna Take It," makes sense. Roaches had conquered kitchen cabinets, trashcans and, after discovering several cockroach shells on top of the ramen, the food supply. Eating ramen is a humbling experience. Every noodle-filled bite is a reminder of poverty. But even more humbling is eating ramen after wiping cockroach shells off the 10/$1 label. This was, as they say in Alcoholics Anonymous, bottoming out.

Several weeks before The Evening, my best friend Andrew moved to New York. Homeless and broke, he took up residence on my linoleum floor. "It's good for my back," he said. But what wasn't good were roaches scurrying across his belly.

"We need to do something, man," Andrew said. "It's freakin' disgusting. I have to put on my shoes to go into the kitchen, and even then I don't want to turn the lights on. I'm scared."

I understood, but had few solutions. By now Steve had developed an obsession with cable TV and Aaron replaced Formula 409 with a girl. These pastimes, combined with a laissez faire-attitude concerning the infestation, had awful repercussions. Our trashcans overflowed with Chinese takeout containers. The shower turned rainbow-hued. The apartment smelled like a New Jersey landfill. Just like parting the Red Sea, roaches poured from walls and into our apartment.

I brought Steve into the kitchen and attempted to explain the inherent wrongness of roaches scuttling across our green plastic cutting board, but he'd have none of it. "I just try to ignore them," he said.

"But Steve," I said, picking up a serrated knife and impaling a plump victim on the green surface,

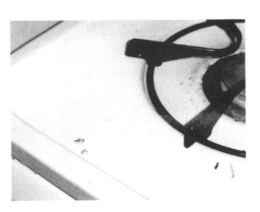

"this is disgusting!"

"We live in New York City, Josh," Steve said. "Roaches are part of city life."

"And car bombings are part of the Middle East, but you don't see people putting up with that, do you? Just because others tolerate bugs as romantic New York bullshit doesn't mean we should agree. These roaches molted in your beer glass!"

It was a lost cause. He shrugged his shoulders and returned to ESPN. I tried pleading with Aaron, but he was talking to his girlfriend on the phone. Andrew resided in my camp but his pressing concern was employment, not killing roaches. I had a job. I had no girlfriend. I rarely watched TV. What was my distraction?

That Sunday evening was a carbon copy of every other—hungover and tired. Andrew had invited a lady friend to our apartment to chat, but I was incommunicado thanks to another night of 32-ounce Budweisers at a Brooklyn dive. So while Andrew, the girl, Steve and Aaron chatted in the living room, I set to scrubbing the dinner dishes.

I placed a dirty pot in the sink. Our inept Greek landlord—whose solution to drafty windows was warmer blankets—had installed the wrong faucets. Cold = hot. Hot = cold. After two years I still forgot, especially when 32-ounce-beer-exhausted. I turned on the hot water. Oops. When I switched to cold I felt pressure on my back, not unlike tapping fingers. I turned around, expecting a roommate. No one. I reached around and there's no sense feigning suspense.

A cockroach.

My fuse was lit.

I lost my shit.

Shaking spastically, I knocked the cockroach to the ground and murderized it with bare feet. I grabbed the roach spray from beneath the sink as well as a large rag. A very large rag. I leapt onto the countertop and flung open my cookbook cabinet. My tofu and Moosewood cookbooks were covered with cockroaches. To my credit, I did not scream. Andrew was attempting mad game on the lass ("When I traveled Europe…" I heard him say), and revealing the extent of the infestation would atom bomb sexual chemistry.

Instead, I quietly, methodically shook the roaches free from the cookbooks and quashed them. I repeated this act in all cabinets, rousting cockroaches from my rice cooker and water boiler and coffee roaster—every useless appliance my parents had given me was infested. But still I kept quiet and kill, kill, killed. The rag turned brown. I sweated. When I exterminated all visible bugs, I opened the window. I doused crannies, crooks and corners with enough bug spray to render my sperm useless.

"What are you doing in there?" Steve asked. That spray hiss was something.

"Cleaning," I answered, squashing another roach.

Oh, okay," Steve said. "Need any help?"

I surveyed the kitchen—not a cockroach was stirring. There was enough poison on the walls to eradicate five generations of insects and several domesticated animals. I was woozy, yet happy. Like shaving my shoulders, I knew this was a feeble salvo, and that the cockroaches would return. In fact, roaches did return the next night. And two months later I moved to another apartment with problems that made cockroaches seem a dream. But I didn't know that yet. All I knew was that tonight victory was mine. ★

I first came to the
Pentridge Children's Garden to
flirt with a girl. Her name was Garlic,
and I'd met her at a show where I was doing my
Punk Rock Stand Up Comedian thing. She was
in town for the summer to work at the Pentridge
Children's Garden, an activist project in West
Philly that a few of my other friends worked at.

She was interning on the summer program there,
teaching kids how to grow vegetables and maintaing
what was the only green space in the neighborhood
(unless you counted the large green crackhouse
across the street). It was a hard thankless job,
really; trying to grow plants and kids in a sort of
desperate environment that wasn't very healthy
for either. I knew about the program, but wasn't
very interested, but I was interested in Garlic,
who wore overalls even in the summer and had
pigtails, so, you know, I got on my bike and rode
over one day.

Arriving at the Garden, I found that she was not
there that day. Nor, it so happened, were any of
the paid staff. What was there was thirty shrieking
Insane kids jumping all over one terrified volunteer
who looked like he was about ready to faint. To
this day whenever I hear the phrase "hell on earth",
I think back to that first moment I had with the
Pentridge Children's Garden. As I said, Garlic
wasn't there, but I got roped into staying and helping
out that day.

contact: 1308 W. Cary St. I Richmond, VA 23220-5463

At first it was just that day they needed a hand with, then two. Then it was a week. The garden was kind of crazy that summer. Eventually all the staff and volunteers got back on track though, and equillibrium and calm returned to the garden, relatively speaking at least.

But I stayed. Not even to flirt with the girl. Me and Garlic barely said two words to each other that summer, so busy were we running around pulling kids out of the pond and giving them piggyback rides and instructing them in pulling out what I sure hoped were weeds.

Sometimes change happens so naturally and organically that you don't even notice. And like a patch of ilanthus can suddenly infest and commandeer an entire garden, the Pentridge Children's Garden sprung up all over my life without me even realizing it. I didn't even notice untiul two months later, when someone said to me "The Garden is really important to you, isn't it?" I hadn't thought of it like that yet, but I had to scratch my head, and realize. "Gee, I guess it is. How about that." It's just weird, because beore I went to the Children's Garden, the two things I liked least in the world were plants and kids.

And bang, here I am still, three years later. A patch of green and a neighborhood of kids and families in southwest philly makes up my life. Who'd have guessed? Not me--- I can still barely believe it in fact. From getting a winter art class started to writing grants, from organizing to get falsely imprisoned folks from the neighborhood out of jail to being welcomed into families' homes and lives, I guess I've made bettering this community my life's work.

And I feel like the luckiest guy on earth. Ending up with such a great life and incredible work, plus a heart full to overbursting with love for this bunch of insane kids. It's not exactly something I can describe, and I even have a tough time writing about it. Like the forest and the trees, it's hard to talk about something that makes up most of your life; hard to even figure out where Pentridge Street ends and I begin anymore. But I ain't complaining. Getting to watch these kids grow up is the best thing that's ever happened to me.

But it's funny; the whole thing can be traced back to that one girl, Garlic. Like how stopping by the garden to flirt with her set the rest of my life in motion, but then I barely talked to her that whole summer we were both working there. Funny because we did start talking to each other in the fall. And by winter were falling hard. And what do you know, we ended up spending some of our second garden summer hiding in the toolshed kissing. I'm still with the Children's Garden, and I'm still with Garlic. Don't see either of those coming to an end anytime soon either. It's just kind of funny. Funny and sweet.

Safety Pin Girl

*mix tape in
your soul*

Mix tapes are strange creatures. They can take a song you hadn't thought about in years, and because it was on the tape you'll want to listen to it all the time. Or it can take a song you wouldn't even normally like, and suddenly the context of the tape will make you love it. Like you could be driving in your dad's car with two of your friends late at night in the summer, when you're completely stoned and you just need to drive too fast and smell the lake breeze and look at the stars blinking down at you because you're too paranoid to go home yet, and the mix tape you're listening to has this U2 song on it, "Lemon." And you really hate U2 and you think Bono is an ass and the song itself is so annoying but at that moment, because it's on that tape, and it's late at night and you're stoned, the song makes perfect fucking sense.

contact: 410 18th St. | Racine, WI 53403

Secret Mystery Love Shoes

by Androo Robinson & Maria Goodman

Hey Kids! Andy here. Take my hand, won't you, as we journey through the mystical land of...

D.I.Y. DIVINATION!

MONKEY MOUTH! WHO DREW THIS?

~When we were staying with our friends Pat + Shannon, Maria and I dug out their dusty ol' ouija board and gave it a spin. Fzr. sftz'z ←Nothing much happened.

Later, after we moved into our own place, we wanted to try it again. We don't have a ouija board, though. SO, as you might expect from the SMLS crew, we made one!

You will need: paper. (taped to table.) sharpie! bottle cap (to use as a pointer.)

You just write out the alphabet in th' middle, "hello", "goodbye", "yes" and "no" in each of the four corners, and the numerals 0-9 if you want. On ours I drew three faces ☺ 😠 ☹ to represent emotional states, since you can't hear the tone of voice of whoever you're talking to.

Okay, back to our story:
~We each laid a finger on the bottlecap, said hello, and we were off! Our homemade board was EXTREMELY talkative. In the beginning, we made the acquaintance of a fella we were to hear a lot from in all our ouija adventures. Out of respect for his privacy, we'll call him Mr. T. At first he told us some very creepy stories. Evidently he'd led a violent life. Also he was a pottymouth. Also he seemed to have a crush on Maria. Fainter hearts would have quailed, but we fear nothing here at Secret Mystery Love Shoes. And, I'm happy to say, our fortitude paid off. In subsequent sessions, Mr. T has calmed down, but still talks plenty. He's willing to answer questions, but if he feels impish or cranky he'll make nonsensical jokes, or rattle off a string of rhymes, at which point we leave him alone. Overall, he seems sad but ultimately hopeful, and the power of love is one of his favorite subjects.

contact: 2000 NE 42nd Ave #303 I Portland, OR 97213

Okay, now to answer some of those questions you are no doubt Just bubbling with:

Q: Does the ouija board predict the future?

A: Not so far, but it does know things we haven't told it, and talks about people we know (but haven't mentioned) with varying degrees of accuracy. (And it spells difficult names correctly.)

Q: Does the ouija board grant wishes?

A: It wishes it could. Wish-fulfillment is one characteristic of its mode of speech...it frequently tells you what you want (or dread) to hear, so rational discretion is advised. Don't go goofy.

Q: How's it work?

A: I dunno. But it makes us sleepy, so I know a lot of energy is involved.

Q: Isn't it dangerous?

A: I don't think so, no. Just don't be gullible, stay balanced in your judgement, and be polite. All life (or whatever) merits your respect.

☞ Do **YOU** have any ouija board stories? TELL US!

And now... **D.i.Y. Divination** part two: The Tarot

↝ I got interested in the Tarot when I was in junior high. (I think I'd just read "The Manitou" or some other junky novel.) I bought a deck from a local bookstore (run by "a bunch of witches" according to their competitors; whose store I also frequented) and snuck it into the house, where I'd study all the cool little pictures and try to puzzle it out.

It was only natural that the Tarot would prove to be a source of fascination for li'l me, because:

A.) Mythological Motifs (LOVE that stuff!)
B.) Symbolism! I'm a sucker for symbolism!
C.) Ancient Mystery~ o°oooooo!
D.) Pictures! Storytelling! I LOVE COMICS!

So here it all was before me... a mute and mutable language languishin' colorfully 'cross my comforter... beckoning me... whisp'ring wisdoms... ➤Okay so whatever. I lost that deck. I dunno what happened to it.

But recently Maria and I went to a university book sale, and : found a beautiful oversized Major Arcana deck.

[Now, for anyone scratching their head over this, The Tarot deck is divided into two sections: The Minor Arcana; which roughly kinda corresponds to a deck of reg'lar playing cards, and the Major Arcana, which, uh, doesn't. There are decks out there, which, for their own esoteric reasons, consist only of the Major Arcana cards, of which there are twenty-two.]

↪Also at the sale was a cheap paperback on the subject, and so I snapped that up too.

: SO I was back in the game after all these years! Of course, I only had the major arcana, so I wasn't playing with a full deck. (har har: So what'd I do? I did what any zinester would do: I took that paperback, which had pictures of ALL the cards in it, and I SCAMMED KINKO's. Made oversized copies on cardstock of all th' Minors, trimmed 'em down to match the Majors I had, and voila!

• Purists (and Kinko's management) may find fault with this meth' od, but I favor the hands-on (and wallet's empty) approach in just about ev'rything, so this deck suits my soul. So back off!

Only thing is, it's HUGE (oversized, like I said) - and what if I wanna play with it at work? Delve for cosmic truths on The Man's time?
    •(I'm at work right now, by the way)•
I need a more portable model ~ a Gameboy tarot deck, if you will. What to do? Well, if you're an obsessive freak like me, you might draw your own deck on a stack of business cards. Yup, that's what I did; had to gather cards from several sources (did you know that business cards come in different sizes? I didn't) until I had 78 I could use, then I drew 'em up, quicky-cartoony/stickfigure style.

This is the sorta thing I figured I could knock out in an afternoon, so of course it ate up an entire weekend. (Just about, anyway.)

THE LOVERS

Oh well. It's all part of the learning process. If you wanna really SEE something, draw it. That's my advice.
        Okay but don't ask me about yer future, I'm new at this.

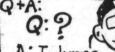

Q+A:
Q: ?
A: I dunno.

Yeah so here are some more cards you can look at if you want. The end.

Tools
by Lu

TOOLS

"there is a proper tool for every job" is a maxim that needs repair. I prefer " the details of every job will expand to require all the tools you own. So if a ship lap joint will suffice, and the carpenter owns a dovetail jig and router, a dovetail joint gets made. Two useful theorems follow from this new postulate: 1. Consider NOT getting the proper tool for the job and just making do with what tool is already here, and 2. If a good tool is being sold cheap, buy it. Soon a job for that tool will magically appear.

We naturally solve problems with whatever tools we have. Going out and buying the "proper tool" with money is just another tool for the rich and unimaginative. Imagination is the tool most people lack. That's why a surgeon always thinks to operate and a nutritionist counsels good diet. A woodworker decides to use wood and a metal fabricator steel, while a lawyer just decides to file a suit. Never get diagnosed by residents, because they always think you have whatever last disease they studied in doctor school.

When money and a client are involved, it almost never pays to be imaginative. I would never suggest to a customer that we try repairing their house with bits of baling wire I pick up on the side of the road while biking . No. I tell them I am charging them for the finest fasteners and the pneumatic device to apply them, and get the job done as quickly and cleanly as possible. Then I keep whatever tools and left over fasteners I charged them for. 150 years ago possessing a saw was the large part of being a carpenter, and you inherited your great grandfather's. In the early 19th century there were only a dozen or so smith's on the entire eastern seaboard who made carpenter's saws, and it was no mean feat to do so prior to modern industrialization. Now for a day's wages a whole set of handsaws and a power saw can be purchased. Tools are getting cheaper and cheaper, both in price and quality, and a cheap, crappy tool is often more economical for the small time operator. This is what I call "the home depot factor". They sell the building materials and the tools at the same place because you can only expect the tools to last about one job. On the other hand, you might not get another job so it makes sense to use the cheap tool and consider it a bonus if it outlasts the job. While in New England I did a tiling job worth a couple thousand dollars. $200 paid for all the tools—scratch cutter, nippers, sheetrock square, level, chalkline, screwgun, and etc. At the end of the job I left the tools in a box in the basement, although they might have been good for a few hundred more square feet of tile. I felt sort of wasteful about abandoning them. Later I found out that huge contracting firms do the same thing with heavy equipment. They buy brand new bulldozers and loaders and earthmovers for a job and then when it's finished they dump all the equipment on the used market. It is more economical to sell it and buy new stuff than to pay for transportation, storage, and maintenance between jobs. Who buys the used equipment? I don't know.

Slouch

Open Letter to Eddie Pepito
by Jef Samp

Hello Eddie.

I've been meaning to write you for some time now, but it's so hard figuring out what to say to you. I think about you weekly, if not daily. In the span of time I've known your name I've gone through nine pairs of shoes, six furniture arrangements and four girlfriends. In this sense, you're a constant for me, a lodestar.

And like a star, you remain both distant and ever-present. Or perhaps not ever-present, but forever, and profoundly, absent. More like a black hole than a living star, I sense your existence only indirectly; I detect you by the space you don't seem to inhabit. I've never met you, I don't speak with you, I don't know you, but I infer you.

The framework for our acquaintance began a few summers ago at the end of a nine-week self-indulgent stint of housesitting and couch-surfing. I found a pleasantly Spartan studio apartment in East Oakland, which appeased my then-fervid desire to live simply, or at least remotely. At the time I never bothered activating phone service, thinking this might enhance the reclusive charm of the place.

I didn't realize what that would mean until a year later when losing my cell phone on a train cut me loose from the human network of personal telephony. The experience was bracing; I alternated between stretches of giddy liberation and sick-to-my-gut, squirming, panicky moments of absolute isolation. I managed without a phone for a little over a month before my resolve weakened; the unarguable convenience of pizza delivery supplanted my taste for solitude.

The PacBell representative explained that although the first three digits of my number were geographically predetermined, I could select from a few different four-digit options to complete the number.

Here, Eddie, I should let you in on a little secret of mine: I enjoy a mild, innocuous, and relatively common form of synesthesia, such that I experience numbers as colors. If you're not familiar with this phenomenon, synesthesia is the condition in which one type of sensory stimulation excites the sensation of another. A synesthetic might perceive pain as a particular color; another individual might register sounds as textures. Words, letters and (as in my case) numbers are also common loci for cross-modal sensation. I've "had" this for as long as I can remember, and it's not the sort of thing I can switch off. In the same way that, upon hearing a cat's meow you might envision its shape, I see or hear a number and the associated color is just immediately present.

When the telephone company representative offered me a number consisting of two tastefully complementary bands – warm tones followed by cool – I couldn't have been happier. So subtly attractive! So pleasing to my jangled senses! At last, a number I could give out to friends, without feeling the obscure urge to apologize for its garishness.

For the first three months with my new number, I received, on average, one wrong-number call per week. It was enough to pique my interest. The intended recipients were diverse, almost perversely so. By October I was accustomed to recounting my latest wrong-number story over beer. By November, I'd cultivated an obsession: I began maintaining a list online for my friends to check.

A few of my earliest efforts:

Sep 10: Answering machine message from the credit bureau presents Shawanda with an ultimatum.
Sep 16: Monolingual Spanish speaker calls six times in one hour asking for "Mitch".
Oct 02: Hopeful fellow asks whether I'm still showing the house on Hawthorne, or if it's been sold.

contact: 733 Baker St. I San Francisco, CA 94115 I momireadslouch.net

Oct 22: Thwarted a call for Leroy. Followed by two hang-ups.

Nov 06: Confused older fellow asks whether this is the International Shipping Office.

Nov 26: Long message on answering machine for Mr. Pepito from his son's parole officer, asking whether the lad has tried contacting him recently.

Dec 02, 4:30am: Collect call from the Phillipines for Laura. I was hung over enough that I almost accepted the charges.

Dec 12 Me: Hello? Caller: Tin bo may hai doan hoa! Me: What? Caller: >Click<

Dec 14 Sadly, there is no Eddie here.

Dec 18 Dante Garcia is not in residence.

Retrospectively, I wish that I had been more thorough in these first few months. What you see above is a healthy subset of the calls I received, though there were several more. I rarely felt it worth noting hang-up calls (I got lots and still do). There's also the problem of the callers who hang up at the sound of my answering machine—I'm usually only home to sleep, eat, shower, and leave. The scope of my surveillance is small, which makes the number of calls I recorded even more remarkable.

But Eddie, I should come clean here about my reasons for keeping the list. It was, at least in part, for the sake of amusement, as I've described. I know enough of psychology to distrust memory, especially my own. I seemed to have stumbled upon a telecommunications Bermuda Triangle, and I wanted the evidence to back up my unlikely stories.

But I had other, more emotionally murky motivations as well. I'm sure I'm not alone in feeling annoyed by the intrusive quality of misplaced calls. In my quiet, dingy, isolated apartment, it's easy to feel put-upon by relatively minor distractions. The phone's jarring ring disrupts, yes, but it also promises. It insinuates an unforeseen connection - with a friend, a relative, perhaps a lover. It tacitly tells you: Someone was thinking of you when you weren't around! You are cared for! If you doubt your significance in this world, here's proof!

Now you can begin to appreciate my position—a man besieged (in his own home!) with a litany of disruptions and broken promises. Without wanting to seem to maudlin about it, I'll remind you of hapless Bartleby, Melville's moribund scrivener whose frail soul was dashed against the rocky face of modernity by the ill winds of a career in the postal service's dead letter office. What is a misplaced call, but a twentieth century manifestation of the same existential bleakness represented in an unredeemed piece of mail?

Perhaps Eddie, you understand me when I explain that part of my motivation for listing the wrong number calls I'd received, was an attempt to bend these tormenting disruptions to my will; to weave the chaotic accidents of my life into the pattern of my own purposes. Perhaps not.

On the morning of December 20th, I received a phone call from a man insisting that I "buzz him up". My apartment has an intercom system separate from our phone lines. I have a little white panel on the wall near my front door with buttons labeled "Listen", "Talk" and "Door". I am also acquainted with another style of intercom: a programmable device that allows the visitor to place a phone call to your line.

After a great deal of idiotic Abbott-and-Costello grade conversation, I surmised that it was on such a device that this man contacted me. I tried explaining to him the absurd futility of the situation. He grew angry, demanding to be let in so he could visit room Two-Oh-Eight (the apartments in my building are only numbered as high as twenty four).

I suppose I could have tried random combinations of key-presses on my phone, but it might have taken hours to let him into the building. Worse, I might have been haunted by the notion that I might have unwittingly helped the fellow do something untoward. For all I know he may have been a would-be burglar, or a kidnapper, or a thief, (or a hapless resident who lost his keys).

I tried getting out of him the address of the apartment where he was at but he didn't seem to understand what I was asking. The best I could get out of him, before he hung up in frustration, was the name on the intercom box next to the number he'd dialed to reach me. I'm sure it won't surprise you to learn that it read "Pepito".

In the last week of the year I got two messages for an "Eddie Pepito"; these from a stern-voiced woman leaving a toll-free number and reference code along with the ominous message that "we have important business" to discuss. I intercepted a third call on New Year's Eve Day from what sounded like the same person, and assured her that you were no longer available at my number.

The calls continued, as did my odd list:

Jan 02, 6am: Elderly latina woman asks "Is Eddie there?" over a very poor (long distance?) telephone connection.

Jan 02, 7:10pm: Man with Japanese accent wonders whether he's reached "Galaxy Realty". He hasn't.

Jan 04: A Voice Very Much Like That of Sesame Street's Snuffleupagus: Halloa! Is this the peh-pee-toe residence?

Me: Nope. I've gotten a lot of calls for him, but he doesn't live here.

A.V.V.M.L.T.O.S.S.S.: Sooorry!

I also began receiving messages that sounded, in content, like the Stern Voiced Lady, but now a recording, with no name attached. The recordings were impossibly loud:

WE HAVE AN IMPORTANT MATTER TO DISCUSS. PLEASE CONTACT US BETWEEN THE HOURS OF 8 AM AND 9 PM EASTERN STANDARD TIME AT [888 number, plus three digit extension]. YOUR REFERENCE NUMBER IS 2-5-3-4-0-0 [ends with a crazy screeching noise].

After the sixth or seventh message, I deigned to return the call.

Automated Message: Welcome to Alliance One. If you know the extension of the party you're trying to...
Me: [Pressing buttons, then long pause]
Woman: Hello?
Me: Hi. I got a message on my machine telling me to call this number, but I have no idea what it's about.
Woman: Hold on. [Long pause, ringing noise.]
New Woman: Hello?
Me: Oh. Hi. Um, I got this answering machine message telling me there's "an important matter to discuss" and telling me to call this number. But I don't know why. What's this all about?
New Woman: Hello?
Me: Hi. Can you hear me?
New Woman: Ah-huh. Go on.
Me: I got a message telling me to call. What's this about?
New Woman: [Click, dial-tone]

I gave up and took a shower. Half an hour later, I began to worry that the recorded screeching messages would continue, so I called again:
Automated Message: [same as before]
Me: [Press same buttons]
AM: This agent is on the line. Would you care to hold? To hold, press the 1 key. To leave a message...
Me: [Press the 1 key, wait about a minute]
AM: This agent is still on the other line. Would you like to continue holding?
Me: [Press 1 key again. This step repeats 6 or 7 times. I distract myself by nervously scraping candle wax off the glass table in the living room]
Woman: Hello, Alliance One.
Me: Hi. I got this message on my answering machine, telling me to call here. I've got a reference number!
Woman: What is it?
Me: Um... 2-5-3-4-0-0
Woman: Ok, hold on. [Series of sounds of being repeatedly put on hold, taken off hold (background office noises) and then put on hold again]
Man: How can I help you?
Me: Hi. I'm calling because I got an answering machine message. It said to call back and give you a reference number. Do you want it?
Man: Yeah, sure. What is it?
Me: 2-5-3-4-0-0
Man: How many zeros?

Me: Two.
Man: [pause] That's not enough numbers. You need to give me seven numbers.
Me: [toying briefly with the idea of making up another number] Oh. Well, I've only got six. Can we make do with that?
Man: Ok, what's your phone number?
Me: [brief hesitation, then I tell him]
Man: [long pause] Ok. I have... Edwards. Are you Edwards?
Me: No...
Man: Peh-pih-toe?
Me: Oh. Edward Pepito. No. I get a lot of calls for that guy, but he doesn't live here. Not sure what that's about.
Man: Oh. All right. And this is your number?
Me: Yeah.
Man: I'll have your number checked out, so we don't call it again.
Me: Thanks. That'd be great.
Man: Ok. Thank you sir.
Me: Wait! Can you tell me what this is all about?
Man: What?
Me: Well, you left a lot of messages on my answering machine. Can I ask what all these calls are about?
Man: Sir, by Federal Law I'm not allowed to share that information with you.
Me: Oh. All right then. Thanks. [We hang up.]

Now I regret not having asked which law. I'm fairly certain he didn't know, and even if he had, I doubt he'd have told me. And of course, the calls didn't stop:
Jan 15, 3:20pm: A call for Marcus.
Jan.16, 7:45pm: Despite assurances to the contrary, I just received another automated call from Alliance One. Apparently, WE [still] HAVE AN IMPORTANT MATTER TO DISCUSS.
Feb 19: Over the month or so, I've received approximately 3 calls per week from the Alliance One Automated message system. Today I finally decided to do something about it (again).

First Call: The automated call system comes on and prompts me for an extension code. I use the code from the message ("3-2-0") which is supposed to connect me with "Mary Collins". The automated system responds, "The person you are trying to reach; CHRISTY SMITH; is still on the line. You are... FIRST... in line. To continue to hold, press 1, to leave a message, press 2, or to try another extension, press the # key." I press 1, and the system answers, "can I ask who's calling?" I say my name, wait a few seconds, and the machine says: "I will attempt to put you through. Please stay on the line." I wait. After a minute, the machine makes some weird clicky noises, then says "You have a call from; [in my voice:] JEF; press 1 to take the call, press 2 to take a message." Puzzled, I press 1. The machine hangs up, and I get a busy tone.

Second call: The automated call system comes on and prompts me for an extension code. I don't give it one. I get a variation on the hold message: "The person you are trying to reach [long pause] is still on the line. You are... THIRD... in line. To continue to hold, press 1, to leave a message, press 2, or to try another extension, press the pound key. You must press a key to remain connected" I press 1, and the system claims that it "will attempt to put" me through. After a minute, I get the "continue to hold" message again, and press one again. This time, I'm SECOND in line. Within a couple iterations, I'm first. Then I continue the loop for about twenty minutes (while watching the Simpsons). Suddenly: "Welcome to Alliance One! If you know the extension of the party you're trying to reach, please enter it now." I go through process again, and the system informs that there are more than TEN callers in line ahead of me. Exhausted, I hang up.

March 07: An errant call for Gerald.

March 16: Me: Hello? Caller: Is this Mr. Ed Pepito? Me: [feeling a little perturbed at having been bothered, while having company over, on an otherwise pleasant Saturday afternoon:] No. It's not Mr. Ed Pepito. Or Edward. Or Eddie. I get a lot of calls for that guy, but he doesn't live here. Actually, he's never lived here. And he's never going to live here, if I have my way. So you can permanently disassociate this phone number from that name. Caller: Okay sir. I'll take care of that.

Around this time I went out of town to visit my grandparents. A few years ago they both retired they had completed a combined 70 years of service in the employ of Pacific Bell (neither of them will brook this new 'SBC' name). Now they've got a lot more time for bumming around with the grandkids.

I mentioned you to my grandfather. I thought that, as a phone company veteran, he might be amused by my tales of wrong-number woe. When I finished relating the highlights of the calls I'd received to date, he furrowed his peppered, bushy brows and pursed his lips with disapproval. "That shouldn't happen," he pronounced.

After a bit of rumination, and confirmation from his wife, he assured me that the phone company took Measures to Prevent These Things from Happening. To wit: no phone number is recycled into use without a six-month fallow period. During this time, callers are greeted with either the standard "out-of-service" announcement, or a forwarding number, at the former owner's request. My grandparents found it hard to believe that I could receive such a profusion of wrong number calls. They shook their heads and shrugged their shoulders at yet another sign of the world's general decline into chaos and nonsense.

When I got home I was surprised to find that I hadn't received single call from your friends and

creditors. I wondered whether my grandparents' collective scorn had been enough to set things right. The respite, however, proved short-lived:

April 01:
Me: Hello?
Guy: Is Marcus there?
Me: Nope. No Marcus.
Guy: Really?
Me: ... Yeah.
Guy: Who is this?
Me: Well, I'm not Marcus.
Guy: What number is this?
Me: What number were you trying to dial?
Guy: I don't know. I didn't write it down or nothin'.
Me: Then I'd try again.
Guy: Marcus ain't there?
Me: Nope.
Guy: Well, I think it's five-five-five-two-six-two-somethin' [number modified for anonymity]
Me: That sounds a lot like my number, but I'm not Marcus.
Guy: Man, just tell me your number.
Me: Uhh... why?
Guy: Who are you?
Me: Why would I give you that information?
Guy: It's not like it's any big - CLICK! - [Dial Tone]

April 13: Answering Machine Message: This message is for Pablo Garcia, this Sue calling from "Eye-Care", and I'm just calling to let you know we received your glasses. They're in; you can come and pick them up at your convenience. Our hours are, from Tuesday to Friday 10 to 6, and tomorrow, Saturday, from 10 to 3. Ok? See you then. Bye-bye.

May 04: Kate from Kaiser Permanente wanted to speak with Mr. and Mrs. Garcia.

May 14: Answering Machine Message:
Hi, this message is for Pablo. I'm calling from Dr. Montami's (?) office for "Eye-Care". I just wanted to let you know we've received your glasses, so you can come in at your convenience to pick them up. Thank you very much. Bye.

Where do all these people get my number?

I tried calling these people back, afraid Mr. Garcia might go forever without his new glasses. I hope the poor fellow's luck was better than mine – I never got a hold of anyone.

This is the last entry I made into my log of misdirected phone calls. In the end, I'd given up any attempt at thoroughness. The calls kept coming, but I just lacked the will to record them. After less than a year of effort, the project had lost whatever life-affirming effect it initially produced. I seem to recall a roughly contemporaneous relapse into the misanthropy that inspired my move into this apartment in the first place. It's possible I stopped enumerating these reminders of my isolation because they no longer stung, or because it was a sting to which I had grown inured.

But Eddie, it's important for me to let you know that the calls have continued. The collections agents began calling again last summer, and continued doggedly through the fall. For a few weeks before and after the nadir of my black spell, I disconnected the phone (leaving my jerry-rigged jack sensibly intact) but the moment I plugged it back in, the creditors were there waiting, undaunted. I gave one or two of them a taste of my bile. They call back less frequently now, but they do call. As does everyone else.

A month ago I got one for "Angel". Moments after hanging up, another call for "Dante". The pattern was unnerving but ephemeral – I've observed no further evidence for a higher power meddling with my phone line.

Last Saturday I got my third call from the intercom outside your old apartment (the second was a message from UPS delivery: Final Notice). This caller was more astute than the first, he understood the (admittedly complicated) situation. He stated he didn't know the address of the apartment he was visiting – he described it as "across from the park on East 16th". Someday I'll look hard at a map and try to deduce the location, so I can find the building manager and get that number changed.

I've learned, instinctively, to differentiate between your creditors and your friends. The bureaucrats have a hard time with Spanish phonology. "Pepito" isn't that hard of a word to get out, but I actually had someone a couple of weeks ago ask for a "Mr. Potato".

Everyone else seems to know you as "Eddie"; I hope you don't think me presumptuous for having taken the liberty. I feel like you owe me that much intimacy, at least. I am, after all, the unintentional victim of your thoughtlessness. Not that I mean to accuse you, for all I know, you may be dead or destitute or somewhere in between.

Or it's possible that you still move purposefully through the same streets as me, and that you simply use this number, my number, when you're confronted with someone you'd rather not hear from. Maybe your name isn't even Eddie Pepito (or Ed or Edward or Eduardo). Perhaps this is a fraudulent alias you employ along with "Marcus" and "Dante Garcia". These are the strange thoughts I endure during my most quiet, paranoid moments. I've also wondered whether you might be an elaborate joke played by some baroquely impish friend of mine. I even considered the Borgesian possibility that I might be Eddie Pepito, secretly arranging these calls to torment conscious myself.

In my quiet, small, East Oakland apartment, waiting to field yet another call on your behalf, I can't rule any possibility no matter how unlikely. For now, I'll remain content to shop this letter around for publication, hoping to find you one way or another. I want a chance to sit down and talk with you and discuss the years of calls you've missed. If you're reading this now Eddie, give me a call, collect if necessary. I'm sure you know the number. ★

Sobaka

Into Somaliland:
An Obscure Road into an Obscure Country
by Sean Rorison

It is eleven years on, over a decade since the collapse of government. Over five years since all attempts at reconciliation from international organizations failed: Somalia. The country, and people, have been abandoned by the world. Our headlines have moved on to other things, as if perhaps by ignoring the problem would make it go away.

For the most part it hasn't. And yet, in the north of the country, something odd has occurred: a government has formed.

A meager infrastructure has begun to take shape. It's being created under the guise of a new country, a place called Somaliland. I had heard rumours that it was reasonably safe to visit this new republic, which no one will admit exists—and which no country will formally recognize. This place in the "black hole" that Kofi Annan called Somalia is a calm bastion in the factional anarchic storm—the only way which the world has known Somalia for over a decade.

I had been told that to enter Somaliland by vehicle, a town called Jijiga in northeastern Ethiopia was the entry point. Hargeisa is the capital of this self-declared state, and Boorama is a larger town just near the border. Reaching one or the other would be my goal.

Desperately early in the morning we took off from Addis Ababa to Dire Dawa, a reasonably busy Ethiopian town graced with a paved runway and new terminal. We were asked to deplane while they refuelled. A curious middle-aged British woman approached me.

"Hi. Who are you working with?"

She was nearly flabbergasted to hear that I was a tourist: a tourist out here, heading for Jijiga, the apparent aid coordination centre of Ethiopia.

Upon arrival in Jijiga: no paved runway. Two tin shacks. Many military men standing around. She offered to get me a lift into town with the people she was meeting.

Jijjga is a reasonably large town for this part of the world, although camels wandering through the town centre are common, and much of the place is made up of dirt road and shacks. The entire area was surprisingly green. "We have been getting rain for the past few weeks," one of the local aid workers told me.

I was taken back to their office with the lady and three local workers. "Only a tourist," I said, as we sat, drinking soda water, chatting; them wondering what I was doing in Jijiga, sort of curious but very friendly.

I was assigned not one but two locals to deal with my itinerary: to the immigration office and get stamped out, but only if I can get back in. And then find a bus to Boorama or Hargeisa. Whisked away in their spiffy Land Rover to the immigration office, I got to talking with one of the men. "This town is where all of the aid groups are centred," he said, "and also where the people come to get food."

"Is there enough for everyone?" I asked, expecting the usual African optimism.

"I don't know."

And I still wonder.

The bus to Boorama had left an hour ago; the only one of the day, which I found quite odd. We went back to their office. "So, I guess you're in Jijiga for today?" one of the men asked.

"Well, perhaps. Let's wait and see if there is another way to get to Boorama or Hargeisa today." And the thought must have clicked in his head, because he suggested that I go to Hartishek, where it was easy to connect to Hargeisa. Before I knew it, I was in a tiny bus screaming across the muddy road to the halfway point between Jijiga and Hargeisa: Hartishek.

Rolling across green fields, it was easy to see that many nomads were going back out to the countryside with their herds and beginning life again. The desert here swallows rain fast and graciously; the plains around Jijiga are rolling green now, when only a few years ago they were fodder for the news as endless tracts of dust.

Before Hartishek, still deep in Ethiopian territory, the bus passed through the first Somali roadblock. Of course, it does not actually block the road: it is merely two sticks on either side of the dirt road with a string hooked across. No one paid any attention to me. But I knew from the features of the people in the bus that I was far from Ethiopia already: these people were almost all Somali.

Hartishek is a refugee camp, surrounded by mounds of garbage. In that garbage children play, and African vultures twice the size of the children scavenge. Thousands of plastic bags have been tied onto the whithered bushes; the dirt road turns into deep mud ruts, and crowds of women sit on the side clutching large tin cans bearing the EU symbol. The dirt, the dust, the garbage, and the multitudes of people in such a tiny, desperate town; thousands upon thousands of little white huts that look like bubbles across the rolling plains: this is Hartishek.

A small boy, the conductor for the bus I was on, led me to a Land Cruiser that was loading up for Hargeisa. I met an older African man there: A bit tired in the eyes, with white hair and beard, he spoke with honest-sounding English. He said he was a refugee.

"I don't know why God created the black man," he confided in me, "all he does is suffer. And they are rude. How many African countries have you visited? Are any of them without suffering?"

He was certainly pessimistic. He also offered the idea that I pay for all of the seats on the vehicle so it could go immediately.

Usually, I don't do this; and the price was high. However, I only had a few days at the most to see Somaliland, and every minute counts at this point. Unfortunately. I have often said to myself that a little time in a place is far better than no time at all, and have had many great experiences this way. So with scant regard for budget I paid the high price—although for the simple fact that it was better security as I was about to enter what is essentially a rogue state, I think it was a smart move.

Another roadblock was not far from the town and a Somali with an AK-47 slung behind him disappeared with my passport and driver into a shed. The old man was still in the Land Cruiser with me.

"Perhaps you need a translator," he said. "I could translate for you."

I offered him a modest sum in Ethiopian currency to come with me. "But I will return immediately, and I need to buy the bus back."

"As you like," I said with a friendly smile. He quietly slipped out the back door and disappeared.

The Somali with the gun came out of the shed and up to my window, one hand holding the end of his AK-47 behind his neck, and grunted at me. He didn't make eye contact, but merely looked in the truck quickly to see if there was anything illegal or valuable he might want. And then, we were on our way.

There is no road from Ethiopia into Somaliland; in fact, there is no formal land connection whatsoever. In Djibouti you have dirt tracks impressed by determined four-wheel-drive vehicles, and in Ethiopia you have the same. Except this time the rains came.

Three years of rain began to fall, and the dry green of this semi-arid land turned into a mudstorm of water and dust. The haze of the raindrops was blasted by the wind, and the ruts cut deep by Land Rovers were turning into rivers. We began sliding, spinning slightly, and eventually—of course—got stuck.

One half hour lost. One mud-drenched driver. But we persisted, and I saw massive turtles crawling across the dirt. They were the only ones who didn't seem to mind, although I am sure the nomads were not complaining too much either.

It was here, moving toward the Somali frontier, that the mood truly changed. There was nothing but us and a general direction. And about two hours later, we reached the real border of Somaliland, another stick-and-string checkpoint. The driver stopped. We stared at the old man who sauntered towards us.

His face was nearly a skull: an older man, decked out in a beige uniform, his AK-47 slung over a shoulder and a hat to die for—a tall and official looking cowboy hat with faded letters on the front that spelled RANGER. The driver explained the usual story of the tourist and the destination, and the string dropped.

Somaliland. Somalia. Whatever you call it, this was not Ethiopia. It hadn't been for over seventy-five kilometres.

The landscape became different: more barren, dry, and somehow surreal. The flat grass shifted into rocky scrub and rolling hills. A dirt track to an ignored republic. An obscure way to an obscure country.

Slowly the nomads began to appear, and then we went through the first town with brick buildings. All were destroyed. The nomads persisted in their tents, though. Their sheep, all with white bodies and black above their neck, wandered and ate the sparse foliage. Old military vehicles, rusted and burned, littered the countryside. And suddenly, two hours after crossing the border: pavement.

A road—and another checkpoint. Four boys dressed as soldiers hopped in the back of our vehicle. The story was told again. We drove in silence to the police station, where we were directed into the city and into immigration. And behold, after a smooth half hour ride, the land dipped into a valley and there lay a large looking town:

Hargeisa. Capital of the country that no one will admit exists. Multitudes of coloured cement houses. Arabic and Somali signs dot the bright yellow and blue buildings. New cars roll by. It is wet, quiet, but it's a city. And the capital of this odd, odd country—Somaliland.

Somaliland had never really been a fluid part of colonial Somalia—before 1960 it was its own country, a territory of Britain, while Somalia was a territory of Italy. British Somaliland became independent in 1960—for four days. After that, it was decided by the European powers-that-be that the two Somalias should become one country, and the capital should be Mogadishu. And of course since it came from the mouth of a white man, it was so.

When the government of Mogadishu collapsed in 1991, Somaliland used the opportunity to declare independence. By no means were things rosy for the new country from the beginning—civil war raged until 1995, but hostilities continued until 1998, and now things are just tense between the west and the east of the country. Those that know the country know that it's safe right now. But so few know the country; no one in Ethiopia really seemed to know anything about it.

A guide in Djibouti was certain that I would be killed if I tried to enter Somaliland via their border—but after he had talked to some of his friends he found out otherwise. Advisories across the world send conflicting reports about the state of the country, not only because they don't want their citizens to go there, but also because no one has an embassy in the country to confirm what's going on. One fellow I spoke to on the internet actually said it was safer than Ethiopia—and yet the Canadian embassy in Addis Ababa insisted that I come down to their office outside of their usual opening hours to get their advisories about the two countries.

Immigration looked at my passport, and told me to come back at nine in the morning when they were open, and could get the stamps out. Taken to a hotel room for the night, I unloaded my bag and a Somali-Ethiopian who was born in Somalia but had lived in Ethiopia but pretty much the Somali region of Ethiopia (get that?) took me to change money. One US Dollar = 3000 Somaliland Shillings. The largest note is 500 shillings—I was given a fat clump of bills that landed on the moneychanger's table with a thump.

Cafeterias lined this road in Hargeisa, and all eyes were on me as throngs of Somalis sat in their plastic chairs and listened to the radios. There were no televisions around. Dinner was three samosas and a Fanta for a whopping US dollar's worth of Shillings. The Somali who led me around, surprisingly, didn't ask for a tip. Just by that gesture I knew he wasn't Ethiopian.

We walked back to the hotel. "May I ask you a question?" he said, and then without waiting for my response, proceeded: "What do you think of Somali people?"

I never had the chance to answer him as we walked to the reception in the hotel and I handed over a wad of money to pay for my room.

But if I had answered his question... The Somalis: physically, they are often rather tall, skinny, with slightly distorted facial features like an overbite, long chins, and deep set eyes. My instincts tell me they are odd; more unpredictable than other African societies, more in tune with ancient associations to clan and tribe than other Africans who have accepted the westernization of their societies. I will go out on a limb here and say they rely more on their instincts than the other, more colonialized, African ethnic groups.

The Somalis are the people in Africa who have most abruptly rejected any colonial influence, with the anarchy in the east a sort of return to ancient tribal warfare. They are a devoutly Muslim people. They are African, and harbour no outsider's interference in their destiny.

Crazy? Perhaps. But the Somalis are Africans at their most base. They want to do things their way. They will learn through their own mistakes. And they will find a purely African solution to their problems.

Hargeisa is a busy town when it's not raining, with a few of those Arabesque attractions a tourist brochure might put in when there isn't really anything of interest: a few mosques, a market, a main street. Buildings appropriated by government. But like most of Africa, it's far more interesting than it looks.

On my way to immigration a babbling man on the street began to follow me, holding his arms out. "Five hundred years ago the slave ships began their way across the ocean," he shouted, "and the chains of west Africa still burn on my wrist!" I gave him a curious look, and he was eventually called aside by some older men, who probably told him not to bug the white man like that. A few minutes later a group of women began to follow me; I felt a pinch on my shoulder. They had thrown a rock at me.

"Have you ever been in a war?" the officer at immigration asked me. His boss wasn't there yet to stamp me in; he was supposed to arrive at nine, and now it's ten thirty. I told the officer I was talking to that I had never been in a war, or at least, not my own. And I've certainly never fought in one.

"It's not good," he replied. "But in 1988—we had to fight."

Tensions were escalating in 1988—the regime down in Mogadishu had ordered several thousand people killed in Hargeisa. Even now war damage is one of the most prevalent sights in the city.

The officers were all decked out in army uniforms, nicely pressed, with clean black berets on their scalps. The officer I had been speaking to grinned. I asked him about the fact that no country recognized Somaliland. He grinned again.

"It makes no difference to us. If they want to recognize us, then let them recognize us. If they don't want to recognize us, then they don't recognize us."

He continued. "We are nomads, you know? Life is simple here. You wake up, eat, chew Qat, tend the animals, eat, and sleep. Political things matter little. If people want to fight us, then they will lose, because we have nothing to lose."

I finally received my entry stamp, and departed the office. I had met a doctor earlier in the day who was looking for a western reference, as Africans often are (no matter that they're also looking to make some cash by helping out foreigners). He invited me for tea after I ran into him a few hours later, and we chatted. He was very interested in studying his PhD abroad, so I offered to mail him a university catalog. He gave me a tour of his hospital: clean but bare, and no sign of any patients or medical supplies. He then offered to arrange me a private car to Boorama, for cheap. But first, there was the matter of lunch.

The doctor, a friend of his and I wandered over to a large open restaurant, with dirt floors and a dingy, dark indoor room. We sat outside. Mango juice, water, a dish of spaghetti with sauce, and a large dish with rice and two loins of goat meat; and also some very awful tasting "animal" soup. All fine and dandy you say. And yes, it was all fine, except that you have to eat all of this with your fingers. And yes, people wash their hands before and after meals. He and his friend directed me toward the private taxi stand after our lunch.

Soon we became surrounded by men—shouting, pulling, pushing, surrounding us. I was asked to sit down while he negotiated. Five minutes later I got up and moved through the throng into a taxi, shrugging off hands pulling at me, always mindful of my bag. The taxi was stuck, we locked the doors as the crowd persisted. One man reached through an open window and tried to unlock my door; I pressed against the lock quickly as the taxi finally sped off. We stopped several blocks away to negotiate a price.

We settled on a sum that was extremely expensive for the region, but my time constraints forced me to accept it. The doctor took down his car number, his name, his tribe's name, his grandfather's name, and the make of his car and threatened to throw him in jail if anything happened to me. Yet another example of how a fellow African does not trust his fellow African.

Off I went to Boorama. I gave the doctor some cash for his help. The taxi driver's cut was such a large amount of bills that he had to stuff several stacks of them in his glove compartment—here, people have an incredible skill which is flipping through dozens upon dozens of bills very quickly using their thumb and forefinger. I never did get the hang of it. ★

This Is Still Not About Your Favorite Band

I love you ...
by Julie Ryan

I love you like I love my family

Sometimes it's really hard to think objectively about what we love- but if we can't criticize what we love and if we can't take constructive criticism- or discern it from hateful criticism- how can we grow? How strong are our positions if we are not willing to put them to the test? A lot of people seem to think it's about asserting whose position is right- about being dominant. For me it's about exploring the idea and having a discussion, thinking aloud, on paper.
I am always wanting to find common ground- to bridge gaps- to reconcile opposing sides- maybe I'm too idealistic- wanting to be some sort of peacemaker- but here's the deal- I can try to include everyone who is willing to be included.

So I went to the peace March on Feb 16th 2003, in San Francisco. I had been to the one in January too. It was amazing! The diversity of the crowd- all these people who want peace, for many different reasons. Both times after the main march there were breakaway marches that I also had a degree of participation in, and both times I had *mixed feelings* about the anarchist led breakaway marches. And I thought about it and talked over with friends, family, and colleagues.

So I made a little public service announcement about it on the radio that went a little something like this:
"The SF Chronicle described the group of people participating in the breakaway march as the **black bloc.** As my boyfriend and I walked in the main march- 4 or 5people handed me flyers for breakaway march- probably because I was wearing black and had patches on my jacket. I noticed that they were not handing flyers to the Black, Chinese, Mexican, Indian people around me, or suburban soccer moms.

contact: Julie Ryan | PO Box 243 | Arcata, CA 95518

I asked a few people if they were planning to
spray paint and smash shit.
The Response: "Why so many questions, are you an
infiltrator?"
His message to me was clear. You're either with
us or against us.

SO I marched 1/2 way to show my solidarity for
the ideas and beliefs:

      -That you don't need a permit to march
      -That freedom of speech should be free
    -That the patriot act is un-American and
              unpatriotic
         - That capitalism is fucked up

That I only marched half way and then ducked into
the curios crowd on the sidewalk didn't have to
do with the police- although the cops were
sneering and I could tell by the way they had us
surrounded from the get go- that they meant to
herd everyone into one place and arrest us!
Not to mention that having the crap beat out of
you is no fun.

What I am not in solidarity with is the
vandalism- ya- that's right- the *vandalism* Not
the act itself-not the intentions- but because of
how it is interpreted by people- people! Not just
the mainstream press, but everyday people.

I hate SUV's, I hate Abercrombie, Citibank,
Starbucks, I hate the Gap, Old Navy, and their
cooperate cousin Hot Topic! Etc. . . .
The General Public doesn't always "Get It" They
don't see that those institutions are specific
targets chosen for very specific reasons (bad
environmental and social justice records on many
counts).
What people see is vandalism- and they compare
these actions to the post super bowl vandalism of
the Raiders Fans. NOW COME ON! Do you really want
to be compared to a bunch of drunk football

rednecks that smashed and set fire to businesses
that have contributed goods and services to the
community? (Ok, so some of them were chain stores)
Sorry Folks. I see the difference because I have
listened to a lot of the same punk records and I
have read a lot of the same books-

But I don't want to be a part of a revolution
that excludes people. My revolution includes my
grandparents and my parents, and the working
class. My revolution is not limited to primarily
young, white, students (student aged) people who
have had the luxury of education and are
privileged to the information that shapes their
points of view.
When I see that- and that's really what I saw
both times:
I don't see revolution- I see elitism.

Why do you protest on the coattails of a peace
march? (I guess for media exposure)

Why don't you/we go to shopping malls in Walnut
Creek and other rich suburbs and stand in front
of stores with banners saying "this store
supports child labor, anti-union, deforestation"
(Or use the crowded mall parking lot to your
advantage and put leaflets on car windows about
how their SUV's give the kids in their own
neighborhood breathing problems- make it close to
home!)
Sure you might get kicked out- but if you act
calm (fuck you is not always the best reply),
well it might piss some people off, but it might
make people think and change."(ENcourage BOYCOTTS)
I ended by saying, "if you have something
intelligent to say call in, but if you're calling
to say fuck you, don't bother."

What I didn't mention when I made my PSA on the
radio. . . How I have told other people about the
anarchists' etc- intentions and actions at the

protest, and explained that it was not random graffiti on random buildings but "spotlighting" organizations that hurt everyday people.

A lot of people I spoke with thought that the breakaway march does unfortunately tarnish the image of the main protest and it does alienate a lot of people. They agree that spray paint is not the best way to reach the masses.
There is more than one way to be radical and I encourage you to do it!!!! Be creative and do it in a way that won't alienate someone who is different than you, or consequently the opportunity to educate and find common ground will be lost.

Things that do work are stickers, stencils, flyers, banners, alterations of billboards, and other forms of subvertising. These are more effective when they have a short but informative message. "Shop with your heart not your credit. card- don't support child labor" "McDonalds burns forests" "Wal-Mart puts Americans out of work" verses "Fuck Wal-Mart" or "Fuck McDonalds" It helps when the design is uncluttered so that it is legible, lacks swearing, and has a book title or web address where people can look up info themselves. Learn lesson from big advertisers- short, sweet, and catchy and credible
(Unlike my ramblings)

How about this for a summary: Effective change often calls for bending and even breaking the rules- but lets do it in a way that is not elitist and includes not alienates people who seem "different" than ourselves. And yes I do believe that every little thing we do makes a difference. Like family- I see more good things than bad and even though I criticize its because I want you to think and I want good things for all of us. Solidarity & Love   Julie

Tight Pants

Tales from the School Front: Mr. Tarnowski
by Madeleine Baran

Tales From the
School Front:
MR. TARNOWSKI

*Note: Inability to draw people who look
like adults. Note: Inability to draw.

What follows is the story of the greatest teacher I have had in my twenty two years of existence. Of course, in this stupid world of ours, we hold up people like Socrates as the greatest teacher in the history of the world. Socrates? A guy who was so stupid as to willfully be executed by the state for "corrupting the youth" because he said that the state was like a parent to him, and therefore he had to do what it commanded? THIS is the guy we respect? Come on! It is the duty of all of us punks, anarchists, and

wierdos (and yes, Ms. Tight Pants is all of the three!) to hold up other, brighter models of scholarly excellence, lest we start purposely locking ourselves up in Athenian prisons! Behold the man I bring before you... Mr. Tarnowski!

Mr. Tarnowski was my Chemistry teacher in tenth grade, and my Physics teacher in eleventh grade, at the dreaded Divine Savior Holy Angels high school. Sticking Ms. Tight Pants into a school containing even ONE of the four words in its name would have been bad enough! But come on! Divine? Savior? Holy? Angels? Overkill, says I! Out of this climate of all-girl Catholicism came one brave soul to liberate poor punk rockers like myself from the boredom of secondary education!

Mr. Tarnowski came to DSHA after leaving being his lucrative job as an engineer, out of a desire to enter the teaching profession. A thirty-something man, average-looking, at first he did not attract much attention. But in a few weeks time, the controversy surrounded this science teacher became legendary!

contact: PO Box 100882 | Milwaukee, WI 53210

Kids of the Black Hole!

Initially, he attracted attention mostly for blowing up things, which, when you think about it, is a pretty damn good way to begin any new job. Huge black holes would appear in the ceiling of the science room, and all signs would point to Mr. Tarnowski. However, he would adopt my favorite lying strategy--complete and total denial. As in, "No, I swear, it wasn't me. It ABSOLUTELY WAS NOT ME." Repeat. After awhile, the administration gave up trying to solve the mystery of who was behind the willfull destruction of their beloved ceilings. But by that time, Mr. Tarnowski had entered into much more risky territory!

Now, at the point at which he started blowing up things, I took interest, and starting talking to him after class occasionally. One day, I was

wearing a Dead Kennedys shirt (as it was a Non-Uniform day, a monthly occurrence allowing for approximately 97.5% of the girls in my school to show off their latest Gap acquisitions), and Mr. Tarnowski came up to me in the hallway and asked, "So, people still like that band?" I informed him of their immense popularity amongst the 15 year-old skater boy subculture, to which he replied, "I used to be into those guys, but around 1984 they got really popular and I stopped paying attention." This man got OUT of the Dead Kennedys before most people ever heard 'em! Wow! I was impressed! We talked for a little about punk rock, and I found out that he had been very into punk/hardcore in the early 80's, but lost interest when it became all about "the pit" and beating people up. Rock and roll! A friend of early 80's hardcore is a friend of mine!

From that day forward, the two of us had an understanding, an unspoken pact, contract, or bond. We were both members of an elite group: people at my high school who were not worthy of having our limbs individually tied to four different horses, and then ripped from our torsos. (Without sounding "judgemental"--oh no! Not THAT!-- I must say that, without exception, all of the cool people in my high school, which

Acid, Trailer Parks & Death!

numbered maybe six people total, were punk, with the exception of my English and Journalism teacher, who did a lot of acid and lived in a trailer park. Look for his story in an upcoming Tales from the School Front!) Our unspoken bond resulted in some much needed support and favors from Mr. Tarnowski. He allowed me to skip his class as many times as I felt like it, and would never mark me absent. If I got a detention for skipping another class, he would sign it, and indicate that I was talking to him about some sort of Chemistry-related problem. If I did come to his class, and felt like reading, sleeping, or writing a letter, that was fine, too! His reasoning was, "You already know the basic principle of science--Always question everything--so you really don't need to know the

specifics." Pressed for more details, he would say, "These idiots here (gesturing to girls passing by in the halls) already know all of the specifics of science, which they memorize for some stupid college application, so that they can get some stupid job, have kids, and then die. And they won't ever know the most basic principle of science! It's so frustrating! Almost everyone here is unbelievably self-centered and stupid!" (Let me say right now that any teacher who wants to openly mock the other students in the class has never failed to become a close personal friend of mine!)

Mr. Tarnowski's basic philosophy resulted in a number of innovative teaching methods. We didn't have homework. We all took the same test over and over again until we got a 100%. There was no clear-cut grading policy. He just graded you on how well you understood and lived the "basic principles of scientific inquiry." Which meant that most of the girls failed the class, even though they knew all of the elements on the periodic table and could recite in their tanning salon of choice the basic safety procedures for a Chemistry lab. And then there was Ms. Tight Pants! I knew NOTHING about Chemistry or Physics! For some inexplicable reason, I CANNOT do word problems. When you start confusing letters and numbers, I get a splitting headache (Ooh! Dickies references galore!) or maybe I get so down I give myself a headache (Ack! Even an unsolicited Frank Black reference! Whatever will I think of next?!). I

Fuck School! (x2) Fuck My High School!

definitely would've failed both Chemistry and Physics if Mr. Tarnowski had not been my teacher for both of those classes. Just think, Ms. Tight Pants could have had a low grade point average! I might not have gotten into, uh, zine college. Oh wait, it really wouldn't have mattered at all! But don't tell that to the nation's youth!

Instead, I consistently received an A+ in Chemistry and Physics, and rarely attended class. Punk rock!

Sadly, the administration did not view Mr. Tarnowski's unorthodox-early-eighties-hardcore-inspired teaching methods with approval. After about two dozen too many complaints from girls who were failing his class, the principal stepped in. She sat in on his classes to make sure that he was teaching what was in the book; she ordered him to assign homework, which SHE then collected to make sure that it was actually being assigned; and she made him give normal tests and have a normal grading method.

All of this, however, was not enough to prevent the Black-Flag-loving Mr. Tarnowski from getting into trouble! He continued to upset the fragile sensibilities of the young ladies, directly accusing them of being selfish, stupid, and idiotic. In one of the finest moments in my entire high school career, he made my least favorite girl in the class cry, simply by suggesting that she was "only interested in her own little rich suburban world." That is a direct quote! I love that man! Especially in the context of my crappy high school, these things were not said! Except by me and two or three other students! Never by a teacher! Until then!

So, up to that point, Mr. Tarnowski had been responsible for the following: blowing up the science room ceiling, violating the school attendance and detention policies, betraying the loyalty to traditional grading and testing systems, and directly insulting his students. What could he possibly do to top all of the above? You shall see!

One normal (read: ungodly early and horrible) morning, I woke up to go to school, only to find out that...the school had been flooded! No school! For THREE DAYS! The entire library had been destroyed, as had the entire administrative offices! Not to mention countless student lockers! Millions of dollars of damage! The cause: Mr. Tarnowski failed to close the windows to the science classroom before leaving for the night, causing the water pipes in the room to get so cold that they burst! The single greatest act committed against my school! Of course, he denied any of my accusations that it was intentional, and blamed the whole thing on sheer forgetfullness. However, I knew better.

Especially when, not more than two months later, he did the same exact thing again! Forgot to close the window, the pipes burst in the middle of the night, and there was more flooding! Only this time, the flooding was

Guns, Deviancy, & Cursed Places!

nowhere near as extensive, and the school didn't even close for a day. But still!

At that point, complaints against Mr. Tarnowski were rising. The pressure was on him to tone down his teaching methods and end his harassment of students. But he refused! At the end of the year, he was asked not to return. He accepted, because it was clear that it was either that or being fired. (And, all of us shitworkers know, it is better to quit a job than be fired, so as best to obtain yet another shit job in the future.)

So Mr. Tarnowski was no more. A few months after he left, someone in my class saw him at some sort of WalMart type store...buying a gun. I took this as a positive sign that perhaps he would return for some sort of retribution on all of his enemies, but that day has yet to come.

And then, about two years after graduating high school, he came into eat at the restaurant where I worked! A grand reunion was had, with lots of talking about how much we both hated Divine Savior Holy Angels, and how glad we both were to be far, far away from that cursed place! I told him that he was, without a doubt, my favorite teacher of all time, and he thanked me and left me a big tip! Alright! Let's hear it for Mr. Tarnowski, flooder of Catholic all-girls high schools and a fan of 80's hardcore from Back In The Day (B.I.T.D.)! Let us raise him up as a living example of punk rock teaching put into practice! Let us encourage his brand of deviancy in hopes that it may multiply, and soon everyone will have a science teacher who knows all the lyrics to "Let's Lynch the Landlord"! Punk rock!

Trouble in Mind

Whatever, Dude
by Erik Ruin

WHAT EVER, DUDE

a critique of the popular anarchist aesthetic

1. FRAMING THE QUESTION

For a month or so before our new house was ready to move into, I wd bike back & forth to work on it. Almost every night on my way home, I'd pass the corner of Rosa Parks & MLK. There's really not much on the corner itself, just some scrubby fields & a few beaten-down houses, a church a lot away, some ugly apartments. And a big grey utility box, standing on it's own. With a great big stencil on it- a 3 foot high hand grenade, with the caption BASK IN YOUR THOUGHT CRIME.

I can't help but wonder what most people in this neighborhood (core city- generally a pretty beat-down part of town) think of the image of a giant hand grenade on their corner. Do they wonder how it got there, who put it there & why? Do they catch the Orwell reference? Do they admire it's photorealistic virtuosity ? Does it make them crack a grin? Does it coax a sigh out of them on their way to pick their kids up from school down the street? Does it make them feel scared?

Do they see themselves throwing that hand grenade or do they see that hand grenade being thrown at them?

Does it just blend in, in their minds, with all the violence they see everyday- the bombs dropping in Iraq, the police harrassing their youth, the movies & video games & toy guns ? Or does it blend in, like it does in my mind, with all the other after-images of violence & upheaval - does it's impact pale in comparison w/ the slow devastation that racism & the whims of capital have wrought on this place? Do they look at it thinking "hell, that bomb's already exploded"?

Did the person who put this here ask themself any of these questions before they reached for that can of spraypaint?

contact: PO Box 44254 | Detroit, MI 48244

2. THINK BEFORE YOU USE THAT CLIP ART

I see this shit all the time. It's on the clothing we wear- those irritating patches that say RIOT-JUST DO IT. It's on record covers- a constant barrage of war casualty photos & gun-toting badasses. It's in the clip art we endlessly recycle in our newspapers & flyers- fighting cops & throwing molotov cocktails. As an anarchist who does art stuff, I'm disturbed by what I see as the unbalanced focus on destruction & violence in anarchist imagery. It's like we're missing half our vision- in my opinion, the more exciting half.

We need to think carefully about what we're putting out there. Not enough people really think of art as a tool, as an ideological weapon. As much lip service as we may pay to that idea, self-expression often comes first. We all need an outlet for the very legitimate anger & frustration we feel towards this system & the violence it inflicts. However, few people consider that graphics (esp. graffiti) are often one of the first ways people come into contact w/ anarchist thought.

I think of a stencil I saw on the sidewalks of Asheville. It said "defend your community" & pictured people hoisting rifles & taking aim. Folks may very well connect w/ that anger. It might feel like a real response to the brutality they witness & endure. But I feel like they could just as easily walk on by, shaking their heads, dismissing it as an unrealistic, irresponsible fantasy. Communities are everyday under assault on many fronts- Their air & water are poisoned. Their homes & livelihoods are pawns in the heartless games of real estate developers & corporate executives. The importance of their lives & identities are belittled by a media that touts highly salable stereotypes.

Is the best way to fight all these battles with a gun? Is the only emotion we have in common our anger? What about sorrow, & fear? Compassion & empathy? Yearning for something better? I have to think a better world must be built on all these things, but first & foremost it must be rooted in joy & love- in the things that make us feel the most free. We're shortchanging not only the people we're trying to reach, but also ourselves, by skimming the surface. By predominately talking about how pissed off we are, we're losing sight of many ways to talk to people, with people.

Likewise, when the same Eric Drooker & Seth Tobocman graphics adorn every zine or newsletter, people only get a very limited glimpse of the range of expression available. Those two artists have very specific (& very powerful) voices. Not everyone is going to hear that. Not enough voices are getting heard.

3. THE NECESSARY DISCLAIMER

Let me state for the record that I'm no pacifist, though I gotta say I'm not too fond of guns or fighting. I believe that nonviolence can be a useful tactic, but it's not the only tactic. There very well may come a time when armed resistance is necessary in order for us to liberate ourselves from the repressive forces of capital & the state. You can rest assured, though, that if I feel the need to pick up a gun, I'm going to be looking for the soonest opportunity to put it back down. Power over life & death is not something to be taken lightly.

This is why I'm so troubled by all the images I see celebrating violence in anarchist propaganda. Violence has pretty inherently authoritarian properties. It's a last resort, to be used against people who leave us no other choice.

4. SMASHING AS FASHION

During the IMF/World Bank protests in Washington, DC, someone in my affinity group approached me. They asked me for help lugging a barrel filled with an unknown liquid across to a nearby intersection. In the haze of adrenaline, I did- I seem to remember they had some intention of creating a flaming barricade or something equally dangerous. Lucky for us, whatever was inside of that barrel wasn't highly flammable.

This is what I'm talking about, the result of this hyper-macho, unreasonably confrontational stance. No, I'm not trying to pull some kind of a Tipper Gore argument here, tracing these actions back to that one flyer with the overturned car graphic on it. But I don't think this kind of imagery & rhetoric helps at all. It only encourages & reinforces an attitude that glorifies this street warrior stereotype. Yeah, that kid throwing the tear gas canister back at the cops in the protest video is a badass. However, we shd be careful we're not turning him into a new Anarchist Rambo. As someone who's taken place in various forms of direct action, I can attest to how exhilarating it all is. But because of that, it's easy to get carried away & forget about tactics, strategy & the safety of yourself & others. We can't forget we're all children of a media-saturated generation. I think deep down, a lot of us wanna be that masked-up daredevil everyone cheers on in the protest video.

Obviously this doesn't just effect the way we view ourselves, it has an impact on the way we are viewed by others. Anarchists are consistently reduced, in the eyes of the general populace, to two-dimensional black-masked vandals with no other agenda than destruction. Sure, the bulk of the blame for this falls squarely on the corporate media & the government. In Philadelphia, during the protests against the Republican National Convention in 2000, the police showed videos of WTO protesters breaking windows to small shopowners in an attempt to scare & distance them from us. It's one way people who offer solutions outside the acceptable margins of thought are demonized & dismissed.

But when I look at the imagery/propaganda put forth by our community, what do I see? Black balaklavas, slingshots, machine guns w/ captions like ARM YOUR DESIRES. We need to be actively showing people that the same people who break windows & spike trees are also urban gardeners, community organizers, & generally caring, compassionate people.

FREEDOM.
I have in mind the only liberty worthy of that name, liberty consisting in the full development of all the material, intellectual & moral powers latent in every man; a liberty which does not recognize any other restrictions but those which are traced by the laws of our nature..

I have in mind the liberty of everyone which, far from itself checked by the freedom of others, is, on the contrary, confirmed by it & extended to infinity. And I have in mind...

...unlimited... all, freedom... freedom in everything... triumphing over... the principle of authority... was ever the ideal... this force); a freedom... having overthrown all heavenly & earthly idols... founded & organized... world, the world of human solidarity, upon the ruins of all the churches & states. —MIKHAIL BAKUNIN

MALCONTENTS MISSIVE 1

5. TELLING PEOPLE WHAT WE WANT

I truly believe that we want people to feel more empowered & less scared. We want people to feel like they can take charge of their own lives, that they can trust their neighbors, that they have a voice that's worth listening to. & yes, that the city is theirs to shut down if they choose to. What are we as radical artists doing to bring this about? How can we do it better?

These are hard questions & I don't pretend to have the answers to them. All I can do is offer a few ideas....

First of all, I think it's pretty obvious we cannot rely on the media to get our message across clearly. I think there's some questions this brings up as to the strategy of property destruction. It may put a clear message across to the corporation chosen (& I don't doubt for a moment that they were carefully chosen.) I think the message that comes across to the passerby is less clear. I think a lot of people think of Starbucks first & foremost as a place to get coffee, not as a corporate megalith that eradicates small businesses & exploits 3rd world coffee growers. They're not necessarily gonna connect the dots unless we give them some help. Can it hurt to paste or stencil that information on the same street, leave a bunch of leaflets in that broken window?

Secondly, there's the challenge of putting across the positive ideals of anarchism. It's difficult to sum up something so complex in a two-dimensional format that will still hold & catch someone's attention. But that doesn't mean it's not worth doing. Focus on the counter-institutions being built, the values that need to be the basis of anarchist society (equality, mutual aid, liberty)- juxtapose that to the value system that capitalism instills (hierarchy, ruthless competition, imprisonment).

I think hope is something that in the end, is a thousand times more compelling & sustainable than anger. It's better to have something worth fighting for than just a reason to fight.

In the summer of 2000, a group I'm involved with, the Street Art Workers, put out a call for people's utopian visions. The responses were incredibly diverse & often very moving- from open-ended visions (corn sprouting from/being swallowed by turning gears) to straight anarchist propaganda (illustrations of quotes from Durutti, Bakunin & Emma Goldman). At first, I remember thinking much of it was only tangentially related to the topic or was too vague. But more & more I feel anything that gets people started dreaming up a better world has got to be good.

GET INVOLVED

STREET ART WORKERS

Every year SAW members pick a theme, make art, and put up each other's work. We aim for the largest possible impact by posting art simultaneously across North America.

ArtTrouble@yahoo.com
1369 Haight St. SF, CA 94117
415-821-7282

With Fire in Our Throats

Towards the Formation and Defense of a Collectivized Flaming Hot Cheetos Factory

by Andrew Cornell

For decades food politics have been a unifying point of struggle for activists working in a wide array of social justice movements. Critics of corporate culture, environmentalists, farm worker unionists, animal rights activists, and others have made strong arguments for the necessity of creating fundamental shifts in the way people in Western industrial countries create food and feed themselves. They point to the sheer brutality of factory farming, the hazardous working conditions under which migrant workers labor, the unhealthy chemicals used in processed foods, and, of course, the obscene power of multi-national agricultural and fast-food conglomerates to shape our desires and our diets.

What all these good-hearted, impassioned activists fail to realize, however, is the sheer grandiosity, the singular delectability, the utter, objective, perfection of the Flaming Hot Cheeto. Before the predictable acrimonious denunciations regarding the negative qualities (the staining-yellow of fingers, the mild gastro-intestinal discomforts caused by reckless accession of recommended serving size) of Cheetos start to fly, it needs to be said that the Flaming Hot Cheeto is as incomparable in grandeur, so demonstrably superior, from the standard Cheeto, as the world's most beautiful peacock is to the filthiest, homeliest pigeon to ever hobble its way through the gutters of the planet. That the two exist within the same culinary phylum, even, is one of the great failures of modern classificatory science. Consequently, standard, nay degenerate, Cheetos, will not be addressed henceforth in this treatise.

Though it takes months of regular consumption for the average person to react to Flaming Hot Cheetos (FHCs) with anything less perfunctory than an immediate impulsive craving, the thinking person will eventually deduce that the true wonder of FHCs lies in the fact that they inhabit the precise intersection of *perfection in texture* and utter *flawlessness in flavor*.

It is hard to deny that part of the pleasure of biting the nape of a lover's neck during the act of lovemaking is the slight pressure doing so exerts on the gums of the biter. Skin is soft, and gives under pressure, but is not punctured so easily as most foodstuffs, thus creating a sensation as interesting, if not as immediately erotic, for the love-biter as for the lucky love-bitee. The unequivocally unique texture of the Flaming Hot Cheeto—not solid, yet certainly not hollow—gives them the structural integrity to create this same gum massaging effect when eaten in a repetitive fashion in large enough quantities. On top of this gratifying sensation, FHCs make an incredibly satisfying crunching sound as they are surreptitiously crushed in that miniature mortar and pestle known as the human mandible. Attempts by imitators can't match this quality. The give too easily, often disintegrating at first contact with saliva, sometimes leaving hard, tiny balls of whatever sick substance they are made from to circulate freely in the mouth like the grit of dirt that accompanies improperly washed leaves of spinach.

Likewise, no imitator can match the taste of a true Flaming Hot Cheeto. The spice combination coating each FHC which performs a function comparable to the machine in Kafka's Penal Colony, were it set not to use its multitude of needles to horrifically and painfully inscribe into the subject's back the indictment for which the prisoner was condemned, but instead to use those same needles to inscribe utter pleasure, unmediatedly, onto the tongue. Clearly, Flaming Hot Cheetos are in class of their own. They are, indeed, one of the great treasures of the modern world.

Having now made the case for world-historic value of FHCs, the task remains for us to point out the flaws of analysis put forward, to elucidate important points overlooked, by the aforementioned coalitions of activists working to create new patterns of food production and consumption. Farm Workers Unions such as the UFW, the Coalition of Imokolee Workers, and the Farm Labor Organizing Committee argue that we must contest the paltry wages paid and the unhealthy conditions under which laborers work, and they are right—but they neglect to mention that some of these workers harvest the corn that that forms the corpus of the FHC. Animal Rights activists declare that "meat is murder, dairy is rape," and they are right—but they fail to point out that one important biproduct of this callous inhumanity is the Flaming Hot Cheeto. The Frito-Lay Corporation is a favorite target for legions of young anti-corporate protestors. Not only is the company owned by PepsiCo, which also peddles grease and sugar to children through its Taco Bell and Kentucky Fried Chicken chains, giving credence to concerns about a "Junk-Food Trust," it exports this trype throughout the world, using the power of a new-breed "junk-food imperialism" to prop up corrupt governments, such as the brutal dictatorship in Myanmar (Burma). These concerns are, once again, just and righteous. But NO WHERE amongst the countless leaflets, posters, websites and educational videos that these protestors invest considerable time and money, is seen as much as a word of acknowledgement, much less appreciation for, the fact that the FritoLay Corporation is the creator and manufacturer of that worthiest of delicacies, The Flaming Hot Cheeto.

One is tempted to make brash and fatuous denunciations. To shout down and heckle and shame such activists. To point out their shallow, unthinking, simple-mindedness. To lay clear the hypocrisy of fighting for a world of beauty and pleasure, and yet denounce (even if only implicitly) Flaming Hot Cheetos—so obviously a necessary component of any such world. The temptation is certainly there to, in a word, "call them on their shit".

But we won't do that. We won't be swayed to stoop to that level. Because we are on the side of good: the side of Flaming Hot Cheetos. We need not accept as simplistic a politics as our supposed comrades in the movements we critique. We call for an expansive politics—a politics that grows out of the fertile soil of broadly-conceived visions for total social, political, and economic change. We call not for the reformist solution of ending all progressive movements that threaten the sanctity of Flaming Hot Cheetos production, as many meek, less visionary ideologues do. Instead we call for the revolutionary solution of linking the struggle for Flaming Hot Cheetos intimately to all other radical, intersecting struggles for peace and justice.

We call, here and now, for the creation of loosely federated, worker-owned, collectivized, Flaming Hot Cheetos factories! FritoLay factories currently producing FHCs are to be appropriated with no compensation to the former stockholders and junk-food trust executive lackeys. Precedent has been set for the appropriation of junk food factories by Guatemalan workers who seized a local Coca-Cola bottling plant in the 1980s. The newly collectivized FHCs factories shall do everything in their power to function holistically on a bio-regional level, obtaining ingredients from small, local, farming cooperatives.

We call on all parties to acknowledge that cheese is in fact only a minor ingredient in Flaming Hot Cheetos— that, in fact, it is found at least three-quarters of the way down the ingredient list, which is arranged by proportion of the ingredient to the whole. Technology to create faux meat and dairy products what it is, we have the utmost confidence that research and development teams could easily replace the actual cheese with a cruelty-free substitute, with a taste difference proven, in a double-blind test even, undetectable to the most well-trained palate. To mark this difference, and to carry-on the struggle for our bovine brothers and sisters, we adamantly support changing the product's moniker to Flaming Hot *Cheatos*.

Finally, but no less importantly, all sizes of Flaming Hot Cheatos packaging shall be altered to permanently and forever exclude any reference or image of "Chester Cheetah," the lanky, spotted mascot of Cheetos under the old regime. Chester has no significance to FHCs and only brings the unwanted baggage of associations with yellow-bastard standard Cheetos. Though the flaming asteroid-man featured on some old FHCs packages is arguably more acceptable than Chester, we argue instead that liberated Flaming Hot Cheatos should prominently feature a flaming, hot, queer boy—the obvious visual pun that homophobic FritoLay would never have considered, no matter how much market share it might have provided in the upscale Gay and Lesbian Snack niche.

These demands are non-negotiable, and if not granted will be obtained through any and all means of struggle at our disposal. In fighting for them we fight alongside all of humanity in the struggle for a classless, anti-racist, anti-sexist, queer-positive, participatorally democratic society. It needs only to be mentioned, in conclusion, that Flaming Hot Cheatos, are, in fact, also the final nail in the coffin of primitivist ideology. They provide the clearest, most defensible argument to date for the importance of maintaining ecologically friendly, community controlled, socially-productive technologies for the betterment of all human and non-human beings.

Join with us as we cry out: Down with regular Cheetos! Down with Frito-Lay! Down with the Pepsi Corporation! Down with Archer Daniels Midland, Supermarket to the World! Down with pesticide laden, genetically modified corn product! Down with cheese and dairy products in miniscule amounts three quarters of the way down the ingredient list! Fuck Chester Cheetah! But Up, Up, we say, with Flaming Hot Cheatos! Up with the little flaming gay guy! Long live Flaming Hot Cheatos!!! Long live Flaming Hot Cheatos!!! Long live Flaming Hot Cheatos!!! ★

Women's Self Defense:
Stories and Strategies of Survival

Dear Friends and Partners
by Kim and Ariel

Dear friends and partners:
(By Kim and Ariel)

It can be challenging to give support to a survivor of violence. A lot of times friends may not know "how to act" or "what to say" and unfortunately just end up avoiding the subject all together. That is mostly what happened in our cases, and it made Ariel feel really isolated, like she was stuck all alone with this horrible experience. And it made Kim feel like she was partly to blame for the incident and irrational for being scared and sad. This kind of isolation is an experience that other types of survivors feel. For instance, some cancer patients stop hearing from friends who feel helpless and scared of death issues.

Ariel: For a long time, I felt like I didn't have anyone to talk with, or any constructive ways to deal with all of the anger and fear that I felt after the assault. I actually ended up cutting myself; something I had never done before. I believe I resorted to this because I felt so isolated, angry, frustrated, and scared from the whole assault and the lack of support, and needed some way to "release" those emotions.

Kim: I didn't actually tell anyone about my first assault so I denied myself support. Much later, after an attempted sexual assault, friends and lovers did not know how to help so I choose to see a therapist.

If you are in a position to support a survivor of violence, there is **no one-way** to act...just be yourself. As a supporter, you don't have to make them "feel better", just be a friend. The healing process is not going to fit some after-school special "3-phase" model. Healing processes are as unique as the person because the event comes in context with a unique set of life experiences.

The following are some actions we wish people had done (or not done!) to be supportive in the early stages of our healing processes after the assaults, and some of them are things that friends did do that really helped. We are talking about our own personal experiences and needs, and we're not implying that every survivor will want the same things we did.

contact: PO Box 2433 | Champaign, IL 61825-2433

- **Provide a safe space.** I wanted there to be time for me to talk about the assault in a place where I felt safe, unrushed, and undistracted.
- **When I talk about the assault, believe me.**
- **Let me express the full range of my emotions** about the assault: rage, sadness, fear etc. Let me be angry and you can be angry with me.
- **Let me use the terms that I feel are most appropriate when describing the assault.** For example, let me use the word "rape" to describe the severity of an assault even if there wasn't "vaginal penetration".
- **Let me define what about the assault was most hurtful; Do not assume that one aspect of the assault was "worse" then another.** This includes not saying stuff like "That's horrible!" when I talk about what specifically happened. What you may think was horrible may not have been a big deal to me. Or something that you didn't think was "that bad" could have been what hurt me most. Let me decide that.
- **Don't "down play" the assault.** For example, I overheard one friend who I'd confided in saying "He messed with her pretty bad". I was not "messed with" I was assaulted! Let me define what happened in my own terms. Let me name the behavior.
- **Be patient.** Don't ask me to provide details I don't feel comfortable/ready to talk about.
- **Place blame where it belongs: on the assailant.** Don't ask me questions like "Why were you there/in that situation?" or "Were you drinking?" or "Didn't you know that was dangerous?" These types of questions imply that I was somehow responsible for the assault. And besides, why I was where I was is not the issue. Negate my feelings of guilt- that I had any responsibility for the situation happening.
- **Don't dwell on my feelings of fear**, but be considerate of situations that would be scary- walking home through a dark neighborhood at night, getting into a dark house at night, going back to the place where the assault occurred for any reason. Offer to accompany me just because I'd like the company, not because you're protecting me.
- **Focus on the positive.** Help me to realize all that I did to keep myself safe, sane, and together in the situation, and all that I did to get away/end the assault instead of focusing on what the assailant did to me.
- **Let me know I've got your steady, active support.** If you're up for being a support person make it clear that I can come to you again in the future for support. Follow this up by creating a safe space where I can bring up the issue if I want to. For example, a party or show is probably not a "safe space". Instead, we could make plans to go to a quiet café.
- **Allow me to take the time I need to heal-- don't rush me.** Healing comes in cycles and I may feel just fine for a while and then feel not so good again later. Allow me that flexibility, and don't think I should be "over it already".
- **Allow me to be alone if I need it.**
- **Let me talk about my dreams.** I've found that even years later I'll have dreams about the assault which leave me with intense/painful emotions, and it really helps if I can talk it over with someone. As a supporter, you could talk about how the survivor could

A Brief list of Resources for Survivors…to start…

For People Struggling With Self Injury
Books:
<u>Women Living with Self Injury</u> by Jane Wegscheider Hyman
<u>Bright Red Scream</u> by Marilee Strong

Web sites:
Self Injury, Abuse & Trauma Resource Directory
http://<u>www.self-injury-abuse-trauma-directory.info</u>

http://<u>www.selfinjury.freeserve.co.uk</u>

For Male Survivors of Sexual Assault
http://www.utexas.edu/student/cmhc/booklets/maleassault/menassault.html

See also the **Resources** section at the end of the zine.

Zine Librarian Zine

The Salt Lake City Public Library
by Brooke Young

Fancy Pants Introduction

The Salt Lake City Public Library has a very nice zine collection. The director of the library actually sets aside a sizable chuck of cash for the sole purpose of buying zines, which is very nice of her. The collection doesn't always look pretty, but I have high hopes that one day it will turn into the most beautiful and well organized collection ever. Oh, well besides the IPRC, of course. Organized bastards, making the rest of us look bad with their fancy "catalog" and "list" of what they have. Oh well.

The Fearless Leader of the collection is a lovely lady by the name of Julie Bartel. In spite of the fact she has a brand spanking new library degree, her hair is never in a bun and she never squints at children or tells them to take their noise somewhere else. She spends loads of her time making sure people know about the zine collection and keeps the *HMS* Zine Collection running. She does all sorts of thankless jobs like organizing workshops and making sure people know about our collection. All of her none existent free time is spent wondering how her entire desk and the surrounding floor came to be covered in zines and kicking ass with Buffy the Vampire Slayer. Email her at jthomas@mail.slcpl.lib.ut.us

I am Captain Bartel's faithful Number One and respond to the name Brooke Young. I get to be the professional scribe of the collection, mainly due to my inability to draw stick figures. I do most of the ordering for the collection and all sorts of other nameless stuff. I have an unmanageable addiction to English soccer and spent the entire month of June staying up all night long watching South Korea knock out Italy and Spain in the World Cup.
Email me at byoung@mail.slcpl.lib.ut.us

Advice for Young Zine Librarians
(Public Libraries Slant)

Back in my day there was no one to consult with. We had to figure things out as we went along. And we had to walk two miles uphill in the snow just to order a zine. If we were late, then grandpappy would give our bottoms a smack with his belt. Things sure were different in my day. Not like the young kids now who expect advice! You young whippersnappers need

some toughening up, that's what I say. Hmm. Well, I guess you can sit down and eat my Worther's Original candy and listen to my pearls of great wisdom.

Julie's Academic Corner
(Why Public Libraries Should Have Zines)

Julie has spent most of the last four convincing important people that zines should be an integral part of libraries. She has worked out all the arguments as to why public libraries should collect zines. Sadly, when she was gathering this information she was often writing academic papers that are interesting and informative, but rather highfalutin. Most of the following arguments come from a five page part of her thirty page article on our zine collection. I mention this because I would hate to be accused of not stating my sources.

Most of you, dear readers, will be sold on zines in public libraries. The hard part is convincing the big wigs of your library system that zines and public libraries go together like ebony and ivory. One great little factoid is that the Library Bill of Rights states that "libraries should provide materials and information presenting all points of view" (www.ala.org) and alternative materials in general, zines in specific, are a great way to provide access to all points of view. With a relatively small budget, a public library can build a great zine collection that "can help libraries create full-spectrum collections which better serve their patrons" (Queen Julie pg 7). The fact that the materials are often challenging to acquire and problematic to catalog is no excuse for self-censorship. As Julie puts it "especially now, when publishing houses are merging, and mainstream media is tightening its grip on the public subconscious, it is imperative that libraries remain (or become) 'information centers' which provide all kinds of information on all kinds of topics". Wow, she is good.

Some Things to Know About Zine Collections in Public Libraries

1. Be flexible. More often then not there are rules governing your library that will not be changed so that you can order a $2 zine. There are also rules that zinesters live and die by that are in direct conflict with the rules and regulations of

your library. For example, our library used to make us send a check for everything we ordered. Each measly $2 check then had to be approved by the administration. Not only did the administration have to approve a $2 check to Fish Piss but they only met once a month, meaning that by the time the check was sent out the zinester had moved. Many zinesters of course, refused to accept our checks for privacy reasons, meaning that they just didn't cash it and sent us zines or we heard no response at all. A no win situation for everyone. After much negotiating, we came to a compromise of the $4 cash rule. The business office will not send more then $4 in cash through the mail, which gives us a lot of leeway. Everyone rejoiced! Fewer checks in board meetings! Fewer checks to cancel! More zines for our collection! Yeah!

2. Cataloging is a nightmare of epic proportions. Frankly, public libraries can't usually afford to spend the money or spare the cataloger to enter each zine in the library's catalog. Often, there isn't even enough information for a cataloger to use. No date, no volume, no real name, the title changes every issue, etc. Zines make catalogers scream out in horror. I think if we made them catalog each zine the catalogers would rise up with their special tape and talk about revolution. Be prepared to find some other method to keep track of your stuff. Some collections use bookkeeping software and the like. We had a colleague create a Microsoft Access database to enter in title information and other important facts. We have had the database for a little less then a year, which means we have five years worth of stuff to enter. We have not gotten very far really. Also if you decide to circulate your zines and they are not cataloged, you have a problem. We have decided to buy manila envelopes that have a barcode on them and the envelope is what actually checks out. We have no record of what leaves the building or what comes back, but people can take them home. But enough of that crazy library jargon. Yucky. Next thing you know I will be talking about the Dewey Decimal System and even my eyes will shut in boredom.

3. Advertising is gold. Once we started our collection we had a hard time getting the word out. This might sound a little unbelievable, but the coolest and hippest people in Salt Lake don't really hang out at the library. Where do cool people hang out? Having never been cool, this was a problem. However we have spent several years studying the elusive cool person in their natural habitat and we think we have a handle on it. Plus, you don't want to exclude people with just normal levels of coolness. Anyway, the point is that you have to flyer like a trooper and court media like there is no tomorrow. We go to schools across the valley, we flyer everywhere we can think of, we go to tattoo parlors and we spend a lot of time on programming. We have "How to Make Your Own Zine" programs regularly and we also just have an open house to display new zines. Self promotion for the greater good of the collection is a good thing.

Thanks for reading this little piece about our collection. Since the last issue of ZLZ we have had an amazing amount of support. I was totally overwhelmed and touched by the number of people who contacted us, everyone of them saying really nice things. So big props to Greig for the incredible job he does in creating this whole zine. Also, in January 2003 we will be moving into a spectacular new library that is a wonder to behold. The zine collection will be out of the smelly basement and on the second floor. We hope to have it organized by that time too. Knock on wood. ★

Brooke Young
Salt Lake City Public Library
Zine Collection
210 East 400 South
Salt Lake City, UT 84111

Debased on Actual Events
by Susan Boren

WELL, IT HAPPENED. I was weak. I backslid.

I started watching television again.

Maybe this doesn't sound like a big deal to you, but for me, it's the difference between being myself and not being myself. When the TV is on, I lose touch with who I am.

It started in earnest on Sept. 11. A friend called me and told me about the disaster, and like most people, I had to see the images for myself. I had to see the amateur videos of hijacked airplanes smashing into the World Trade Center towers. I had to watch the rolling clouds of toxic smoke flood Manhattan's streets. When the "haunted" firefighters emerged from the "cathedral in hell," shuffling through office paper, concrete, and women's shoes, I needed to hear them evoke movie titles to describe the scene.

I needed it to be real because, like the firefighters, all I could see was cinema in this enormous tragedy. The whole series of events sounded painfully scripted to me. Faithfully, the satiric newspaper **The Onion** reported: "American Life Turns Into Bad Jerry Bruckheimer Movie." It was true. Reality had caved in.

In the months that followed, the narrative got uglier, but no less imaginative. Transfixed, I turned in for the reports on box cutters, anthrax, carpet bombing, state-sanctioned torture, and the sexual sadism of Saddam Hussein's eldest son. I saw power-grabbing Washington elites gleefully use this unprecedented tragedy to funnel public money to Big Business, and I watched them shred the Bill of Rights in the name of "homeland security." In the end, television only heightened the fictional quality of these events. The unthinkable was happening from moment to moment on the TV screen, just like in a boring action movie.

I tried to warm to my role a "protester." Being a writer, I planned many essays, the most savage one beginning with a quote from James Madison – "Perhaps it is a universal truth that loss of liberty at home is to be charged to provisions against danger, real or pretended, from abroad." – but my critique never materialized. For one thing, I couldn't even keep track of the plot. New horrors mushroomed out of old ones, spurred largely by an apocalypse of bombs on Afghanistan and Iraq. While flag-waving Americans cheered this gory feast of special effects, evidence from international news sources began to trickle in that we were bombing civilians on purpose

then mercilessly withholding life-saving provisions from them. Military objectives aside, we needed the region's oil reserves, and these people were in the way. As the atrocities mounted with each newscast, my sense of horror began to grow numb. Without my outrage, my ability to develop a convincing war protest faded away.

Before I knew it, I was doping myself with televised sporting events. Enthusiastically, I cheered the home team, forcing the war to compete with a din of crowd noise. This active denial required a constant flow of distractions, however, and soon I was looking for other things on TV to watch.

It was during a rerun of **The Real World**, several months down the road, that consequences caught up with me. All through the program, I had entertained myself by deriding the show. This isn't real, I thought with satisfaction. These people are clearly playing to the camera, and anyway, can't they see that the context they're in is designed to bring out certain tensions and highlight certain assumptions about human behavior? How can they mistake their situation for reality?

This last question kickstarted a whole new series of thoughts about my own situation. Long-suppressed emotions started leaking into my mind, particularly shame. I realized – consciously – that watching TV had been an ideal way for *me* to 'play to the camera,' an accepted way to participate in 'reality' without actually feeling my horror. When I cheered with the crowd and laughed with the studio audience, I had effectively reduced my complicated inner life to a heavily censored caricature of myself.

Even the tension that I felt as I watched television wasn't mine. It was the product of TV production, often transparently bad production. I allowed myself to be drawn in, however, and the emotional connection to what I watched was very real. I actually cared about contrived, fictional representations and cheered them on to forced, inevitable conclusions. I was viewing genuine human reality as a contrived state, detached from my own experience. I turned off **The Real World** and sat with that thought. Television programming, I realized, was in many ways an accurate microcosm of the larger social environment. In 'the real world,' just like on TV, people are assumed to be ready-made for roles within a larger, rigidly controlled context. The freedom of each individual to make choices outside of the governing context is not considered – in fact, this

contact: PO Box 330156 | Murfreesboro TN 37133-0156 | www.undergroundpress.org

basic freedom is suppressed. The cast of **The Real World** do not cultivate lives outside of the camera's eye, and grudgingly, I admitted that I was guilty of the same thing. By allowing myself to be drawn into the formulaic world of accepted assumptions and two-dimensional feelings, my mind framed my real life as television. In this state, at some level, I ceased to exist. When I rejected free choice, I was reduced to exploited images on a flickering screen.

Once I began to care whether or not I viewed myself – and by extension, my world – as real, a ravenous appetite for reading returned to me.

What I needed was riveting, present-day writing that reaffirmed my shaking faith in the existence of unscripted human life. I scoured my library for suitable material, and finally found what I was looking for among my collection of personal zines. Through perzines like **Xtra Tuf**, **Inspector 18**, and **Doris**, I found a way out of cheap, televised reality. These zines exposed people individually, often completely at odds with their social environment. In this way, they were essentially opposed to the idea of a rigid

social construct. The authors of these zines – Moe, Michael, and Cindy – are notoriously 'real people' in full possession of all the conflicting emotions and experiences that make them unmistakably human. I didn't have to deny, reduce, alter, or conform myself to identify with their stories. In these perzines I found a community of people waiting for me to embrace my own perspective.

It's always embarrassing to be reminded that TV doesn't speak for me, but I understand now why I allow myself to get confused. If I admit that I exist apart from television, then I must accept that I exist apart from that other popular fiction, 'the real world.' That's a disturbing conclusion to come to about yourself, particularly at a time when our social environment is saturated with demands for "unity." It makes sense that I'd want to hide in a crowd of seated spectators, but I also know that I can't hide indefinitely. Eventually, I must find a way to yell at the screen, and personal zines helped me remember that one of the most effective protests available to me is simply standing up and telling my story. ★

HONORABLE MENTIONS ★

Thousands of zines come out each year, and hundreds get nominated for the yearbook. Here are a few that didn't make the final yearbook cut, but certainly merit your attention and well-concealed cash. Drop 'em a line to get a copy! All of these are print zines, though some requested we print their email or web site only.

12 Items or Less
112 Muir Ave, PMB 1057, Hazleton, PA 18201

Al Alavio
www.revolutionvideo.org/alavio

Allah Makes My Ass Tired
PO Box 070674, Milwaukee, WI 53207

Alt.Culture.Guide
826 Old Charlotte Pike East, Franklin, TN 37064

Always in Season
PO Box 380403, Brooklyn, NY 11238

Animal Workers
PO Box 510214, Milwaukee, WI 53203

Arcane Candy
PO Box 230370, Encinitas, CA 92023

Attempted Not Known
PO Box 64522, Sunnyvale CA, 94088

Attic Wit
3148 Hartwick Lane, Fairfax, VA 22031

Bandoppler
PMB #P506, 6201 15th Ave NW, Seattle, WA 98107

Big Q Zine
UCSC GLBTIRC, 1156 High St, Santa Cruz, CA 95064

A Brooklyn Diary
426 Sterling Place #3C, Brooklyn, NY 11238

Bummers & Gummers
PO Box 66, Yoncalla, OR 97499

Cathedral
138 Overland Rd #3, Montevallo, Al 35115

Chain-Breaker
621 N Rendon, New Orleans, LA 70119

Chord Easy
PO Box 190, Phm. OR 97370

Clip Tart
PO Box 66512, Austin, TX 78766

Cold Hands Dead Heart
www.angelfire.com/ill/miketwohig

Coming to Amerika
guiltyexpat@yahoo.com

A Companion Guide to Rooftop Films
info@rooftopfilms.com

Confessions of an Unattractive Man
iliketodrawpictures@hotmail.com

Crack The Sidewalk
22-52 36th St, Astoria, NY 11105

Cytronic
132 Liberty St, Bowling Green, OH 43402

Diatribe
17853 65th Ave, Tinley Park, IL 60477

The Door Was Never Locked
PO Box 4964, Louisville, KY 40204

Durga
PO Box 5841, Eugene, OR 97405

Dwan
Box 411, Swarthmore, PA 19081

East Village Inky
PO Box 22754, Brooklyn, NY 11202

Evasion
xevasionx@hotmail.com

Everyday Resistance
everydayresistance@yahoo.com

Faesthetic
www.faesthetic.com

Fanorama
109 Arnold Ave, Cranston, RI 02905

Foul
3231 N Kenmore #2F, Chicago, Il 60657

Full Unit Hookup
622 West Cottom Ave, New Albany, IN 47150

The Growing Upheaval
375 Hudson St 5th Floor, New York, NY 10014

H2S04
PO Box 423354, San Francisco, CA 94142

Hip-Hop Hymnal
Central City Lutheran Mission, 1354 N G St, San Bernardino, CA 92405

Hungover Gourmet
PO Box 5531, Lutherville, MD 21094

I Defy
614 S 48th St #1, Philadelphia, PA 19143

Ingleside News
5591 St. Laurent, Levis, Que, G6V 3V6, Canada

Interstitial
118 N Columbus St, Lancaster OH 43130

In The Van
PO Box 1299, Boston, MA 02130

In Your Room
PO Box 1514, Bellingham, WA 98227

I Spent the Summer Traveling in Europe
startla_mayhem@yahoo.com

Jape
12033 Lumpkin, Hamtramck, MI 48212

Kerbloom
PO Box 3525, Oakland, CA 94609

Ladies Liberation Handbook
PO Box 3023, South Brisbane, BC Q1D 4101, Australia

Les Gens Affluent dans les Rues.

Lower East Side Librarian
521 E 5th St #1D, New York, NY 10009

Low Hug
112 Muir Ave, PMB 1057, Hazelton, PA 18201

Maggot Zine
23 Veteran's Drive, Fredericton, NB, E3A C4, Canada

Make Something!
PO Box 12409, Portland, OR 97212

Manufacturing Dissent
c/o APLAN, 818 SW 3rd Ave, PMB 354, Portland, OR 97204

The Match
PO Box 3012, Tucson, AZ 85702

Media Reader
PO Box 220386, Chicago, IL 60622

Media Whore
37 Home st, Malden, MA 02148

Meniscus
1573 N Milwaukee, PMB 464, Chicago, IL 60622

Message from the Homeland
PO Box 1725, Westfield, MA 01086

Mishap
PO Box 5841, Eugene, OR 97405

Monkey Dust
PO Box 40242, Albuquerque, NM 87196

Move on
PO box 8131, Pittsburgh, PA 15217

The New Formulation
2620 Second Ave #4B, San Diego, CA 92103

One Fine Mess
71 Strom St #2C, Tarrytown, NY 10591

One World Freedom Journal
PO Box 50217, Baltimore, MD 21211

Penny Dreadful Travel Guides

The Perfect Mix Tape Segue
PO Box 14332, Portland, OR 97293

Personality Liberation Front
PO Box 3023, South Brisbane, BC Q1D 4101, Australia

Pixelthis
www.pixelthiszine.com

The Pornographic Flabbergasted Emus
PO Box 770332, Lakewood, OH 44107

Prison Music
PO Box 184, Yoncalla, OR 97499

Prisoners Speak
PO Box 721, Homewood, Il 60430

Problem Child
PO Box 460310, San Francisco, CA 94146

Random Life in Progress
1214 N Damen #2, Chicago, IL 60622

Resident Alien
1810 Sealy, Galveston, TX 77550

Rocket Queen
PO Box 64, Asheville, NC 28802

Rock Out! Ideas on Booking DIY Shows
PO Box 5027, Chicago, IL 60680

Show me the Money
PO Box 48161, Coon Rapids, MN 55448

Sister Friend
PO Box 4539, Fairview Heights, Il 62208

Slave
PO Box 10093, Greensboro, NC 27404

Slither
www.221colab.org/kelly-Froh

Smut Peddler

www.saucygoosepress.com

Songs About Ghosts

PMB #5, 302 Bedford Ave, Brooklyn, NY 11222

Space 4 Machines

PO box 635, Urbana, Il 61803

Stainless Steel Lens

PO Box 070674, Milwaukee, WI 53207

Stolen Sharpie Revolution

PO Box 14332, Portland, OR 97293

Subject to Change

girl_exile@hotmail.com

Subversive Notions

2817 West End Ave #126-102, Nashville, TN 37203

Subways

845 43rd St #2A, Brooklyn, NY 11232

Switcheroo

PO Box 2443, Richmond, IN 47375

Tangent

PO Box 27, St Mary's City, MD 20686

Tanglefoot

superfrida@earthlink.net

Tenacious: Writings from Women in Prison

1414 Lincoln Place, Brooklyn, NY 11213

This!

The_beard_emporium@yahoo.com

Totally Gamez

3941 Mintwood Ave, Pittsburgh, PA 15224

Tranzilla

www.xantippe.com/tranzilla

Verbicide

32 Alfred Street, New Haven, CT 06512

War Against the Idiots

1731 Cleveland St, Evanston, IL 60202

We Ain't Got No Car

PO Box 3824, Portland, OR 97208

What God has Revealed to Man

PO Box 106, Danville, OH 43014

Wonkavision

PO Box 63642, Philadelphia, PA 19147

Xerography Debt

PO Box 963, Havre De Grace, MD 21078

You Idiot

PO Box 8995 Minneapolis, MN 55408

Zinester's Guide to Portland

PO box 14185, Portland, OR 97293

Zisk

801 Eagles Ridge Rd, Brewster, NY 10509

NOTES

NOTES

NOTES

NOTES

NOTES

NOTES

NOTES

NOTES